GRAMMAR
in many voices

GRAMMAR
in many voices

Marilyn N. Silva
California State University, Hayward

NTC Publishing Group
Lincolnwood, Illinois USA

Executive Editor: John T. Nolan
Developmental Editor: Marisa L. L'Heureux
Cover design: Ophelia M. Chambliss
Cover illustration: *The Pedestrian Crosswalk,* Allen Garnes/Stock Works
Interior design: David Corona Design
Production Manager: Rosemary Dolinski

Published by NTC Publishing Group
© 1995 NTC Publishing Group, 4255 West Touhy Avenue
Lincolnwood (Chicago), Illinois 60646-1975 U.S.A.
Manufactured in the United States of America.
Library of Congress Catalog Card Number: 94-66705.

4 5 6 7 8 9 ML 9 8 7 6 5 4 3 2 1

Contents

Chapter Four   Infinitive Clauses   88

Chapter Five   Participle Clauses   115

Chapter Six   Taking Stock—A Midterm Review   139

Chapter Ten Adverbial Subordination 228

Appendix A Summary of Syntactic Tests 253

Appendix B Pronoun Paradigms 256

Appendix C Glossary of Syntactic Terms 259

Preface

Grammar in Many Voices investigates the grammar—the syntax—of written English—that is, the system that underlies the construction of possible sentences in the language. Although you have been using a grammar all your life—for surely you would not be able to read this page, otherwise—you probably have not thought much about the system you use every time you speak, listen, read, or write. Yet that system is quite complex, even though it is essentially invisible to us in our day-to-day communications through speech and writing. That system, in fact, is the focus of this book.

Students often don't know what to expect from a course in English grammar. Some expect to be confronted with sentences that they will have to "correct." Others fear that the grammar of their own writing will be subject to scrutiny. Be assured that you will encounter neither of those scenarios in this book. Instead, you will be asked to look at the world of language in a new way, examining the structures that make up what we think of as the English language and the grammatical functions those structures serve. The sentences you will examine— sentences produced for the most part by published writers—contain *no* errors and typically are exemplary. You will learn to analyze these sentences in detail.

As with the acquisition of any new area of knowledge, you will find yourself faced with a "learning curve." That is, it will take time to develop your skill in analyzing the sentences presented to you in this book. At first you may find yourself somewhat perplexed, being new to thinking abut language in the way required here. As you progress, however, the skills that at first seemed so elusive will become familiar, and you will grow increasingly comfortable in confronting new material.

The Organization of the Book

In Chapter One, you will learn the structure of the basic English sentence, and in Chapters Two and Three, you will learn to analyze the details of that basic sentence. Chapter Three will challenge you to make some very fine distinctions among differing sentence patterns. Devote adequate time to studying Chapters Four and Five, understanding that after mastering them you will be equipped with all the basics you need for studying the grammar of English. To help you assess your developing skills, Chapter Six provides a midterm review with plenty of sentences for you to analyze in great detail. Given this, do not attempt to do all of this chapter at once. Instead, complete the first three exercises, the chapter quiz, and some of the sentences whose analysis you are to perform from scratch. Thereafter, do several more of these sentences each time you sit down to study. In this way, you will keep up with new material and review the old at the same time. You will be surprised just how much the "old stuff" helps you to understand the new. Occasional review of Chapter Three, in particular, is advised. You cannot allow yourself to forget previous lessons, because they will be essential in understanding the next lesson. Each new unit of study presupposes prior units.

Features

Throughout this book, you will find technical terms written in boldface type. These terms are defined briefly at the end of each chapter and in the glossary at the end of the book. In addition, you will find that answers to most of the exercises are provided. But you must recognize that the answers to the exercises will do you no good at all if you look at them before attempting to do the exercises yourself, or, worse, if you do not do the exercises at all. To get the greatest benefit from this course, always read the discussions carefully, and then try to do the exercises on your own. Only when you are satisfied that you have done your best should you consult the solutions. It is always a good idea to consult these solutions—even if you are convinced that you have the correct answer—because you will find they include a few more tips to help you work through the material and, perhaps, an alternative solution you had not considered. Another strategy that may help you master the material is to construct sentences of your own analogous to those you are studying, or to keep at hand a favorite book, essay, or short story and find therein sentences containing the structures you are studying at any particular point in the course.

How This Book Differs from Other Grammar Books

In covering the material in this book, you will encounter several features that make this book distinct from other books on English grammar. The first of these is its focus on the syntax of the language (the arrangement of words)—not its sound system or word structure or its discourse properties, although these features clearly are significant and often interact with the syntax in critically important ways. This approach allows us to limit the field of inquiry so that we can study one facet of the language in depth within the confines of a single term of study.

The second feature is the focus on standard written English, rather than the spoken language. This focus saves us from worrying about whether one spoken form (read: *dialect*) is to be considered "superior" to other spoken forms. It also provides you with an important service. Intuitively, you already know about talking and conversing; however, the written language still may be somewhat enigmatic to you. And the more literary the prose, the more enigmatic it tends to be. Studying the grammar of written English, then, may enable you to improve your writing style since it will broaden your knowledge of syntactic options for expressing an idea.

The third feature—and one that diverges from common practice—is the analysis of "real" passages from published writers rather than *ad hoc* sentences manufactured to exemplify particular syntactic constructions. To be sure, I often do make up simple examples to illustrate a point, but these artificial sentences are immediately followed by exercises comprised of scores of sentences culled from a variety of literary sources. In my opinion, using sentences designed for communication rather than for exemplification results in more interesting and colorful exercises that often have value in themselves because they are funny (such as sentences taken from Bill Cosby's *Fatherhood*), macabre (like those taken from Bram Stoker's *Dracula* or Anne Rice's *Interview with the Vampire*), informative (such as passages from Jacob Bronowski's *The Ascent of Man* and from newspaper and magazine articles), artistic (such as sentences from Louise Erdrich's *The Beet Queen*), and just downright silly (from Dr. Seuss).

Finally, the writers whose sentences provide the substance for the exercises come from a variety of ethnic backgrounds and include both males and females (thus the title of this book, *Grammar in Many Voices*). We analyze the prose of published men and women writers who are "Anglo" (though not necessarily of British descent), African American, Hispanic, American Indian, Asian American, and so on. By choosing the prose of a rainbow of authors, I hope to convince you that writing Standard English *is* politically correct. In addition, you will be exposed through these examples to a variety of viewpoints and experiences. Excerpts from Jung Chang's *Wild Swans,* for example, provide through pristine prose a glimpse of what it has been like to be a woman in China during the tumultuous changes in the twentieth century.

What You Will Learn

So just what will you learn from working through this book? You will learn that grammar is not merely a discipline in the service of writing. You will learn that language is far too elusive to be caught in any trap we might devise for it. You will learn that interesting and provocative prose is worth reading and fun to analyze. You will learn to think critically, and to apply your powers of analysis to new situations in your reading, and indeed in your own writing. And you will learn, implicitly, that regardless of one's ethnic background, English belongs to all of us.

Acknowledgments

I thank Professor Linda Coleman of the University of Maryland, College Park, and Professor Dan Alford of California State University, Hayward, for using earlier drafts of this book in their English grammar courses and providing substantive recommendations for improvements. I also thank Christine Frondoso, one of Professor Coleman's students at Maryland, who sent me her helpful suggestions for revision. I am grateful to Professor Carol Franks of Portland State University and to Professor Mary Sue Ply of Southeastern Louisiana University for their perceptive reviews of the manuscript, and to Marisa L. L'Heureux, my editor at NTC Publishing Group, whose advice guided the final version of the book.

I am of course immensely indebted to the students at Cal State who served as my subjects for this experimental-text-in-progress. I value their patience, their enthusiasm, and their hard work, and I thank them for teaching me about how they understand language and how to teach them. I am also indebted to my colleagues in the English Department, Professors Mary Cullinan and E. J. Murphy, who provided unwavering encouragement for this project, and to California State University, Hayward, which awarded me a sabbatical leave and other opportunities for release time so that I could complete this book.

Marilyn R. Silva

Chapter One

Thinking About Sentences

Introduction

In many schools of thought about grammar (and here we mean specifically the **syntax**—or word arrangement—of a language), the *sentence* is considered the appropriate unit of analysis, although you may have at best only a fuzzy understanding of what a sentence actually comprises. When pressed, you may say that a sentence is a complete thought. However, it is likely that your thoughts are complete and yet are not sentences. In fact, you probably think much the way you talk—in capsules of information, in spurts of consciousness that, strictly speaking, are less than a sentence. That is, your thoughts are more likely to come in fragments than in sentences.

The human world—particularly the world of print—is nevertheless full of sentences. To prove this assertion to ourselves all we have to do is peruse any newspaper. There we find many language units beginning with a capital letter and ending with the punctuation mark we call the period—visual cues delineating the boundaries of written sentences. Of course, the exact nature of the content these visual cues capture remains a question.

Grammarians define the sentence in terms of its structural characteristics, that is, in terms of the kinds of pieces that comprise it. So, after having examined many examples of English utterances and texts, grammarians contend that a sentence—a basic language unit—is made up of two major chunks of information, and that—when pressed, a native speaker can determine the boundaries of these chunks. To see to what extent these contentions describe the facts, let us examine the following sentences:

1

1a. The child bounced the ball.

2a. The chef cut the meat.

Now, draw a slash mark after the word that ends the first chunk (or, alternatively speaking, before the word that begins the second chunk).

If you think the way grammarians do, you will have indicated your decision as follows, dividing the sentences along the lines of actor and action:

1b. The child / bounced the ball.

2b. The chef / cut the meat.

Perhaps you split the sentences in a different way. Some students claim that it makes more sense to divide the sentences in the following manner:

1c. The child bounced / the ball.

2c. The chef cut / the meat.

You may argue that it makes no sense to separate an actor from an action, that in (1a), for example, the action of bouncing is what makes a child an actor in the first place, and thus it is the ball that is the separate entity.

Although this argument may have psychological or philosophical value, it is not supported by grammarians. When they carry on the enterprise we call grammar, grammarians look for generalizations that hold across a number of instances—the few rules that govern the many possibilities for English sentences. So, while students who would group agents and actions together may claim excellent psychological and philosophical grounds for doing so, from the point of view of grammarians their analysis is *ad hoc.* In other words, it applies only to a specific instance and not to the vast array of possible English sentences.

To demonstrate the logic of the grammarians' position, let us examine some other English sentences:

3a. John ran.

4a. The dog barked.

5a. The baby was sleeping.

If you try to break each of these sentences into two basic components, it's likely that you will do so in the following way:

3b. John / ran.

4b. The dog / barked.

5b. The baby / was sleeping.

Notice that the slashes for (3b), (4b), and (5b) come between an actor and some activity (3b, 4b) or state (5b). Grammarians contend, then, that the best way to treat sentences (1a) and (2a) is to divide them into actor/action in the same manner. In this way, the structural similarities that all English sentences share is revealed, and a generalization about the nature of sentences can be made. Thus, a sentence in which some entity follows the action word is seen as structurally similar to a sentence in which nothing follows the action.

We have now discovered the two basic parts for all English sentences. Grammarians call these parts **sentence constituents**—a technical term for sentence components. The first of these two constituents is called a **noun phrase** and the second is called a **predicate phrase.** We can now give a technical definition of the sentence: *A sentence is a linguistic entity consisting of a noun phrase and a predicate phrase.* That is, a sentence is a language unit that **predicates** (predicate phrase) something about some concrete or abstract person or thing (noun phrase). Sentences tell us who is doing what to whom. Grammarians graphically represent this information through the following **phrase structure tree:**

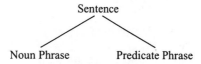

An abbreviated form of this tree—in fact, the more usual form—looks like this:

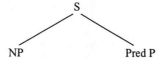

When we talk about such trees, we say that the **S** *dominates* (i.e., is above) the **NP** and **Pred P** *nodes.* (A **node** is a point in the tree.) The phrase structure tree given above is merely a way of indicating visually that a sentence includes an **NP** (noun phrase) and a **Pred P** (predicate phrase). Using the abbreviations shown in boldface as symbols is the norm in doing grammar.

Noun Phrases

Thus far we have avoided any discussion of "parts of speech" such as *noun, verb,* or *adjective,* primarily because thinking like a grammarian involves thinking about chunks of information, or **phrases.** Accurate naming of the part of speech of every word in a sentence, a paragraph, or even an entire book does not comprise a grammatical analysis of that text; nevertheless, a basic knowledge of the parts of speech is necessary in order to be able to describe the structural units that constitute sentences. For example, we define **noun phrase** (NP) as a structural unit comprised of a noun (the head element) plus any additional elements modifying the noun's meaning in some way. Thus, at minimum we need to understand that a noun is the name of a person, place, thing, state, idea, or condition. Although this definition is inadequate, it will serve until we have more understanding of the structure that determines noun status.

What sorts of elements "modify" a noun? In general, **modifiers** are elements that fine-tune the meaning of the word they modify; they limit it, describe it, or characterize it in some way.

The two basic noun modifiers are *determiners* and *adjectives*. A **determiner** typically is the first element to occur in a noun phrase and has little inherent meaning. Instead, it serves to identify the noun as an entity known to both speaker and addressee, or known only to the speaker (an **article:** *the* or *a*); to locate the noun as spatially or emotionally near or far from the speaker (a **demonstrative:** *this, these, that, those*); or to indicate ownership (a **possessive pronoun:** *my, your, his, her, its, their*). In short, a determiner modifies a noun by specifying the noun's *relationship* to the speaker/writer or to some other sentence element. It does not provide a characteristic of the noun. An **adjective** is a noun modifier with a descriptive function. Words such as *red, large,* and *ugly* are adjectives. Such modifiers often indicate an NP and, by extension, indicate the element that is functioning as a noun. In other words, the structure provided by these elements can uniquely identify another element as a noun.

All of the following, then, are noun phrases:

6. John

7. The man

8. The happy man

9. Happy men

10. Your brother

In addition, a **pronoun** can substitute for a noun-headed phrase on subsequent mention, and can be an NP in its own right. Pronouns include "personal" pronouns such as *I, me, you, he, she, it, they,* and *them,* and "indefinite" pronouns, such as *anyone, no one,* and *someone,* which do not have a specific **antecedent,** or NP, that the pronoun replaces in subsequent mention of the NP. (See the Appendix for a list.) Thus, the italicized elements in (11) and (12) also are noun phrases:

11. John brought home the bacon and *he* cooked *it.*

12. *She* sells sea shells by the seashore.

The varying types of noun phrases (NPs) have structures that can be represented by trees. Symbols are used as follows: NP = noun phrase; Det = determiner; N = noun; Adj = adjective; and Pro = pronoun.

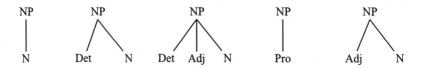

The modifying elements in a noun phrase are tightly *bound* to their nouns. This means that the words that precede a noun generally cannot stand alone, nor can they be moved to other positions within a sentence. Consider the noun phrases of sentence (1a):

1a. The child bounced the ball.

It's a good bet that when you were making your decision about where to divide this sentence, you did not proceed as follows:

1d. *The / child bounced the ball.

1e. *The child bounced the / ball.

In all likelihood, you never even considered these possibilities. Native speakers may not all think alike about language, but they do seem to agree on one point in particular: a word like *the* is closely tied to the word that follows it, and so divisions like those given in (1d) and (1e) are not natural. The asterisk (*) printed in front of these strings of words indicates that the solution, or even the string of words itself, is deviant from ordinary English usage. That is, the string is *ungrammatical.* The notion of what is grammatical and what is not depends not on some grammarian's opinion, but rather on what ordinary speakers of the language consider to be acceptable sentences. The **asterisk notation** is a convention used in studies of grammar to identify such impermissible strings of words, and we shall use it throughout this book. A question mark in the same position indicates marginal or questionable acceptability.

The Predicate Phrase

The other basic structural unit of the sentence is the predicate phrase. A predicate phrase consists of a *verb phrase* and sometimes one or two NPs, adjectives, or certain modifiers called **adverbs,** that temper or intensify the meaning of the verb in some way. The **verb phrase (VP)** consists of a meaningful verb (the **lexical verb**), preceded by any helpers, or **auxiliaries** (*be, have, do, can, must,* etc.), which often but not always co-occur with it. A verb can be most accurately defined as a word that may be systematically **inflected** (changed by suffixes) to show changes in the time of an event. (For example, an *-ed* can be added to a verb to show past time.) A verb phrase functions as a single structural unit (e.g., *had been working, must be leaving, was eating,* etc.), although verb-phrase-based adverbs such as *never, not,* and *always* may occur within the chain of auxiliaries.

The Declarative Sentence

Thus far we have learned that an English sentence consists of a noun phrase and a predicate phrase. In addition, in a basic sentence these two elements are ordered with respect to each other, with the noun phrase (NP) preceding the predicate phrase. This word order is the order for a particular sentence type, the *declarative* sentence, which is used for statements (e.g., *John closed the door.*) and generally is considered by grammarians to be the basic sentence type. Other sentence types are the *interrogative* sentence (the question: *Did John close the door?*), the *imperative* sentence (the command: *Close the door!*), and the *exclamatory* sentence (the exclamation: *What a beautiful day it is!*). The declarative sentence is regarded as basic because it is the simplest to describe in terms of structure and is the most commonly occurring type in written prose. In addition, once we define declarative structure, we can describe all other sentence types in terms of it.

Exercise 1.1

The following sentences come from *Going to Meet the Man,* a novel by James Baldwin. For each sentence, insert a slash mark between the initial NP and the predicate phrase. Then underline *all* the NPs you encounter in each sentence, no matter where they occur. Try to describe the makeup of each NP: for example, determiner-adjective-noun. Make a note of any difficulties you encounter.

1. We live in a housing project.

2. The big windows fool no one.

3. She was humming an old church song.

4. Tears were gleaming on my mother's face.

5. She was crying again.

6. A man fumbled in his pockets for change.

7. He played with the notebook.

Answers to Exercise 1.1

1. <u>We</u>/live in <u>a housing project</u>.
   1. pronoun; 2. determiner-noun

2. <u>The big windows</u>/fool <u>no one</u>.
   1. determiner-adjective-noun; 2. pronoun

3. <u>She</u>/was humming <u>an old church song</u>.
   1. pronoun; 2. determiner-adjective-noun

4. <u>Tears</u>/were gleaming on <u>my mother's face</u>.
   1. noun; 2. determiner-noun

5. <u>She</u>/was crying again.

   1. pronoun

6. <u>A man</u>/fumbled in <u>his pockets</u> for <u>change</u>.

   1. determiner-noun; 2. determiner-noun; 3. noun

7. <u>He</u>/played with <u>the notebook</u>.

   1. pronoun; 2. determiner-noun

Possessives, Compounds, and Other Puzzling Items

Several elements in the preceding exercises should have caused you to consider whether what has been discussed thus far was sufficient to allow you to complete the exercise. In particular, you may have puzzled over analyzing the NPs *a housing project, an old church song,* and *my mother's face.* Also, you may have wondered about the status of the expression *no one,* and the category to which the word *again* belongs.

Expressions such as *housing project* and *church song* are examples of English *compound nouns* and are not adjective-noun combinations. That is, two nouns occur together to form a new concept, with the first serving as a kind of modifier to the second, without being an adjective. To clarify the nature of such constructions, let us examine a bona fide adjective-noun combination occurring in the above exercise: *the big windows.* This construction is an NP composed of a determiner, an adjective, and a noun. If I read the string aloud, I likely will stress the most prominent syllable of the word *windows,* which is the *head* noun of the NP. In addition, I can convert the NP into a sentence of its own by using an appropriate form of the verb *be:* (*be, am, is, are, was, were, being, been*):

13. The windows are big.

If an NP construction contains a compound noun such as *housing project* or *church song,* however, I cannot formulate such a sentence with acceptable results:

14. *the project is housing

15. *the song is church

Compound nouns function as single nouns and can then be modified further by adjectives:

16. an old church song

The NP in (16), then, is a determiner-adjective-noun combination, but the noun is *church song,* and not merely *song.*

A related problem is the treatment of possessive constructions. Possessive pronouns such as *my, your, our, his,* etc. function like determiners in English, and they precede any adjectives that may occur in the NP. Possessive nouns—those marked with the inflection - *'s*—similarly occur in the determiner position in an NP:

17. Mary's violet eyes

18. Joe's ancient bicycle

In fact, entire NPs with their own determiners and adjectives can function as determiners in other NPs. For example, consider the NP *my mother's face,* from Exercise 1.1. The possessive pronoun *my* clearly is not a modifier of the noun *face,* since the narrator of the sentence does not intend the reader to understand "my face." Instead, the pronoun is the determiner of the noun *mother,* here inflected for possessive case. The result is that the entire NP *my mother's* serves as the determiner to the noun *face.* In fact, if one were to modify further the NP headed by *face* with the addition of an adjective, that adjective would have to be inserted between the determiner NP and the head noun:

19. my mother's *sad* face

20. my mother's *happy* face

Any number of adjectives may be added, but the possessive NP always is the first element in the "higher" (or more inclusive) NP. Thus, possessive NPs generally function as determiners.

Next, we come to the question raised by the expression *no one* in sentence (2) of Exercise 1.1. This term and terms similar to it, such as *someone, anyone, something, anything,* and so on, are members of the class of *indefinite pronouns.* These pronouns are "stand-ins" for indefinite **referents,** or entities in the physical world to which the pronouns point. As such, these indefinite pronouns behave as NPs and should be considered accordingly.

Finally, we reach the problem of *again. Again* indicates the repetition of an event. Because it modifies the VP, it is an adverb.

The Prepositional Phrase

A modifying element that often occurs in sentences is the *prepositional phrase.* It consists of a **preposition** followed by an NP that functions as the *object of the preposition.* In order to recognize prepositional phrases, it follows that first we must be able to recognize prepositions.

By definition, a preposition is a word or group of words functioning as a unit that signals a relationship of time, space (location or direction), or association between the object of the preposition and some other entity in the sentence. Some commonly occurring examples are *in, on, to, from,* and *of.*

The ability to perform a grammatical analysis requires the ability to recognize the prepositional phrase. Since an NP serving as the object of a preposition is bound to that preposition within the prepositional phrase, it is not available by itself to relate directly to the verb of the sentence as a *subject* (the NP that typically precedes the predicate phrase in the declarative sentence, i.e., the NP immediately dominated by S in a tree) or as an *object* or other verb *complement* (which we shall learn about in Chapter Three). Thus, the ability to recognize prepositional phrases is helpful for determining the status of other elements in the sentence.

Exercise 1.2

In contrast to nouns and verbs, there are only a limited number of prepositions in English, and with a little reflection, you probably can think of many of them. In the space below, list all of the words and phrases you think are prepositions. After you are finished, compare your list to Table 1. Be sure to memorize those few prepositions that may be unfamiliar.

Table 1: The Most Frequently Occurring English Prepositions

(based on *English Grammar* by George O. Curme, New York: Barnes & Noble, 1947)

aboard	between	like
about	betwixt	of
above	beyond	off
according to	by	on
across	by dint of	on account of
after	by means of	on behalf of
against	by reason of	on top of
along	by virtue of	onto [*or* on to]
alongside (of)	by way of	opposite (to)
along with	concerning	out of
amid [*or* amidst]	considering	outside (of)
among [*or* amongst]	despite	over
apart from	down	owing to
around [*or* round]	during	past
as	ere	pending
as against	except	regarding
as between	for	regardless of
as compared with	for the sake of	short of
as for	from	since
aside from	in	through
aslant	in accordance with	throughout
astern of	in addition to	to
as to	in case of (= in the event of)	toward(s)
at	in the case of	under
athwart	in front of	underneath
barring	in lieu of	until [*or* till]
because of	in opposition to	unto
before	in place of	up
behind	in regard to	upon
below	inside (of)	via
beneath	in spite of	with
beside	instead of	within
besides	into	without

Exercise 1.3

These sentences appeared in Exercise 1.1. This time, underline all the prepositional phrases you find.

1. We live in a housing project.

2. Tears were gleaming on my mother's face.

3. A man fumbled in his pockets for change.

4. He played with the notebook.

Answers to Exercise 1.3

1. We live <u>in a housing project</u>.
2. Tears were gleaming <u>on my mother's face</u>.
3. A man fumbled <u>in his pockets</u> <u>for change</u>.

   There are two separate phrases here; notice that their positions are interchangeable: *A man fumbled for change in his pockets.*
4. He played <u>with the notebook</u>.

Thinking Further about Prepositional Phrases

All of the prepositional phrases in Exercise 1.3 occurred as constructions inside the predicate phrase. To prove this to yourself, just compare your answers to Exercise 1.1 to your responses for Exercise 1.3. Throughout, the prepositional phrase served as a modifier of the verb phrase. Grammarians call this kind of prepositional phrase an **adverbial** prepositional phrase. An adverbial differs from an adverb in that the term *adverb* refers to a particular part of speech. The term *adverbial,* on the other hand, is used to describe the *function* of a particular entity, whether or not it is an adverb or even a construction having any adverbs in it. A quick glance at the prepositional phrases we have encountered thus far should convince you that prepositional phrases do not typically have adverbs in them. Nevertheless, they are *adverbial* in function because of their status as modifiers within predicate phrases. As we shall see in later chapters, other kinds of constructions in addition to adverbs and prepositional phrases may have adverbial functions.

However, a prepositional phrase may also serve as a modifier inside an NP. When it does, it *follows* the noun and is called an **adjectival** (as opposed to an *adjective,* which is a label for a part of speech). To more clearly understand the distinction between adverbial and adjectival uses of the prepositional phrase, let us investigate the prepositional phrase in the first exercise sentence you encountered:

21. We live in a housing project.

The predicate phrase of this sentence is *live in a housing project.* The verb phrase of the sentence is *live,* and the prepositional phrase *in a housing project* locates this verb spatially. That is, the prepositional phrase modifies the verb phrase and is an adverbial. Letting the symbol PP = prepositional phrase and the symbol P = preposition, we can schematize this information as follows:

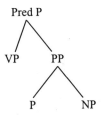

This tree indicates that the **PredP** *node dominates* the **PP** node and that the PP consists of a preposition (P) and a noun phrase (NP). This NP functions as the "object of the preposition." Notice that in the partial tree shown above, we use shorthand symbols for the phrases and parts of speech. This usage constitutes the norm in analyzing syntax, and is the procedure used throughout this book. Please keep this fact in mind as you continue to work your way through this chapter.

An example of a different kind of prepositional phrase occurs in the following sentence taken from a short story by Richard Wright:

22a. A gust of wind dashed rain against the window.

The prepositional phrase *of wind* identifies the kind of gust the author wishes to indicate and thus modifies the noun *gust.* It is therefore an **adjectival prepositional phrase** occurring within an NP. The NP having *gust* as its head noun consists of a determiner, a noun, and a prepositional phrase, in that order. In turn, the prepositional phrase consists of a preposition followed by an NP.

We can schematize this information as follows:

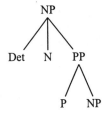

This phrase structure tree indicates that a higher-order construction, the NP, is made of a determiner (Det), a noun (N), and a prepositional phrase (PP). The prepositional phrase (PP) is a higher-order construction at the second level; that is, it has a structure that can be broken down into a preposition (P) and a noun phrase (NP). The PP is a modifier of the head noun. Another way of expressing this relationship is to say that the PP node *is dominated by* the NP node. As opposed to prenominal (preceding a noun) modifiers such as determiners and adjectives, which are "left-hand" modifiers, postnominal (following a noun) modifiers such as PPs are "right-hand" modifiers. As we shall see in subsequent chapters, modifiers other than PPs may be right-hand modifiers.

It is important to understand that not all prepositional phrases following nouns actually modify those nouns. Examine Sentence (22a) again:

22a. A gust of wind dashed rain against the window.

The prepositional phrase *against the window* does not modify *rain,* in spite of its position immediately following this noun. Rather, *against the window* stipulates the location of the rain after the action of the verb and therefore occurs within the predicate phrase, but *not* within the NP headed by *rain.* One test for whether a PP occurs outside or within an NP is the movability test: *elements occurring outside of NPs typically have a greater degree of mobility than elements occurring inside, which tend to be tightly bound to the nouns they modify.* Notice that it is possible to rephrase sentence (22a) in either of the following ways:

22b. Against the window, a gust of wind dashed rain.

22c. It was against the window that a gust of wind dashed rain.

These paraphrases do not introduce a distortion of meaning or cause a loss of syntactic acceptability. The fact that moving the PP *against the window* away from the N it immediately follows *(rain)* results in a paraphrase suggests that the PP does not belong to the NP containing the N. Compare the result if we try to move the PP *of wind*—previously identified as part of an NP—in an analogous manner. We produce gibberish:

22d. *Of wind a gust dashed rain against the window.

Because any NP may contain a PP, it is often the case that prepositional phrases are modifiers within NPs of other prepositional phrases. As an example, let us examine the following sentence taken from Edgar Allan Poe's "The Fall of the House of Usher":

23. The valet . . . ushered me into the presence of his master.

It is important to keep in mind that postnoun PPs can occur within any NP whatsoever, *even within* NPs *functioning as objects of prepositions.* Thus in Sentence (23), *of his master* is a PP modifying *presence.* Thus, *the presence of his master* is the complete NP functioning as the object of the preposition *into.* Sentence length often is directly attributable to many such prepositional phrases occurring as modifiers within NPs. Sentence (23) has the following phrase structure tree, which should enable you to see the locations of the two types of prepositional phrases:

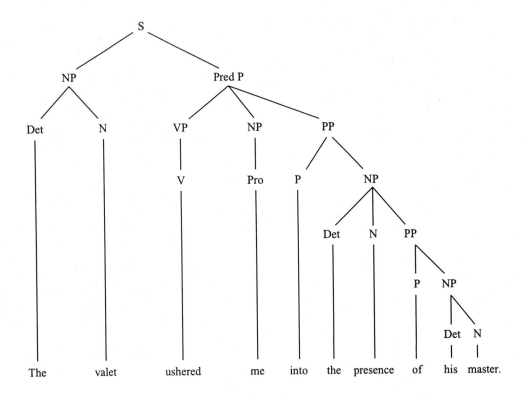

Exercise 1.4

Examine the following sentence taken from Poe's "The Fall of the House of Usher." Make a list of all the prepositional phrases you encounter and determine whether they are adverbial or adjectival. Then compare your answers to those given below. Make a note of any new or difficult elements.

> A valet, <u>of stealthy step</u>, thence conducted me, <u>in silence</u>, through many dark and intricate passages <u>in my progress to the studio of his master.</u>

Answers to Exercise 1.4

of stealthy step: adjectival (*valet* is head N)
in silence: adverbial
through many dark and intricate passages: adverbial
in my progress to the studio of his master: adverbial
to the studio of his master: adjectival (*progress* is head N)
of his master: adjectival (*studio* is head N)

Problems in the Preceding Exercise

If you are observant, you will have noticed several new structures in the sentence from Poe's "The Fall of the House of Usher." Why, for example, are there commas around the prepositional phrases *of stealthy step* and *in silence*? How are we to deal with elements *coordinated* with *and,* such as *many dark and intricate passages*? And, finally, what are we to make of the word *thence*?

Commas surround two of the prepositional phrases in the sentence because these two modifiers are *nonrestrictive* modifiers. We shall have much more to say later about the distinction, but for now it is enough to understand that while **restrictive modifiers** limit the meaning of what they modify, **nonrestrictive modifiers** simply add nonessential information without actually changing the meaning. Nonrestrictive modifiers are always set off from what they modify by a comma; restrictive modifiers are not set off by commas. To illustrate this distinction, let us look more closely at *A valet, of stealthy step.* This NP is headed by the N *valet.* The prepositional phrase *of stealthy step* does not identify which valet the author means; rather, it gives descriptive information without functioning to select the valet out of a range of valets. Such modification is *nonrestrictive* modification. In contrast, we have the prepositional phrase *of his master,* which helps the reader determine which studio the narrator intends the reader to understand. This prepositional phrase is therefore *restrictive.*

Any two or more elements of equal status in a sentence may be coordinated by the use of *and.* Such a coordination occurs in the NP *many dark and intricate passages*. In this NP, the adjectives *dark* and *intricate* are coordinated. Other elements of equal weight may be similarly conjoined: Nouns may be coordinated with other nouns, verbs with other verbs, and so on. As we shall see later, the similarity that allows such coordination may occur on the structural level (the coordinated elements share the same structure) or on the functional level (the coordinated elements do not share the same structure, but function similarly within the sentence, perhaps as adverbials).

Finally, we come to the adverb *thence,* which means "from that place." Adverbs are, generally speaking, modifiers of the verb phrase and therefore logically belong to the predicate phrase. However, adverbs are among the most mobile of sentence elements, and here we find one that has migrated to pre-verb position. Is such movement grammatical? Absolutely!

Exercise 1.5

On the basis of what you have learned so far, underline all the prepositional phrases in the following sentences from "The Fall of the House of Usher" and determine what they modify. Make special note of unfamiliar elements and determine which elements are coordinated when the conjunction *and* appears.

1. But many years had elapsed since our last meeting.

2. A letter had lately reached me in a distant part of the country.

3. The MS [manuscript] gave evidence of nervous agitation.

4. The discoloration of ages had been great.

5. No portion of the masonry had fallen.

6. A servant in waiting took my horse, and I entered the Gothic archway of the hall.

7. On one of the staircases, I met the physician of the family.

8. His countenance wore a mingled expression of low cunning and perplexity.

9. Dark draperies hung upon the walls.

10. A glance at his countenance convinced me of his perfect sincerity.

Answers to Exercise 1.5

1. But many years had elapsed <u>since our last meeting</u>.
    elapsed

2. A letter had lately reached me <u>in a distant part of the country</u>.
    of the country modifies *part; in a distant part of the country* modifies *reached*

3. The MS [manuscript] gave evidence <u>of nervous agitation</u>.
    evidence

4. The discoloration <u>of ages</u> had been great.
    discoloration

5. No portion <u>of the masonry</u> had fallen.
    portion

6. A servant <u>in waiting</u> took my horse, and I entered the Gothic archway <u>of the hall</u>.
    1. *servant;* 2. *archway*

7. <u>On one of the staircases</u>, I met the physician <u>of the family</u>.
    on one of the staircases modifies *met; of the staircases* modifies *one; of the family* modifies *physician*

8. His countenance wore a mingled expression <u>of low cunning and perplexity</u>.

   expression

9. Dark draperies hung <u>upon the walls</u>.

   hung

10. A glance <u>at his countenance</u> convinced me <u>of his perfect sincerity</u>.

    1. *glance;* 2. *convinced*

The Verbal Particle

Now that we understand the workings of the prepositional phrase, we are in a good position to investigate a peculiarity of English syntax called the **verbal particle.** Let's begin by examining two sentences from John Steinbeck's short story "The Chrysanthemums":

24. Elisa . . . pulled on the gardening glove again.

25. Elisa took off her gloves. . . .

In both of these sentences, we find an element that looks prepositional in character, but that in fact is not prepositional at all. Consider Sentence (24). Does *on the gardening glove* constitute a conceptual unit? Does *the gardening glove* function as object of a preposition in this sentence?

In fact, **on the gardening glove* does *not* constitute a conceptual unit. The preposition-like entity is actually a verbal particle—a limited adverb attached to the verb itself semantically, but not physically. Particles differ from ordinary adverbs (and are therefore limited) in that they are more positionally restricted than other adverbs. Particles always *follow* the verb, although they may "jump over" the free NP that constitutes part of the predicate phrase. This property provides a nice test to determine whether the preposition-like entity is a true preposition or a verbal particle: *If the preposition-like entity can be moved to the right of an NP that follows it without resulting in gibberish, the entity is a verbal particle and not a preposition.* If it cannot be moved over a following NP, then it is a preposition, and the NP is its object. Such a movement test applied to (24) results in (26), a perfectly acceptable English sentence.

26. Elisa . . . pulled the gardening glove on.

Notice, however, that if we try to apply the same movement rule to (27a) below, the resulting string (27b) is not a possible English sentence:

27a. The strangers were getting into their Ford coupe.

27b. *The strangers were getting their Ford coupe into.

Remember, if a preposition-like entity is found following an NP as in sentence (26), or following a verb with no NP after it (see Sentence 4 in Exercise 1.6 below), it is certainly a verbal particle.

Try to determine whether Sentence (25) above contains a verbal particle or a prepositional phrase. What techniques will help you decide?

Exercise 1.6

In each of the following sentences from James Baldwin's *Going to Meet the Man*, circle the word that may be a preposition or a particle and determine which it is. When you find a preposition, underline the prepositional phrase that it heads and decide whether it is adjectival or adverbial.

1. It looks like a parody of the good, clean, faceless life.

2. Maybe a kid is lying on the rug half asleep.

3. Maybe somebody's got a kid on his lap and is absentmindedly stroking the kid's head.

4. In a moment, someone will get up and turn on the light.

5. She was quiet for a long time.

6. She stopped and took out her handkerchief and dried her eyes and looked at me.

7. She stood up from the window and came over to me.

8. On the sidewalk across from me, near the entrance to a barbecue joint, some people were holding an old-fashioned revival meeting.

9. The revival was being carried on by three sisters in black, and a brother.

10. The tambourine turned into a collection plate again.

11. The furious man dropped in his coins and vanished.

12. He stood up and walked to the window and remained silent for a long time.

13. We went to the only nightclub on a short, dark street downtown.

14. I read about it in the paper, in the subway, on my way to work.

15. I stood up and walked over to the window and looked down into the courtyard.

Answers to Exercise 1.6

Both particles and prepositions are shown in italics. Prepositional phrases are underlined; particles are only italicized.

1. It looks *like* a parody *of* the good, clean, faceless life.
   like a parody of the good, clean faceless life is adverbial; *of the good clean faceless life* is adjectival

2. Maybe a kid is lying *on* the rug half asleep.
   adverbial

3. Maybe somebody's got a kid *on* his lap and is absentmindedly stroking the kid's head.
   adverbial

4. *In* a moment, someone will get *up* and turn *on* the light.
   adverbial

5. She was quiet *for* a long time.
   adverbial

6. She stopped and took *out* her handkerchief and dried her eyes and looked *at* me.
   adverbial

7. She stood *up* *from* the window and came *over* *to* me.
   both PPs are adverbial

8. *On* the sidewalk *across from* me, *near* the entrance *to* a barbecue joint, some people were holding an old-fashioned revival meeting.
   across from me and *to a barbecue joint* are both adjectival; the larger phrases which contain these are both adverbial

9. The revival was being carried *on* *by* three sisters in black, and a brother.
   in black is adjectival; *by three sisters in black, and a brother* is adverbial

10. The tambourine turned *into* a collection plate again.
    adverbial

11. The furious man dropped *in* his coins and vanished.

12. He stood *up* and walked *to the window* and remained silent *for a long time*.

    both PPs are adverbial

13. We went *to the only nightclub on a short, dark street downtown*.

    on a short, dark street downtown is adjectival; the larger PP, which contains it, is adverbial

14. I read *about* it *in the paper*, *in the subway*, *on my way to work*.

    to work is adjectival; all the other PPs are adverbial

15. I stood *up* and walked *over to the window* and looked *down into the courtyard*.

    both PPs are adverbial

Some Problems You Probably Encountered

For most particle verbs, the verb and the particle seem to form a semantic unit. That is, although the verb phrase of a particle verb is at a minimum composed of two units, on the conceptual level there is only one idea. For example, the particle verbs in the following list have one-word paraphrases:

Particle Verb	Single Word Paraphrase
call up	telephone
give up	surrender
put on	don
stand up	rise
throw out	discard
throw up	vomit
turn off	extinguish
turn on	ignite

However, the formation of a semantic unit by a preposition-like element and a verb will not uniquely identify a lexical verb as a particle verb. Let us consider, for example, Sentence (1) from the preceding exercise:

28a. It looks like a parody of the good, clean, faceless life.

The string *looks like* forms a semantic that can be paraphrased by the verb *resembles*. However, *looks like* is *not* a particle verb. Notice that the purported particle *like* is not movable.

28b. *It looks a parody of the good, clean, faceless life like

The ungrammaticality of the string (28b) provides strong evidence that *like* is functioning as a preposition and not a particle in sentence (28a). In referring to verbs such as *looks like*, some grammarians apply the tag *prepositional verbs*, because the lexical verb can convey its meaning only when it co-occurs with a prepositional phrase introduced by a particular preposition associated with it. We shall consider prepositional verbs in more detail in Chapter Two.

An associated problem is determining the status of verbs not followed by NPs but by independent preposition-like elements. Consider Sentence (7) from the preceding exercise:

29. She stood up from the window and came over to me.

This sentence contains a pair of coordinated predicate phrases, *stood up from the window* and *came over to me*. Each of these predicate phrases has a structure that can be illustrated by the phrase structure trees below:

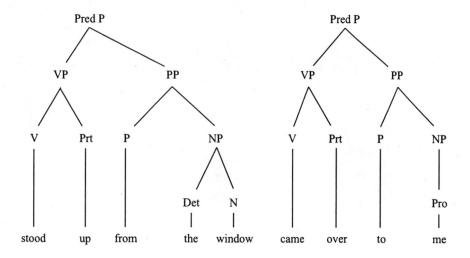

There are, of course, NPs in each of these predicate phrases, but because they are tied to prepositions in the structure we call the prepositional phrase, they are *not* available to complement the verb directly. Thus, there is no free NP over which the particle can jump in either case. Nonetheless, the verb in each predicate phrase is a particle verb. That is, if we find a preposition-like element following a verb having no *free* NP following it, then we can be certain that we have a particle verb. Particle verbs, like many other lexical verbs that we will study in the next chapter, sometimes are followed by an associated free NP—and sometimes are not.

Exercise 1.7

The following sentences come from John Steinbeck's short story "Chrysanthemums." On a separate sheet of paper, draw a phrase structure tree for each sentence. Carefully study the solutions to the first two. Make a special note of the way conjunctions are handled. (Conjunctions combine two elements of equal status into one "super" element.)

1. Elisa cast another glance toward the tractor shed.

2. She tore off the battered hat and shook out her dark pretty hair.

3. He smiled for a second.

4. He leaned confidentially over the fence.

5. Her eyes hardened with resistance.

6. He changed his tone quickly.

7. The gloves were forgotten now.

Answers to Exercise 1.7

1.

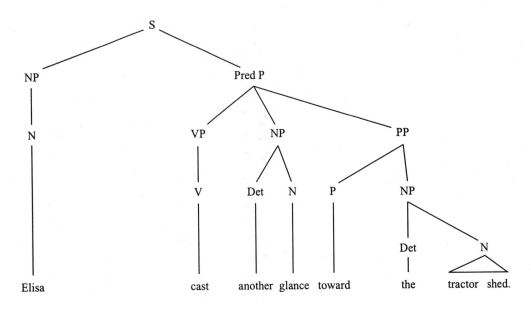

2.

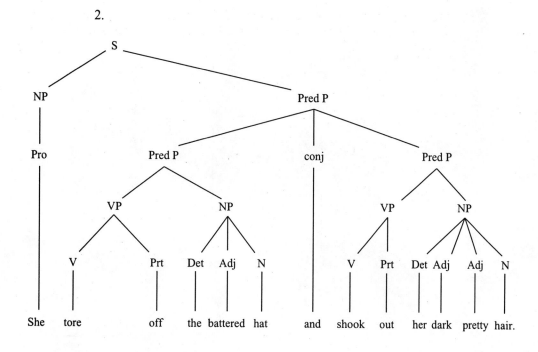

3.

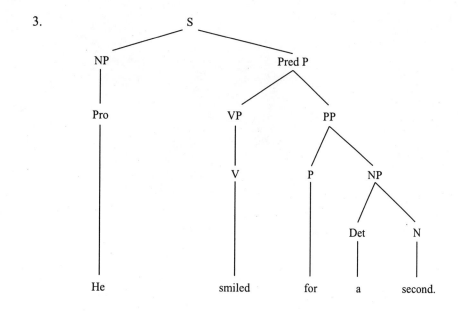

4.

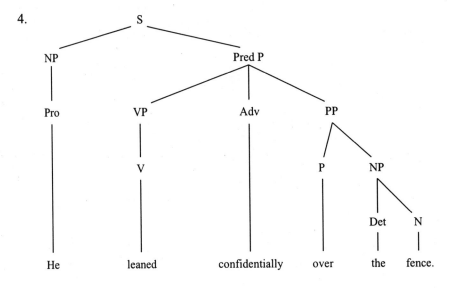

5.

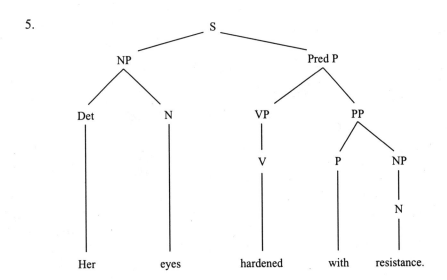

6.

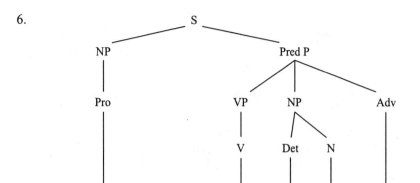

7.

Another Way of Modifying NPs—The Appositive

Sometimes an NP is modified, not by an adjective or an adjectival phrase, but by another NP that serves to rename it, or further identify or describe it. These modificational NPs are called *appositives*. They may provide limiting information about the NP **(restrictive appositives)** and follow it immediately, or they may provide additional but nonessential information about the NP **(nonrestrictive appositives)** and be set off from the head NP by commas. For example, examine the following sentence from "The Fall of the House of Usher":

30. Its proprietor, Roderick Usher, had been one of my boon companions in boyhood.

In Sentence (30), the NP *Roderick Usher,* is an appositive to *its proprietor.* It is nonrestrictive because it gives additional information about the head NP without limiting the meaning. If the appositive were omitted the sentence meaning would not change; however, the reader would not know the name of the proprietor (additional, non-essential information). Examples of both restrictive and nonrestrictive appositives occur in (31) from Jacob Bronowski's *The Ascent of Man:*

31. Among those who came to see Galileo at Arcetri was the young poet *John Milton* from England preparing for his life's work, *an epic poem.*

John Milton is a restrictive appositive to *the young poet.* After all, there may be many young poets from England. *An epic poem* is a nonrestrictive appositive to *his life's work.*

Exercise 1.8

Underline all the appositives in each of the following sentences, and in the space below each indicate whether the appositive is restrictive or nonrestrictive. These sentences come from Jung Chang's *Wild Swans.*

1. At the age of 15, my grandmother became the concubine of a warlord general, the police chief of a tenuous national government of China.

2. The liaison was arranged by her father, a clerk in the small provincial town of Yixian in southwest Manchuria, about 100 miles north of the Great Wall and 250 miles northeast of Beijing.

3. My great-grandfather, Yang Ru-shan, never had enough to buy himself a lucrative position in a big city, and by the time he was 30 he had risen no higher than senior clerk in the police station of his native Yixian, a provincial backwater.

4. My grandmother, Yu-fang, was a beauty.

5. Gen. Xue was promoted to deputy commander of the Beijing garrison, but within weeks his old ally Gen. Feng, the Christian warlord, changed sides.

6. On the seventeenth day of the third moon, in spring 1931, she gave birth to a baby girl—my mother.

7. [Dr. Xia] was not a Han Chinese, . . . but a Manchu, one of the original inhabitants of Manchuria.

8. During the summer my grandmother would put out her favorite annuals: white-edged morning glory, chrysanthemums, dahlias, and garden balsam.

9. On his departure, as on his arrival, he showered jewels on my grandmother—gold, silver, jade, pearls, and emeralds.

10. These two animals were chosen for their lucky sounds: in Chinese the words "elephant" and "high office" have the same sound . . . , as do "monkey" and "aristocracy."

Answers to Exercise 1.8

1. At the age of 15, my grandmother became the concubine of a warlord general, <u>the police chief of a tenuous national government of China</u>.

   nonrestrictive appositive to *a warlord general.* Notice that the entire complex NP functions as the appositive.

2. The liaison was arranged by her father, <u>a clerk in the small provincial town of Yixian in southwest Manchuria, about 100 miles north of the Great Wall and 250 miles northeast of Beijing</u>.

   nonrestrictive appositive to *her father.* Because the phrase beginning with *about* nonrestrictively modifies *Manchuria,* it is part of the NP that includes *Manchuria,* and similar observations can be made for the other prepositional phrases in the appositive NP.

3. My great-grandfather, <u>Yang Ru-shan</u>, never had enough to buy himself a lucrative position in a big city, and by the time he was 30 he had risen no higher than senior clerk in the police station of his native Yixian, <u>a provincial backwater</u>.

   Yang Ru-shan is a nonrestrictive appositive to *my great-grandfather; a provincial backwater* is a nonrestrictive appositive to *Yixian.*

4. My grandmother, <u>Yu-fang</u>, was a beauty.

   nonrestrictive appositive to *my grandmother.*

5. Gen. Xue was promoted to deputy commander of the Beijing garrison, but within weeks his old ally <u>Gen. Feng, the Christian warlord</u>, changed sides.

   This one is rather complex: *Gen. Feng, the Christian warlord* is a restrictive appositive to *his old ally; the Christian warlord* is a nonrestrictive appositive to *Gen. Feng.*

6. On the seventeenth day of the third moon, in spring 1931, she gave birth to a baby girl—<u>my mother</u>.

   nonrestrictive appositive to *a baby girl.*

7. [Dr. Xia] was not a Han Chinese, . . . but a Manchu, <u>one of the original inhabitants of Manchuria</u>.

   nonrestrictive appositive to *a Manchu.*

8. During the summer my grandmother would put out her favorite annuals: <u>white-edged morning glory, chrysanthemums, dahlias, and garden balsam</u>.

   nonrestrictive appositive to *her favorite annuals.*

9. On his departure, as on his arrival, he showered jewels on my grandmother—<u>gold, silver, jade, pearls, and emeralds</u>.

   nonrestrictive appositive to *jewels.*

10. These two animals were chosen for their lucky sounds: in Chinese the words <u>"elephant" and "high office"</u> have the same sound . . . , as do "monkey" and "aristocracy."

    restrictive appositive to *words.*

Terms Used in Chapter One

adjective: a word that modifies a noun.

adjectival: a phrase that may or may not contain an adjective, but that functions to modify a noun.

adverb: a word that modifies a verb, adjective, or another adverb.

adverbial: a phrase that may or may not contain an adverb, but that functions to modify a verb, adjective, or adverb.

antecedent: the particular noun phrase to which a pronoun points.

article: one of the function words *the* and *a (an)* that often begin noun phrases.

asterisk notation: the use of an asterisk in front of a string of words to show that the string does not constitute an acceptable phrase or sentence.

auxiliary: a helping verb that has little inherent meaning.

complement: a phrase that serves to "complete" another entity because without the complement the entity has little meaning.

demonstrative: one of the function words *this* and *that* or their plural forms *these* and *those.*

determiner: those function words such as articles and demonstratives that introduce noun phrases.

free NP: a noun phrase that is not caught up being the object of a preposition.

function word: a word signaling primarily grammatical information, such as a preposition or a conjunction.

head: the chief or defining element of a phrase—e.g., a noun is the head of a noun phrase.

indefinite pronoun: a pronoun without a specific antecedent, e.g., *someone.*

inflected: the property of a word that allows it to indicate its function, usually via a suffix.

lexical verb: the verb within a verb phrase that indicates a specific action or state.

modifier: a word or phrase that limits or describes another word or phrase.

nonrestrictive: the property of providing additional, but nonessential information. Only modifiers may be nonrestrictive.

noun phrase (NP): a phrase whose head element is a noun. It may also include a determiner and adjectives.

object: a noun phrase or its equivalent that enters into a relationship with a preceding verb or preposition.

phrase: a sequence of words functioning as a unit.

phrase structure tree: a schematic representation of a sentence.

possessive pronoun: a pronoun inflected to show that the pronoun possesses the noun that follows, e.g., *his, its, their.*

predicate: when used as a verb (i.e., *to predicate*), to predicate is to assert an action or a quality of an entity.

predicate phrase: the part of the sentence that includes the verb, its auxiliaries and modifiers, and any noun phrases or other constructions required by the verb.

preposition: a word or group of words functioning as a unit that signals a relationship of time, space, or association between the noun phrase that follows it and some other entity in the sentence.

pronoun: a function word that replaces a noun phrase on subsequent mention of the noun phrase.

referent: the real-world entity to which a word refers.

restrictive: the property of providing essential and limiting information. Only modifiers may be restrictive.

sentence constituents: the major structural divisions within a sentence.

subject: the noun phrase that serves as the prime topic in a sentence—often the instigator of the action or experiencer of the state.

syntax: the arrangement of words in a sentence.

verb phrase: a structural unit containing a lexical verb and any auxiliaries or particles associated with it.

verbal particle: a word, usually selected from the class of prepositions, that has lost its prepositional function and behaves instead as a component of the verb phrase.

Chapter Quiz

Part I. On a separate sheet of paper, draw phrase structure trees for each of the following sentences from Dr. Seuss's *The Five Hundred Hats of Bartholomew Cubbins.*

1. A pleasant breeze whistled through the feather in his hat.

2. The sound of silver trumpets rang through the air.

3. Hoof beats clattered on the cobbled streets.

4. Bartholomew quickly snatched off the hat.

5. The executioner leaned across the chopping block and flipped off Bartholomew's hat. (Be careful to deal with the conjunction.)

Part II. Underline the appositive in each of the following sentences from Amy Tan's *The Joy Luck Club,* and indicate whether it is restrictive or nonrestrictive.

6. And Auntie Lin, my mother's best friend, moves to the turquoise sofa, crosses her arms, and watches the men still seated at the table.

7. And next to it is a floor lamp, a long black pole with three oval spotlights attached like the broad leaves of a rubber plant.

8. [T]he other bag contained the most ridiculous clothes, all new: bright California-style beachwear, baseball caps, cotton pants with elastic waists, bomber jackets, Stanford sweatshirts, crew socks.

9. I was one month older than Waverly Jong, Auntie Lin's prized daughter.

10. But he could not stop my mother from giving me her *chang,* a necklace made out of a tablet of red jade.

Chapter Two

An Outline of the English Verb Phrase

Introduction

With our understanding of the workings of the basic English sentence as background, we are ready to turn our attention to the most important element inside the predicate phrase—the verb phrase. As you already know, the VP consists of a lexical (meaningful) verb preceded by perhaps one or more auxiliary (helping) verbs. Sometimes a VP-based adverb will occur within the VP itself. A verb phrase may consist, then, of a single word (such as *walked*) or of several words (such as *was not eating*).

To begin, we need to be certain that we understand the verb and its function. In general, a verb is a word that specifies an action or a state. That fact alone does not make a word a verb, however. Strictly speaking, a verb is a word that may be inflected (systematically varied via suffixes) for *tense* or *aspect* (i.e., varied for conditions of time). We will learn more about tense and aspect in the pages ahead.

Let's begin our analysis of verbs by looking first at lexical verbs—those verbs that actually have a meaning in themselves. There are three major categories of lexical verbs in English: **transitive** verbs, **intransitive** verbs, and **copular** (linking) verbs.

Structurally speaking, **transitive verbs** are verbs that are followed by at least one free NP (that is, an NP not already bound to a preposition within a prepositional phrase). Semantically speaking, this free NP indicates a sentence participant directly affected by the action expressed in the verb itself. Moreover, this NP does not serve as a descriptor of the first NP of the sentence (from now on, to be called the *subject*), although it may be a **reflexive pronoun** (a pronoun ending in *-self*).

A sentence whose verb is transitive typically indicates that an **agent** is doing something to someone or something, as in Sentence (1) below:

1. Horatio sliced the bread.

A partial phrase structure tree for this sentence indicates that within the predicate phrase, a free NP follows the VP:

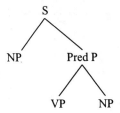

Moreover, the NP in the predicate phrase is in no way equivalent to the subject NP; that is, *bread* is not an alternate label for *Horatio,* but is in fact the sentence element affected by Horatio's action (we can call *bread* the "affected participant").

Sentence (1) demonstrates what might be called the *prototypical transitive event.* Semantically speaking, it conveys the notion that an actor brings about a change of state in some other entity. Not all cases of transitivity are so clear-cut, however. A verb that expresses the notion of an action performed by an agent is a clearer example of transitivity than one that does not. Therefore (1) provides a better example of a transitive verb than either (2) or (3):

2. My cat had five kittens.

3. The research involved dolphins.

Nonetheless, even though (2) and (3) do not precisely fit the semantics of transitivity, syntactically they are transitive sentences. Each has a free NP in the predicate phrase that is clearly distinct from the subject NP.

Intransitive verbs are not followed by free NPs in the predicate phrase. A sentence whose verb is intransitive indicates that a subject NP is doing something that directly affects only itself, as (4) will illustrate:

4. Horatio slept.

The addition of adverbials to such sentences does not affect the status of the verb. In (5), the VP remains intransitive.

5. Horatio restlessly slept on the sofa for a long time.

Copular verbs typically are followed by an NP or adjective that either assigns the subject NP to a class, as in Sentence (6), or assigns an attribute to the subject, as in (7):

6. Horatio is a baker.

7. Horatio is competent.

Notice that *baker* is not an affected participant in the same sense as *bread* in the transitive example. It is more nearly a class to which *Horatio* belongs. And of course *competent* is not an NP at all, but an adjective assigning an attribute to *Horatio*.

The status of a verb with respect to its transitivity or copularity cannot generally be determined by examining the verb in isolation. In other words, we cannot simply draw up a list of verbs for each category and memorize the resulting charts. In order to ascertain the status of a given verb, we must examine that verb in relation to the other elements occurring with it in the predicate phrase and determine the relationship of these elements to the subject of the sentence. Consider, for example, the use of the verb *grow* in each of the following sentences:

8. Mary grew tomatoes in her garden.

9. The tomatoes grew rapidly.

10. The tomatoes grew ripe in the warm sunshine.

Let's consider these sentences and the elements within them. How, for example, does the character of the verb change in each sentence? Does the verb shift from lexical category to lexical category? If so, which use is transitive, which intransitive, and which copular? How did you make your decisions? Think carefully about these questions before going on.

An Analysis of Verb Type

If you are beginning to think in a syntactically motivated way, you will have recognized that the verb *grew* changes somewhat from sentence to sentence. In fact, you may wonder how a single word can seem so different. The answer is not an obvious one, nor is it likely that you have given this problem much thought previously. After all, language is an embedded skill. In other words, we rarely pay much attention to language itself but concentrate instead on the events and interactions to which language is attached. (Have you ever noticed how paying attention to the *way* people speak, perhaps their accents or their pronunciation, causes you to lose track of *what* they are saying?) Now we must acquire a new approach to language; we must reflect on its structure.

Yes, *grew* is a verb, and if one were to attempt to determine its meaning, one would probably say that it is the past form of a word indicating "increase" or "change in a positive direction." That definition is essentially correct and belongs to a part of language that language scholars call **semantics.** There is another level of meaning, however, and that is **relational meaning**—the meaning achieved by a word through its relationship to other words with which it occurs. Relational meaning is brought about through syntax, which is an essential feature of language. How much words in themselves mean is an open question; words in isolation seem to have little existence outside of the dictionary. It is through the grammatical relations given by the syntax of the language that words come to achieve their status as a bona fide part of human language. So, just what does syntax do for the verb *grew* in Sentences (8)–(10)?

In Sentence (8), we find three elements within the predicate phrase: the verb phrase *grew,* the NP *tomatoes,* and the prepositional phrase *in her garden.* We discover that the free NP *tomatoes* does not constitute an identification of the subject NP *Mary.* On the purely syntactic level, then, *tomatoes* is an NP free to interact directly with the VP. These two details fit the criteria for transitivity in English and provide sufficient evidence that the verb is in fact transitive. Notice that in this sentence, *Mary* emerges as an "agent"—or at least a facilitator—whereas *tomatoes* is an NP clearly affected by Mary's intervention. *Tomatoes* is an "affected participant."

The situation in Sentence (9), on the other hand, is somewhat different. The predicate phrase of this sentence contains a VP followed by a lone adverb (rapidly). We have here the classic intransitive situation: The subject NP *tomatoes* is doing something that does not affect another NP in the sentence, if for no other reason than there is no other NP for it to affect. In spite of that fact, the string is a wholly acceptable English sentence. Moreover, one can observe that the subject is in some sense both the instigator of activity *and* the affected participant. This relational evidence clearly points to an intransitive usage of *grew* in sentence (9).

Sentence (10) provides us with yet another possibility for *grew.* As in Sentence (9), we find no free NP to interact with the VP. We do discover, however, an adjective that assigns an attribute *(ripe)* to the subject NP *the tomatoes.* All evidence points then to a copular usage of *grew* in this case.

Using the Decision Procedure

Figure 2–1 is a decision procedure that you can use to determine the transitivity of verb phrases. This tool should be used only in the beginning of your endeavors, since applying it to more complicated sentences may result in error. Think of it as you would a set of training wheels on a bicycle: useful in the beginning, but not over the long haul.

To use the decision procedure, begin in the upper left-hand corner and ask yourself the yes/no questions given in the diamond boxes. Follow the arrow that represents your answers and continue until you reach a stop sign. Occasionally you may encounter a verb whose transitivity may be uncertain. In these cases, the application of a grammatical rule called *passivization* may help you make your determination. Here's how it works. Imagine that you have a sentence such as

"The Irish comprise 10 percent of the population of New York City." It may seem to you that *10 percent of the population of New York City* constitutes a class for the subject NP, and thus you would think the VP *comprise* copular. However, we can interchange the position of the subject and the predicate phrase NP by making the sentence *passive:* "10 percent of the population of New York City is comprised of the Irish." *This sort of change indicates that the original* VP comprise *is transitive, because only transitive verbs may occur in the passive form.* To make a sentence **passive,** interchange the subject and the predicate phrase NP, add the auxiliary *be* to the VP and, in general, add *-ed* to the lexical verb; finally insert the preposition *by,* or occasionally *of,* in front of the original subject NP. Thus, "The chicken crossed the road" becomes "The road was crossed by the chicken." See Figure 2–1.

Figure 2–1

Decision Process for Determination of the Transitivity of Verb Phrases

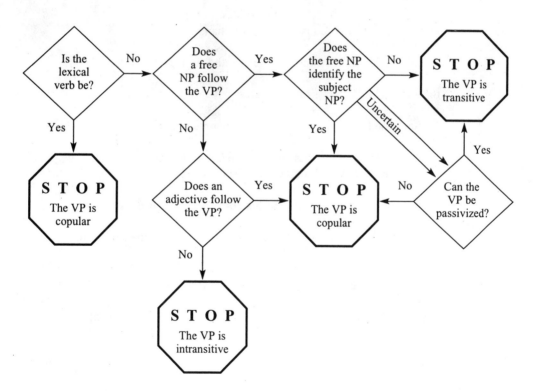

Exercise 2.1

The following sentences appeared in Chapter 1, so you can use the information you have already discovered about them to assist you in this exercise. Underline the verb phrase (or verb phrases in cases of coordinated elements) and, in the space below each sentence, write whether the VP is *transitive, intransitive,* or *copular.* Keep in mind that what you underline here would have appeared under VP in the trees you drew in Chapter 1. Remember, too, that NPs functioning as objects of prepositions are not free to interact directly with the VP in the predicate phrase. In addition, when a sentence has more than one VP, you must evaluate each VP individually (this situation will arise when you have two VPs or predicate phrases combined through the use of a conjunction).

1. The big windows fool no one.

2. She was humming an old church song.

3. She was crying again.

4. A man fumbled in his pockets for change.

5. In a moment, someone will get up and turn on the light.

6. She was quiet for a long time.

7. She stood up from the window and came over to me.

8. On the sidewalk across from me, near the entrance to a barbecue joint, some people were holding an old-fashioned revival meeting.

9. The furious man dropped in his coins and vanished.

10. He stood up and walked to the window and remained silent for a long time.

11. But many years had elapsed since our last meeting.

12. A letter, however, had lately reached me in a distant part of the country.

13. The MS gave evidence of nervous agitation.

14. The discoloration of ages had been great.

15. No portion of the masonry had fallen.

16. A servant in waiting took my horse, and I entered the Gothic archway of the hall.

17. On one of the staircases, I met the physician of the family.

18. His countenance wore a mingled expression of low cunning and perplexity.

19. He smiled for a second.

20. Her eyes hardened with resistance.

Answers to Exercise 2.1.

1. The big windows <u>fool</u> no one.
   transitive

2. She <u>was humming</u> an old church song.
   transitive

3. She <u>was crying</u> again.
   intransitive

4. A man <u>fumbled</u> in his pockets for change.
   intransitive

5. In a moment, someone <u>will get up</u> and <u>turn on</u> the light.
   1. intransitive; 2. transitive

6. She <u>was</u> quiet for a long time.
   copular

7. She <u>stood up</u> from the window and <u>came over</u> to me.
   1. intransitive; 2. intransitive

8. On the sidewalk across from me, near the entrance to a barbecue joint, some people <u>were holding</u> an old-fashioned revival meeting.
   transitive

9. The furious man <u>dropped in</u> his coins and <u>vanished</u>.
   1. transitive; 2. intransitive

10. He <u>stood up</u> and <u>walked</u> to the window and <u>remained</u> silent for a long time.
    1. intransitive; 2. intransitive; 3. copular

11. But many years <u>had elapsed</u> since our last meeting.
    intransitive

12. A letter, however, <u>had lately reached</u> me in a distant part of the country.

    transitive

13. The MS <u>gave</u> evidence of nervous agitation.

    transitive

14. The discoloration of ages <u>had been</u> great.

    copular

15. No portion of the masonry <u>had fallen</u>.

    intransitive

16. A servant in waiting <u>took</u> my horse, and I <u>entered</u> the Gothic archway of the hall.

    1. transitive; 2. transitive

17. On one of the staircases, I <u>met</u> the physician of the family.

    transitive

18. His countenance <u>wore</u> a mingled expression of low cunning and perplexity.

    transitive

19. He <u>smiled</u> for a second.

    intransitive

20. Her eyes <u>hardened</u> with resistance.

    intransitive

The Principal Parts of English Verbs

Treatments of English grammar have traditionally provided the specification of the *principal* (or elemental) *parts* of each verb, regardless of the verb's status with respect to transitivity. These parts are called the *infinitive,* the *past,* the *present participle,* and the *past participle.*

The **infinitive** is the barest form of the verb, having no "endings" or suffixes attached. Essentially, an infinitive is the form you are likely to think of first if you are asked to provide a particular verb. That is, if you were asked to list verbs that indicate locomotion on the part of human beings, you would probably think of forms such as *walk, run, move, jog, jump, hop,* etc. It is not likely that forms such as *walks, moved,* and so on would have occurred to you. The *uninflected* form—the form with no grammatical suffixes—is the basic form to which specific **inflections** may be appended.

The **past** is the form of the verb which indicates past time **(past tense)**. For the overwhelming majority of English verbs, the past form consists of the infinitive form with the inflection *-ed* attached: *walked, moved, jogged, hopped, jumped,* etc. However, a small but quite important number of verbs signal past tense through a change in the vowel of the infinitive form. Here are a few of them:

Infinitive	Past Tense
choose	chose
come	came
draw	drew
eat	ate
fall	fell
grow	grew
hide	hid
ride	rode
ring	rang
shake	shook
sink	sank
sit	sat
swim	swam
throw	threw
write	wrote

Some others signal past tense through a more radical change in the infinitive, for example:

bring	brought
buy	bought
catch	caught
leave	left
say	said
stand	stood
tell	told

And still others do not change form at all. The pastness of the verb must be determined from context, for example:

burst	burst
cut	cut
fit	fit
hit	hit
let	let
set	set

Verbs that form the past through the addition of -ed to the infinitive are often called *regular* verbs; those that signal past through some other process are generally called *irregular*. English grammarians generally use different nomenclature, however. For them, the "regular verbs" are **weak** verbs, whereas the "irregular" ones are **strong**. If you examine the partial list of irregular verbs given above, you will notice that they typically describe ordinary everyday activities. These words constitute some of the oldest words in the English language, and because they describe the everyday and the commonplace, they are highly frequent. Their frequency of use has helped them retain the older English process (in fact, a **Germanic** process) of changing tense by internal sound change and thus resist the widespread (and more recent) process of adding -ed. This resistance has led to their being dubbed *strong* verbs. By contrast, then, regular verbs are *weak*.

The **present participle** is the infinitive form with the suffix -ing added to it. All verbs—weak and strong, transitive, intransitive, and copular—form the present participle in the same way: *running, eating, living, thinking,* etc.

The **past participle** looks exactly like the past tense for all weak (regular) verbs and for some strong (irregular) verbs: *walked, moved, jumped, brought, caught, said,* etc. Occasionally, a strong verb will have a special form for the past participle: *eaten, written, thrown, chosen, fallen, ridden, shaken, rung, gone,* etc. Regardless of form, however, the past participle differs from the past syntactically in one of its uses in that it combines with the auxiliary verb *have* to create what is sometimes called a compound tense (*have eaten, have fallen, had gone,* and so on); the past tense, in contrast, uses no auxiliary in affirmative contexts. The past participle of transitive verbs combines with the auxiliary verb *be* to form the *passive voice,* which we will soon examine in detail.

The present participle and past participle of verbs sometimes function in pre-noun adjective slots as straightforward adjectives, for example:

11. The *climbing* monkey reached the top of the tree.

12. The *weakened* building crumbled after the strong aftershock.

Sometimes, the present participle may serve as a simple noun:

13. *Jogging* is good aerobic exercise.

Many grammarians call present participles functioning as nouns **gerunds.**

The Auxiliary

A critically important element in English verb phrases is the auxiliary, even though not all VPs have one. However, when one or more auxiliaries do appear in an English sentence, the first to occur will take over many of the responsibilities of the verb itself. That is, the first auxiliary will **agree** with the subject in person and number, and the auxiliary verb, not the lexical verb, will be inflected for tense. Before we get too far into these issues, let us see just what sorts of elements function as auxiliary verbs in English.

English auxiliary verbs can be divided into two basic subclasses, *primary auxiliaries* and *modal auxiliaries.* The class of **primary auxiliaries** includes the verbs *be, have,* and *do,* which are all irregular verbs. That means that the different forms of each of these verbs are created by processes that differ from the highly principled formation processes used for the vast majority of English verbs. In fact, these verbs are even more irregular than other irregular (strong) verbs. The past of *be,* for example, is formed neither by the addition of -ed to the infinitive (thus the unacceptability of **beed*), nor by the change of a vowel; instead, *was* and *were* are the past forms of this verb. Even the present tense involves radical change from the infinitive: *am, are, is. Have* and *do* are somewhat less idiosyncratic; they form the past in irregular ways *(had, did),* and even the third person singular of their present tense is irregular *(has, does).* Still, we can see the relationship of these irregular forms to the infinitive. Each of the primary auxiliaries has important work to do in English sentences, as we shall see.

In contrast to the primary auxiliaries, the **modal auxiliaries** are invariant in form. Tense, person, and number are not indicated by change in the form of the modal at all, nor in the lexical verb that co-occurs with it—only the infinitive of a lexical verb may be supported by a modal auxiliary. Modal auxiliaries include the following: *can, could, will, would, shall, should, may, might,* and *must.* Moreover, if a verb phrase includes a modal auxiliary, the modal is always the first auxiliary, no matter how many other auxiliaries also appear. In addition, modal auxiliaries cannot be chained together. For example, (14), (15), and (16) are permissible verb phrases in Standard Written English:

14. may have left

15. must have been eating

16. should have been being interviewed

but (17)–(21) are not:

17. *have may leave

18. *have must be eating

19. *have should be being interviewed

20. *may can leave

21. *might must return

The ungrammaticality of strings such as (20) and (21) would seem to leave English without the flexibility to express more than one modal notion at a time. However, English gets around this problem in an interesting way, through the use of devices called *periphrastic* forms. Most of the modals have associated with them a paraphrase—a multi-word equivalent—that allows a speaker or writer to express notions that are syntactically disallowed by constraints on modal syntax. For example, (20) and (21) above may quite acceptably be rendered as (22) and (23):

22. may *be able to* leave

23. might *have to* return

Below is a list of the common modals and their corresponding paraphrases.

Modal	Paraphrase
can, could	be able to
shall, will	be going to
should	ought to
must	have to

Functions of the Primary Auxiliaries

Each of the primary auxiliaries combines with a form of the lexical verb to produce a VP that signals specific nuances of meaning. You have learned already that the auxiliary *have* combines with the past participle of a lexical verb to create a kind of past form. But the pastness of a verb such as *have eaten* is quite different from the pastness of a verb such as *ate*. A speaker is far more likely to use the *have* form to communicate a past event that has some relevance to a current point of reference. For example, suppose someone invites you to lunch. If you refuse, you might say, "No thanks. I have already eaten." This response implies that you had lunch (a recent past event), and not that you ate dinner last night (a more remote past event). The exact nuances of meaning associated with the *have* + past participle form of the verb phrase are matters of **semantics** (meaning) and **pragmatics** (language use), and need not concern us here, for we are dealing with syntax—the combining properties of words and phrases. What *is* relevant to the syntactic approach and of interest is that the auxiliary *have* always combines with the past participle of any lexical verb, regardless of its classification with respect to transitivity.

Like the modals, the auxiliary *do* combines with the infinitive of the lexical verb, but it typically surfaces only in particular syntactic circumstances: *do* is used to make an auxiliary-less sentence negative and to turn a statement lacking an auxiliary into a question, as well as to add emphasis, as we shall see in a while. For example, examine the various forms for Sentence (24):

24a. Horatio sliced the bread.

24b. Horatio did not slice the bread.

24c. Did Horatio slice the bread?

Because the verb phrase of the affirmative declarative sentence given in Example (24a) is in the past tense, the corresponding negative (24b) and interrogative (24c) sentences also have past tense verb phrases. But since (24a) has no auxiliary, (24b) and (24c) require the *do* auxiliary, and it is this verb, not the lexical verb, which is inflected for past tense (thus the form *did,* the past of the strong verb *do*). Notice that the appearance of the *do* auxiliary requires a change in the form of the lexical verb. Whereas the verb *sliced* in (24a) is inflected for tense (and thus is **finite**), the verb *slice* that appears in both (24b) and (24c) is not; in form, it is an infinitive.

The resemblance of *do* to the modals ends with this requirement, however. Not only does the *do* auxiliary have no real meaning beyond its syntactic function, it also must be inflected for person, number, and tense. In addition, if a sentence already has an auxiliary, *do* cannot appear. Thus, if a sentence has the auxiliary *have* in the affirmative declarative version, it cannot take the auxiliary *do* to signal negation or interrogation, as the examples in (25) amply demonstrate. That is, if we have Sentence (25a):

25a. Horatio has sliced the pie.

it would be rendered in the negative as Sentence (25b), and not Sentence (25c):

25b. Horatio has not sliced the pie.

25c. *Horatio does not have sliced the pie.

The same sentence is converted to a question by inverting (or interchanging) the auxiliary *has* and the subject NP *Horatio:*

25d. Has Horatio sliced the pie?

We do not typically use *do* in the affirmative declarative mode, except for emphasis. *Do* will appear as an auxiliary in an affirmative declarative sentence if a speaker or writer wishes to contradict or clarify a previous statement. For example, imagine a scenario in which Amanda and Gertrude are preparing a buffet dinner, with the help of their friend Horatio. Most of the food has been set out, but they are still preparing the desserts. An apple pie that previously has been mentioned has once again become the topic of discussion. The following conversation ensues:

> AMANDA: Now, where did that pie get off to?
>
> GERTRUDE: Horatio took it into the kitchen. He was going to slice it.
>
> AMANDA: I'll bet! Horatio is probably digging into that pie right now.
>
> GERTRUDE: Nonsense, Amanda. Horatio *did* slice the pie. I saw him doing it myself.

The *Be* Auxiliary

We come now to what is probably the most important auxiliary in English, *be*. The most irregular verb in English, the forms for *be* generally look nothing like the infinitive. The forms of *be* are as follows: *be, am, is, are, was, were, being,* and *been.* If you do not recognize these forms as variants of the verb *be,* it is *essential* that you memorize them.

The principal use of the *be* auxiliary is as a *tense, person,* and *number* carrier for the *progressive aspect.* To avoid becoming too mystified by these technical terms, you should familiarize yourself with the following explanations.

Tense

Tense is an inflection on a verb that indicates whether an event is *present* or *past.* Only these two tenses are indicated by inflectional suffixes in English, and only the past tense inflection (*-ed* for weak verbs) consistently appears regardless of person and number (see below). In most instances, the present tense of the verb is indistinguishable from the bare infinitive, with one exception: When the subject

NP can be replaced by the pronouns *he, she,* or *it* (i.e., when it is *third person singular,* as described below), the present tense is indicated by the inflection *-s* or *-es.* Although we use the term "present" to describe this tense, the simple present tense does not usually indicate present time. In fact, with the exception of verbs of mental experience such as *know, think, believe, hope,* and *want,* verbs that carry the present tense inflection typically signal habitual or usual behavior. If I say, for example, *Mary drives to work,* I do not mean that she is driving in her car right now. English accomplishes this meaning in other ways, through the progressive, which we will soon discuss.

A common myth about English is that it has a future tense. Although English can express futurity, the future is indicated through the use of the modals *will* or *shall,* or their periphrastic equivalent *be going to,* or through the use of some present form accompanied by appropriate adverbs or adverbial phrases (e.g., *I leave for Europe on Wednesday.*). There is not, however, a future inflection similar to the past and present tenses in the English language.

Person

Person is a property of verbs and of pronouns that indicates whether the subject NP (in the case of verbs) or the antecedent (in the case of pronouns) is the speaker or writer *(first person),* the addressee *(second person),* or the entity spoken about *(third person).* Typical subject pronouns are *I* (first person), *you* (second person), or *she* (third person).

Number

Number is a property of verbs, and of nouns, and of pronouns. It indicates whether an entity is singular (one) or plural (more than one). In the present tense of most third-person verbs, singular number is marked by adding *-s* or *-es* to the infinitive, e.g., *runs, eats, walks. Be* is a special case, however, because it distinguishes number in both the present and past tenses:

Present		**Past**	
singular	plural	singular	plural
am	are	was	were
is			

Note that there is no singular form for the second person, present or past tense of *be.* Perhaps it is more accurate to say that there is no distinction in written English between singular and plural forms of the second person. In any case, the plural verb form is always used with *you.*

Aspect

Aspect is a particularly important property of English verb phrases, but you have probably never heard of it before because most authors of grammar texts call it *tense*. **Aspect** indicates the nature of events, whether they are ongoing *(progressive)*, complete *(perfective)*, habitual, or happening at a single point in time *(punctual)*. Here is a real-life explanation to help you understand the difference between tense and aspect. My dog, like virtually all dogs, becomes quite excited when I return home after an absence. She will jump up and down, wag her tail, and attempt to lick me. One day, I went out the front door of my house to take out the trash. I was probably gone for a minute or less. When I reentered the house, Susie-Pooch displayed the usual exuberant greeting behavior she exhibits when I return from work or from a shopping expedition. My husband chuckled, "Susie-Pooch, you silly dog! Mommy has only been gone for a minute." I replied, "You're the silly one; she doesn't understand tense—only aspect." What I meant was that the time elapsed since I had left was not significant to the dog, but the nature of the event was. She understood that I had reentered the house.

Many aspectual notions are inherent in the particular lexical verb one uses, but only some are *grammaticalized,* that is, appear as an inflection on the verb. The most important grammaticalized aspect is the **progressive,** which occurs as an inflection on the lexical verb in English verb phrases: *The suffix -ing attached to a lexical verb indicates that an event is or was ongoing. This aspect is called the English progressive.* English verb forms bearing the *-ing* inflection are called **present participles.**

The English progressive occurs frequently, but it does not occur alone. You see, English inflections all occur on the ends of words, as suffixes, and English does not allow suffixes to pile up, one after the other, as many other languages do. Instead, English allows one inflection per word. When the inflectional slot on an English verb already is filled by the progressive inflection, English must look elsewhere to indicate the obligatory categories (i.e., notions that must be explicitly indicated for a sentence to be grammatical) of *tense* and *person* in the verb phrase. English had to find a way to carry these categories, and it did so by pressing into service the auxiliary *be*. Thus, when *be* co-occurs with the present participle of an English verb, *be* is inflected for person, number, and tense (categories conflated into single inflections, for the most part) and the lexical verb is inflected for aspect. Together they signal an ongoing activity.

A second important grammaticalized aspect is the **perfective,** signaled via the past participle of the lexical verb, together with the auxiliary *have,* which is inflected for tense, and perhaps person and number. The English perfective generally indicates a past time that has some relevance to another event that is more recent. For example, *I have eaten* is more likely to be used to refer to the recent past than is *I ate.* And when one event precedes another in the past, we say something such as the following: *By the time he arrived, I had already left.*

Analyzing Verb Phrases

You have seen the following sentences in Exercise 2.1. This time, I have underlined the verb phrase (or verb phrases, in cases of coordinated elements) and have described the verb phrase in terms of person, tense, number, and aspect, and whether a modal occurs. I have indicated whether the lexical verb is weak or strong. You will notice that not all categories apply to all verbs; only explicit inflections are noted.

26. The big windows <u>fool</u> no one.
Weak verb; present tense. Note that the verb is *uninflected* for number and person. We can tell that the verb is *not* third person singular, but beyond that we cannot say what it is, inflectionally speaking.

27. She <u>was humming</u> an old church song.
Weak verb; past tense, progressive aspect, singular. The auxiliary *was* is not specifically inflected for person, since this form can occur with first or third person singular.

28. She <u>was crying</u> again.
Weak verb; past tense, progressive aspect, singular.

29. A man <u>fumbled</u> in his pockets for change.
Weak verb; past tense. Weak verbs inflected for past tense are *not* also inflected for person and number.

30. In a moment, someone <u>will get up</u> and <u>turn on</u> the light.
Get up is strong; *turn on* is weak. These VPs share the auxiliary *will;* they have a modal only and no tense, since modals are invariant. These VPs are uninflected for aspect, but they could be (e.g., *will be getting up*).

Exercise 2.2

The following sentences appeared in Exercise 2.1. This time, underline the verb phrase (or verb phrases in cases of coordinated elements) and in the space below each sentence, describe the verb phrase in terms of person, tense, number, aspect, and whether a modal occurs. Indicate whether the lexical verb is weak or strong. (*Note:* Not all categories apply to all verbs; look for explicit inflections. Examine grammatical aspect rather than lexicalized [word-inherent] aspect.)

1. She was quiet for a long time.

2. She stood up from the window and came over to me.

3. On the sidewalk across from me, near the entrance to a barbecue joint, some people were holding an old-fashioned revival meeting.

4. The furious man dropped in his coins and vanished.

5. He stood up and walked to the window and remained silent for a long time.

6. But many years had elapsed since our last meeting.

7. A letter, however, had lately reached me in a distant part of the country.

8. The MS gave evidence of nervous agitation.

9. The discoloration of ages had been great.

10. No portion of the masonry had fallen.

11. A servant in waiting took my horse, and I entered the Gothic archway of the hall.

12. On one of the staircases, I met the physician of the family.

13. His countenance wore a mingled expression of low cunning and perplexity.

14. He smiled for a second.

15. Her eyes hardened with resistance.

Answers to Exercise 2.2

1. She <u>was</u> quiet for a long time.
   strong verb; past tense, singular

2. She <u>stood up</u> from the window and <u>came over</u> to me.
   1. strong verb, past tense; 2. strong verb, past tense

3. On the sidewalk across from me, near the entrance to a barbecue joint, some people <u>were holding</u> an old-fashioned revival meeting.
   strong verb, past tense, progressive aspect, plural

4. The furious man <u>dropped in</u> his coins and <u>vanished</u>.
   1. weak verb, past tense; 2. weak, past

5. He <u>stood up</u> and <u>walked</u> to the window and <u>remained</u> silent for a long time.
   1. strong, past; 2. weak, past; 3. weak, past

6. But many years <u>had elapsed</u> since our last meeting.

   weak, past tense, perfective aspect. The verb *elapsed* is particularly interesting because its semantics will only allow third person subjects; however, the VP here carries no third person inflections.

7. A letter, however, <u>had lately reached</u> me in a distant part of the country.

   weak, past tense, perfective aspect

8. The MS <u>gave</u> evidence of nervous agitation.

   strong, past

9. The discoloration of ages <u>had been</u> great.

   strong, past, perfective

10. No portion of the masonry <u>had fallen</u>.

    strong, past, perfective

11. A servant in waiting <u>took</u> my horse, and I <u>entered</u> the Gothic archway of the hall.

    1. strong, past; 2. weak, past

12. On one of the staircases, I <u>met</u> the physician of the family.

    strong, past

13. His countenance <u>wore</u> a mingled expression of low cunning and perplexity.

    strong, past

14. He <u>smiled</u> for a second.

    weak, past

15. Her eyes <u>hardened</u> with resistance.

    weak, past

Voice

There is one other important usage of the *be* auxiliary—the *passive voice.* As you now know, lexical verbs may be transitive, intransitive, or copular. And you know that a typically transitive event is one in which an agent brings about a change of state in some entity through the action of the verb. Transitive sentences have the following structure

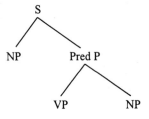

with the condition that the NP dominated by (i.e., occurring under) Pred P *does not* identify (or assign to a category) the NP dominated by S (the subject NP).

Thus, as we have seen, (1) is a transitive sentence,

1. Horatio sliced the bread.

and it is a sentence that is in the **active voice.** When a sentence is transitive and **active,** the subject NP of that sentence is, semantically speaking, the agent—or instigator—of the action. Active voice is the common or usual voice for English transitive sentences.

Speakers and writers of English have available to them, however, an alternative way of expressing the same idea using different syntax. In the **passive voice,** the affected participant—and *not* the agent—occurs in the subject NP slot:

31. The bread was sliced by Horatio.

In comparing (31) to (1), we find that in addition to the exchange of positions by the NPs, the verb is inflected differently: The *be* auxiliary appears, together with the past participle of the verb; the tense of the auxiliary matches the tense of the verb in the original sentence; and the auxiliary now agrees in number with the new subject NP. The VP is now said to be in the *passive voice.* In addition, the NP that served as the subject of (1) now functions as the object of the PP introduced by *by.* In the passive sentence, this PP is optional—it may or may not occur and the sentence remains grammatical. Thus (32) is a perfectly acceptable sentence of English:

32. The bread was sliced.

Sentences such as (32) allow a speaker or writer to make a statement about a transitive event without mentioning the agent, who may not, after all, be known—or be relevant to the current discussion. That is, making a sentence passive allows the NP of the predicate phrase to be "promoted" to subject position; this NP now has a higher position in the phrase structure tree because it occurs just under the S node. The sentence remains inherently transitive, however, even though an NP does not follow the VP. You see, transitivity is a semantic notion that has consequences for the syntax. And only transitive sentences may have passive counterparts. Calling an example such as (32) intransitive is therefore a distortion, since intransitivity typically involves an actor doing something that affects only himself or herself, such as (33):

33. Horatio jogs.

It is best to think of passive sentences as having a passive transitive VP, or possibly a **detransitivized** VP.

Think again about the statement above: *Only transitive sentences may have passive counterparts.* The accuracy of this statement can be demonstrated by examining sentences that are not transitive and observing what happens when one tries to force them into passive form. Review for a moment the following copular sentence presented in (4):

4. Horatio is a baker.

Now try to make it passive. The bizarre result is (34):

34. *A baker is been by Horatio.

Intransitive sentences, of course, lack free NPs in the predicate phrase, but let us imagine a situation involving something that is an NP but that functions as an adverbial because it is actually a PP with an understood preposition (such as *on* or *during*):

35. Horatio bakes every day.

If we try to make this example passive, we get a peculiar result:

36. *Every day is baked by Horatio.

The property of English grammar that allows only transitive sentences to occur in the passive form gives us a handy test for transitivity. That is, if we are in doubt about the category of the lexical verb in a given sentence, we can see whether the sentence can be made passive. If it can, the verb is transitive. If not, then, with very few exceptions, the verb is not transitive in the particular instance.

Exercise 2.3

Underline the complete verb phrase in each of the following transitive sentences. Then, in the space following, write the word *active* or *passive,* depending on the voice of the verb. All sentences in this exercise come from Jacob Bronowski's *The Ascent of Man.* [Note: Present participles without accompanying auxiliaries and infinitive forms of verbs preceded by the word *to* do not function as the verb phrase of the principal clause. Therefore, do not underline them. They are doing other kinds of syntactic work, which we shall explore in Chapters 4 and 5.]

1. An undertaking as large as this, though wonderfully exhilarating, is not entered lightly.

2. Man is distinguished from other animals by his imaginative gifts.

3. So the great discoveries of different ages and different cultures, in technique, in science, in the arts, express in their progression a richer and more intricate conjunction of human faculties, an ascending trellis of his gifts.

4. Two million years ago *Australopithecus* made rudimentary stone tools.

5. And for the next million years, man in his further evolution did not change this type of tool.

6. Theoretical discoveries with radical consequences can usually be seen at once to be striking and original.

7. The aqueduct at Segovia in Spain was built by the Romans about AD 100, in the reign of the emperor Trajan.

8. Three inventions sustained the network of authority: the roads, the bridges (in a wild country like this), the messages.

9. [The masons] carried with them a kit of light tools.

10. Even very primitive peoples have a number system.

Answers to Exercise 2.3

1. An undertaking as large as this, though wonderfully exhilarating, <u>is not entered</u> lightly.
    passive

2. Man <u>is distinguished</u> from other animals by his imaginative gifts.
    passive

3. So the great discoveries of different ages and different cultures, in technique, in science, in the arts, <u>express</u> in their progression a richer and more intricate conjunction of human faculties, an ascending trellis of his gifts.
    active

4. Two million years ago *Australopithecus* <u>made</u> rudimentary stone tools.
    active

5. And for the next million years, man in his further evolution <u>did not change</u> this type of tool.
    active

6. Theoretical discoveries with radical consequences <u>can usually be seen</u> at once to be striking and original.
    passive

7. The aqueduct at Segovia in Spain <u>was built</u> by the Romans about AD 100, in the reign of the emperor Trajan.
    passive

8. Three inventions <u>sustained</u> the network of authority: the roads, the bridges (in a wild country like this), the messages.
    active

9. [The masons] <u>carried</u> with them a kit of light tools.

active

10. Even very primitive peoples <u>have</u> a number system.

active

Exercise 2.4

Underline the complete VP in each of the following sentences from Jung Chang's *Wild Swans.* Then, in the space following the sentence, identify the VP as *transitive, intransitive, copular,* or, in the case of passive transitive verbs, *passive.* If you find more than one VP, number them to avoid confusion. Remember that the decision procedure you have learned does *not* accommodate the passive voice. Therefore, after you locate the VP, ask yourself *first* whether it is passive. If it is not, then you can safely use the decision procedure in Figure 2–1.

1. Her father had been promoted to deputy chief of the local police because of his connection to General Xue, and had acquired land and property.

2. Even her physical and psychological submission was mulled over nostalgically.

3. In fact, all this time the general had not been far away at all.

4. The warlords and their fief system had collapsed and most of China was now controlled by a single force, the Kuomintang, or nationalists, headed by Chiang Kai-shek (*headed* is not acting as a main VP in this sentence; ignore it for the moment).

5. General Xue's visit to my grandmother did not last long.

6. Her heart missed a beat.

7. She was invaded by a wave of panic.

8. The next day she packed his things and he left, alone.

9. A happy year passed.

10. The journey was an adventure.

11. The area had been convulsed yet again.

12. At first [Pu Yi] was called Chief Executive; later, in 1934, he was made emperor of Manchukuo.

13. My grandmother hired a horse-drawn cart and drove north along a bumpy, dusty road to General Xue's mansion. . . .

14. My grandmother's sister was not allowed into the room. . . .

15. This was nothing personal: the relatives of a concubine were not treated as part of the family.

16. My grandmother called out to him, but his eyes remained shut.

17. She picked my mother off the bed and hugged her tight.

18. As a concubine, her whole future and that of her daughter were in jeopardy, possibly even in mortal peril.

19. Even the garden was designed with security rather than aesthetics in mind.

20. There were a few cypress trees, some birches and winter plums, but none near the walls.

Answers to Exercise 2.4

1. Her father <u>had been promoted</u> to deputy chief of the local police because of his connection to General Xue, and <u>had acquired</u> land and property.
   1. passive; 2. transitive

2. Even her physical and psychological submission <u>was mulled over</u> nostalgically.
   passive

3. In fact, all this time the general <u>had not been</u> far away at all.
   copular

4. The warlords and their fief system <u>had collapsed</u> and most of China <u>was now controlled</u> by a single force, the Kuomintang, or nationalists, headed by Chiang Kai-shek.
   1. intransitive; 2. passive

5. General Xue's visit to my grandmother <u>did not last</u> long.
   intransitive

6. Her heart <u>missed</u> a beat.

   transitive

7. She <u>was invaded</u> by a wave of panic.

   passive

8. The next day she <u>packed</u> his things and he <u>left</u>, alone.

   1. transitive; 2. intransitive

9. A happy year <u>passed</u>.

   intransitive

10. The journey <u>was</u> an adventure.

    copular

11. The area <u>had been convulsed</u> yet again.

    passive

12. At first [Pu Yi] <u>was called</u> Chief Executive; later, in 1934, he <u>was made</u> emperor of Manchukuo.

    1. passive; 2. passive

13. My grandmother <u>hired</u> a horse-drawn cart and <u>drove</u> north along a bumpy, dusty road to General Xue's mansion. . . .

    1. transitive; 2. intransitive

14. My grandmother's sister <u>was not allowed</u> into the room. . . .

    passive

15. This <u>was</u> nothing personal: the relatives of a concubine <u>were not treated</u> as part of the family.

    1. copular; 2. passive

16. My grandmother <u>called out</u> to him, but his eyes <u>remained</u> shut.

    1. intransitive; 2. copular

17. She <u>picked</u> my mother off the bed and <u>hugged</u> her tight.

    1. transitive; 2. transitive

18. As a concubine, her whole future and that of her daughter <u>were</u> in jeopardy, possibly even in mortal peril.

    copular

19. Even the garden <u>was designed</u> with security rather than aesthetics in mind.

    passive

20. There <u>were</u> a few cypress trees, some birches and winter plums, but none near the walls.

    copular

Terms Used in Chapter Two

active voice: a form of the VP of particular verbs that have subjects serving as agents acting upon another sentence entity.

agent: the role played by the subjects of active verbs. An agent causes a change of state in some person or thing.

agree: a verb is said to agree with its subject, and a pronoun is said to agree with its antecedent. These statements mean that the forms of verbs and subjects and of pronouns and antecedents match in their person and number.

aspect: the property of VPs by which they indicate the nature of events, e.g., whether an event is ongoing or occurs at a single point in time.

copular verb: a verb that sets up a kind of equation between its subject and its complement. The complement either assigns the subject to a class (when the complement is an NP) or assigns an attribute to the subject (when the complement is an adjective). The best example of a copular verb is *be*.

detransitivized verb: a transitive verb that has undergone the passive operation.

finite verb: a verb inflected for tense.

Germanic: the language subfamily to which English belongs. Other languages in this group include German, Dutch, and Norwegian. Languages belonging to the same family have a common ancestor language.

gerund: a present participle serving as a noun; e.g., *swimming* is my favorite sport.

infinitive: the uninflected or base form of a verb.

inflection: a suffix indicating vital grammatical information about a word.

intransitive verb: a verb that is not followed by free NPs.

modal auxiliaries: the verbs *can, could, will, would, shall, should, may, might,* and *must;* the verb that follows a modal must appear in the infinitive form.

number: markings on verbs, nouns, and pronouns that indicate whether the form in question is singular or plural.

passive voice: the form of the VP indicated by the combination of the auxiliary *be* and the past participle of the lexical verb. Only inherently transitive verbs have passive forms in English.

past participle: one of the principle parts of the verb, the past participle usually ends in *-ed* or *-en,* and when part of the VP of the predicate phrase, it is accompanied by an auxiliary.

past tense: the form of the verb signaling time past, most often indicated by *-ed.*

person: an indication in a verb or pronoun as to whether the subject of the verb or the antecedent of the pronoun is the speaker, the addressee, or whatever is spoken about.

perfective aspect: a VP made up of *have* and the past participle of the lexical verb.

present participle: a verb form ending in *-ing*.

pragmatics: the study of how language is used to get things done in the world.

primary auxiliaries: the verbs *be, have,* and *do* in their function as helpers preceding another verb.

progressive aspect: signaled by *be* plus the present participle of the lexical verb; indicates ongoing action.

reflexive pronoun: a pronoun form ending in *-self.* It cannot serve as the subject of a sentence.

semantics: the meaning component of language.

strong verb: a verb that forms its past tense by changes inside the base form, usually a vowel change.

tense: the time reference of a verb—in English, past or present.

transitive verb: a verb that is followed by a free NP that does not identify the subject. Usually the subject acts upon this free NP.

weak verb: a verb that forms its past tense by adding *-ed.* The vast majority of English verbs are weak verbs.

Chapter Quiz

Part I: Underline the VP in each of the following sentences. Then, in the space following, indicate the *voice* of the verb by writing the word *active* or *passive.* If clauses coordinated with *and* occur, treat each VP separately. All sentences in this quiz come from *A Leg to Stand On,* by Oliver Sacks.

1. I could have been used as a classroom demonstration of this rare and singular "neuro-existential" pathology.

2. My teapot was whisked away before my third cup, and Nurse Sulu brought me a basin.

3. I must have presented a strange sight to the good therapists.

4. Previously I had passively awaited his calls.

5. Now the moral obscurity and darkness was lifted, as well as the physical darkness, the shadow.

6. A newcomer, low on the totem-pole, I was assigned to a table in the corner, an object of curiosity, concern and perhaps some contempt to the veterans.

7. All of us were enjoying an extraordinary Sabbath of the spirit.

8. Muscles must be exercised, or they lose strength and tone.

9. I ordered almost everything on the menu—from anchovy toast to rum-balls and meringues.

10. Everywhere, and in myself, I discovered a Rabelaisian gusto—a coarse, but festive, and perfectly chaste gusto.

Part II: Underline the VP in each of the following sentences and, in the space following, describe the character of the VP by writing *transitive, intransitive,* or *copular.*

11. The huntsman gave me some aquavit from a flask.

12. The burning liquid was indeed the "water of life."

13. I phoned my brother, a doctor in London.

14. Obsessive fears gnawed at my mind.

15. My perceptions were unstable.

16. I had a splendid evening—a celebration really.

17. The violence of my sudden movement jerked me awake.

18. Even in coma the muscles retain some activity.

19. Very early in life, at Charcot's suggestion, Freud wrote a classic paper on the distinction of organic and hysterical paralyses.

20. A man with a phantom—a phantom leg—could not kick a stone.

21. My encounter with the young surgeon in Odda had been perfect in its way.

22. A sense of utter hopelessness swept over me.

23. In the hospital we lost our sense of the world.

Part III: Underline the VP and, in the space below each sentence, describe the VP in terms of person, tense, number, aspect, and whether a modal occurs. Indicate whether the lexical verb is weak or strong. (Remember that not all categories apply to all verbs. Examine grammatical aspect rather than word-inherent aspect.)

24. My father, and old friends, would be dropping in soon.

25. We had met by chance.

Chapter Three

Elements in the Predicate Phrase

Introduction

In previous chapters we focused on the structure of basic English declarative sentences, leaving for later discussion much about the function of the various NPs that occur. We have, however, studied the functioning of VPs as far as transitivity, voice, tense, and aspect are concerned. And we know that VPs head the predicate phrases of sentences. In addition, we have learned about the functions of one very important NP, the subject. However, other NPs, as well as other types of phrases, occur in the sentence—in the predicate phrase as *objects* or *complements* (i.e., entities that bring about completion) of the verb phrase. Our goal in this chapter is to learn to identify by function all of the objects and complements that can occur in the predicate phrases of the basic English sentence types. From the point of view of understanding how English grammar operates, this chapter is the most important chapter in the book.

Structure and Function—The Visible and the Invisible

In understanding the workings of even simple English sentences, we need to be clear about the distinction between *structure* and *function*. A **structure** is a particular coherent grouping of elements in a sentence that can be described in terms of the components that constitute it. For example, as we recognized as early as Chapter One, we can identify the NP structure fairly easily by the presence of certain elements, such as determiners, that are uniquely associated with it. In fact, we could write a formula that could serve as a general identification mechanism for NPs. In an important sense, we identify an NP by examining it carefully, looking for particular signals (such as determiners) that the item under consideration is indeed an NP. Similarly, other structures in grammar such as VPs and PPs are amenable to identification by inspection.

However, knowing that a particular grouping of words is a particular kind of structure such as NP or PP tells us nothing about how it is used in a given sentence, because the same kind of structure may have several different kinds of functions. By **function,** we mean the use to which any given structural element is put in a particular sentence. To familiarize ourselves with the notion of grammatical function, let's review a familiar one, that of *subject.*

By designating a particular construction the subject of the sentence, we assign to it a functional description. Given its position in an ordinary declarative sentence, a subject is generally easy to spot. Typically, a subject is a free NP or something else that behaves like one, and it occurs before the verb, making it the first element we meet in a simple declarative sentence. But most importantly, the subject NP is generally the element that performs the action (i.e., the agent) in an active transitive sentence (e.g., *Horatio sliced the bread*), experiences the action or state in an intransitive sentence (e.g., *Horatio slept*), or is described in a copular one (e.g., *Horatio was quiet*). Subjects of English sentences therefore present little difficulty regarding their identification.

We already know that NPs also occur in positions in which they cannot be sentence subjects—objects of prepositions being one obvious example. We know, too, that free NPs can occur as companions to the VP in the predicate phrase. In addition, elements other than NPs also may occur in the predicate phrase. In an important way, the function of a particular constituent is not immediately available to our senses and is therefore "invisible" because we can't determine function merely by looking. Instead, we must analyze the sentence in order to figure out how the structure is used in the sentence.

Types of Elements

Any structural entity (such as an NP, adjective phrase, or adverbial phrase) that completes a VP (i.e., that occurs with that VP in the predicate phrase, such as the NP following an active transitive VP) is either an object or complement (that is, a necessary element that is not an object) of the verb phrase, and the process by which a sentence is completed by such entities is called **complementation.** Some elements are NPs—structurally speaking—serving as objects of transitive verbs. Other elements are either NPs, Adjective Phrases (AP), or Adverbials (ADV), and occur with copular or certain transitive and intransitive verbs. The elements that are absolutely required by the verb as a condition of grammaticality are generally called **obligatory** constituents, and elements that can be omitted without a loss of grammaticality are generally called **optional** constituents. This distinction between optional and obligatory elements is purely a syntactic one, based on the notion of ideal forms. For example, if I were to ask you how John cut the cake, you might answer: "John cut the cake with a knife." And surely, we would all agree that from the point of view of communication, the prepositional phrase *with a knife* is absolutely essential. However, from the point of view of syntactic acceptability (grammaticality), this PP is an optional element, for omitting it from the sentence does not alter grammaticality one bit: *John cut the cake* is a perfectly acceptable English sentence. Note that the NP *the cake* is absolutely obligatory because omitting it yields an unacceptable string of words that English speakers would agree does not constitute a sentence; **John cut with a knife* is not acceptable. The distinction between optional and obligatory elements is an important one in the analysis of the syntax of any language. However, as we shall see, there are occasions when the boundary between optional and obligatory is not so clear.

The Patterns of Basic English Declarative Sentences

English sentences can be categorized into five basic sentence types, all based on variation in the predicate phrase. Each one of the five basic types has two or more subtypes, and assignment to one or another category is usually quite straightforward, although there are times when the boundaries between categories become somewhat indistinct or "fuzzy." We will examine each of these categories and investigate solutions to those cases that are problematic.

Pattern 1a: The Intransitive VP, Part I

In what is probably the simplest sentence type, the VP of the predicate phrase has no free NPs following it. If any NPs occur, they serve as objects of prepositions within PPs. These VPs are called *intransitive* verbs. Examine the underlined portions of sentences (1a) and (2a) taken from Bram Stoker's *Dracula* and (3a) from Jacob Bronowski's *The Ascent of Man:*

1a. The wind <u>came now in fierce bursts</u>.

2a. Before our very eyes, and almost in the drawing of a breath, the whole body <u>crumbled into dust</u>. . . .

3a. The rudiments of astronomy <u>exist in all cultures</u>.

You will find in the underlined portions of the predicate phrases of these sentences absolutely *no free NPs*. Whatever follows the VPs in these sentences is either an adverb (e.g., *now*) or an adverbial prepositional phrase (e.g., *in fierce bursts*). Moreover, we can tinker with these sentences by omitting the adverbials, and we will find that although the process results in a rather lean version of the original, the string of words remains an acceptable sentence, as Sentences (1b–3b) attest:

1b. The wind <u>came</u>.

2b. The whole body <u>crumbled</u>. . . .

3b. The rudiments of astronomy <u>exist</u>.

Thus, grammatically speaking, the only *obligatory* element in the predicate phrase is the VP itself. The pattern of the predicate phrase may therefore be given as follows:

    IV   where **IV** stands for "intransitive verb."

This structure may be represented by the following tree diagram:

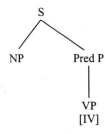

Pattern 1b: The Intransitive VP, Part II

A number of intransitive VPs are problematic because, although they have no free NPs as their companions, they seem to require certain adverbials. In particular, we find sentences such as (4a) and (5a) from Tina Marie Freeman-Villalobos's short story "The Way it Was." The predicate phrases in these sentences are underlined:

4a. We <u>went into the kitchen</u>.

5a. He <u>was lying on a blanket on the floor</u>.

Both predicate phrases contain true prepositional phrases, *into the kitchen* and *on a blanket on the floor*. Notice that if we tinker with these sentences in a way analogous to the omissions in Sentences (1b–3b), the result is the peculiar set of strings given in (4b) and (5b):

4b. ?We went.

5b. ?He was lying (ignore the meaning "he told an untruth").

Sentence (4b) could be used only if the path of the action of the verb was previously mentioned, and would certainly be ungrammatical for a sentence uttered or written out of the blue. Sentence (5b) clearly is unacceptable if we mean by *lying* "to position oneself in a reclining manner." Thus, Sentences (4a) and (5a) have intransitive verbs with *obligatory* adverbials.

Determining whether an adverbial is obligatory or optional is not always obvious. Consider, for example, Sentence (6) from the same short story as Sentences (4) and (5):

6. My matchbox landed by his feet.

Would Sentence (6) be just as grammatical without the prepositional phrase *by his feet*? If so, does its omission yield a sentence with essentially the same meaning? Undoubtedly, you are uncertain about your answers to these questions. For our purposes, then, we will merely identify the VP of intransitive sentences and mark nothing else.

Pattern 2a: The Copular VP, Part I

A second sentence pattern in English involves a copular VP followed by an NP or an adjective phrase. The underlined portions of example Sentences (7) from *Dracula* and (8) from *The Ascent of Man* illustrate copular VPs and their complements:

7. The two men <u>might be Dr. Seward and Mr. Morris</u>.
8. Astronomy <u>became a model for all the other sciences</u>.

The VP in Sentence (7) is *might be,* and that in Sentence (8) is *became.* The complements are the compound NP *Dr. Seward and Mr. Morris* and the complex NP *a model for all the other sciences.* Notice how in each case the complement is essentially another designation for the subject. Sentence (9) below, also from *The Ascent of Man,* illustrates a copular verb followed by an adjective phrase (AP) complement. In this case, the AP *unnatural to his age* assigns a characteristic to the subject NP:

9. The system of Copernicus <u>seemed unnatural to his age</u>.

The verbs *be* and *seem* are always copular, and *appear* and *become* usually are. Sometimes *feel, act, look, taste, smell,* and *sound* are copular, as well. To determine the status of the verb, remember to examine the entire sentence.

Traditionally, complements of copular verbs have been called "subject complements." This designation is somewhat problematic, because as we shall see in Chapter Four, copular verbs complemented by NPs or APs are sometimes subjectless, so the grammarian has to reconstruct the implied subject. In addition, for sentences in general, it is the verb that actually requires the complement, and so the term "subject complement" distorts the situation somewhat. Therefore, in this book, we shall designate all such NPs and APs that sometimes follow copular verbs *copular complements.*

Pattern 2b: The Copular VP, Part II

Sometimes a copular verb is complemented, not by an NP or an AP, but by an adverbial or adverbial prepositional phrase that *locates* the subject. As an example, consider the following sentence from Anne Rice's *The Witching Hour:*

10. The doctor had never been inside an antebellum mansion.

In Sentence (10) the adverbial prepositional phrase *inside an antebellum mansion* locates—albeit negatively—the subject of the sentence. Of all the copular verbs, *be* is unique in its ability to be complemented by this kind of obligatory adverbial, which we shall also call a copular complement.

You may be wondering right now if perhaps Sentence (6), repeated below, wouldn't be more accurately identified as having a copular verb whose complement locates the subject:

6. My matchbox landed by his feet.

Such an analysis may be preferred by some grammarians, but it is not one I favor. For one thing, unlike the verb *be,* such verbs do not admit NP or AP complements, and it seems really to stretch the point to say that such verbs have the equational characteristics of a true copular verb. In such cases, fuzzy though they may be, we can say with certainty that the verb clearly is not transitive because it takes no objects, and by default is intransitive rather than copular. What we have here is an area of uncertainty—a fuzzy boundary between copular and intransitive verbs. A competing analysis to the one presented here might group together in one category copular and intransitive verbs, with copularity constituting a special case of intransitivity. However, since most grammarians continue to pursue a three-way distinction (among copular, intransitive, and transitive), we shall adhere to that distinction throughout this book.

The pattern for copular sentences is as follows:

CV-CC   where **CV** means "copular verb" and **CC** indicates "copular complement."

This structure may be represented by one of the following tree diagrams:

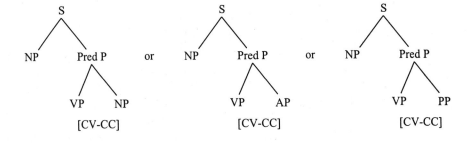

Pattern 3: The Monotransitive VP

Another simple sentence pattern is that of a VP followed by a single NP that does not identify or describe the subject, but serves instead as the **affected participant** in the sentence. In this situation, the verb is said to be *monotransitive.* Example (11) from *Dracula* provides an example of a monotransitive sentence pattern:

11. They, too <u>were pursuing the party with the cart</u>. (Read *with the cart* as modifying *party.*)

The predicate phrase of this sentence, indicated with underline, has the monotransitive VP *were pursuing* and the NP *the party with the cart.* This NP is called the *direct object* of the verb *pursuing.* The pattern of the predicate phrase may therefore be given as follows:

TV-DO   where **TV-DO** stands for "transitive verb—direct object."

This structure may be represented by the following tree diagram:

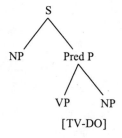

Remember that a good test for transitivity—and also for object status of a predicate phrase NP—is the application of the *passive* rule: If a sentence has an acceptable passive voice paraphrase, the NP that becomes the *subject* in the passive version starts out as the *object* in the original active counterpart.

Pattern 4: The Ditransitive VP

When a transitive VP has more than one free NP following it, and the verb involves a physical or verbal transaction in which some entity is transferred between the parties to the transaction, we call that verb *ditransitive.* Probably the best example of a ditransitive verb is the verb *give.* In fact, the special kind of object that occurs with the ditransitive verb—the *indirect object*—is sometimes called the "dative," which was the name given to the indirect object in Latin grammar. The word *dative* comes from the Latin *datus,* the past participle of the Latin verb meaning "give," and the indirect object probably received this title in honor of the verb most likely to have one. The underlined portions of Sentences (12a) and (13a), again from *Dracula,* illustrate nicely the ditransitive sentence pattern:

12a. Presently she woke, and I <u>gave her food</u>.

13a. He <u>handed me his glasses</u> and pointed.

In (12a) the VP *gave* is ditransitive, the NP *her* is the indirect object, and the NP *food* is the direct object. In Sentence (13a), *handed* is ditransitive, the NP *me* is the indirect object, and the NP *his glasses* is the direct object. That is, the *semantic* function of the indirect object is "receiver of the transferred entity"; the semantic function of the direct object in ditransitive cases is that of "transferred entity."

A good test for ditransitivity is as follows: If we can insert the preposition *to* in front of the first of two successive NPs in the predicate phrase and move the new prepositional phrase to the end of the sentence, and the result is acceptable, then the NP that before movement occurred first is the indirect object and the second is the direct object. This test works well for most ditransitive verbs, although some (e.g., *buy*) work better with the preposition *for*. Sentences (12b) and (13b) below show the results of applying the *to*-test to Sentences (12a) and (13a):

12b. I gave food *to her.*

13b. He handed his glasses *to me.*

Not only has the *to*-test yielded grammatical results, it has done so without any distortion of meaning. We are therefore certain that our original analysis was correct. By the way, current thought among many grammarians is that the entire prepositional phrases given in (12b) and (13b) remain indirect objects, in spite of the fact that they are not bona fide NPs and in spite of their moved position. One way of looking at this seeming anomaly is that position determines function only in the absence of some explicit indicator of function, such as a preposition. Given the equivalence in function of the first of two NPs in the predicate phrase and the corresponding prepositional phrase, one can see the justification for such an analysis.

There are some ditransitive verbs that fail the *to*-test, however. Sentence (14a) from *Dracula* gives a good example of one of them:

14a. I asked him a few questions on Transylvanian history.

If we apply the *to*-test to (14a), the result is (14b) or (14c), depending on our choice of preposition:

14b. *I asked a few questions on Transylvanian history to him.

14c. *I asked a few questions on Transylvanian history for him.

Clearly, Sentence (14b) is ungrammatical. Sentence (14c) is potentially grammatical, but not if we want it to mean what (14a) means. The preposition *of* would of course work, but since it does not have the general applicability of *to,* we certainly can't rely on it as a test. Nonetheless, *asked* is a ditransitive verb in (14a), because, given the fact that two NPs follow the verb, there is only one other sentence pattern (pattern 5a) that it possibly could fit, and as we shall see, clearly it is not an example of that pattern. In addition, the transaction is a verbal one (*ask*, like *tell* and *promise*, is a **speech act verb**, whose action involves talking rather than physical activity), and the situation is that *him* receives "transferred entities"—*a few questions on Transylvanian history.*

The sentence pattern for basic ditransitive sentences is as follows:

TV-IO-DO   where **IO** and **DO** represent indirect and direct objects, respectively.

The ditransitive structure may be represented by the following tree diagram:

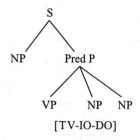

[TV-IO-DO]

It will come in handy for you to remember that ditransitive VPs may have passive counterparts, and when they do, either object—direct or indirect—may be "promoted" to subject (for example, *I gave her food* can be rendered *Food was given to her* or *She was given food*). When the indirect object becomes the subject through such a process, the VP *will continue to take a direct object, in spite of its passive status (She was given food).* Try playing with a few ditransitive sentences by making them passive. What happens to the indirect object when the direct object is promoted into subject position?

Pattern 5a: The Complex Transitive VP, Part I

The fifth basic sentence pattern involves a third subcategory of transitivity, called *complex transitivity.* In this pattern, a transitive VP is followed by an NP— which is its direct object—and a second NP or AP, which is its predicate complement. (You may know this complement as an "object complement"; however, in this book, we shall use the term "predicate complement" in order to collect into one category a number of slightly differing but related phenomena.) The underlined portion of Sentence (15a) from *The Ascent of Man* provides an example of a complex transitive predicate phrase containing two NPs:

15a. I <u>call that brilliant sequence of cultural peaks *The Ascent of Man*.</u>

In (15a), the complex NP *that brilliant sequence of cultural peaks* is the direct object, and the second NP (which just happens to be the title of the book, thus the italics), *The Ascent of Man,* is the predicate complement. It is critical to understand that the predicate complement is not merely something optional added onto the end of an ordinary transitive sentence; complex transitivity is qualitatively different from monotransitivity. Examine (15b) to prove this assertion to yourself. It is obvious that (15b) is not acceptable because it lacks the predicate complement:

15b. *I call that brilliant sequence of cultural peaks.

The relationship between the two NPs in the predicate phrase is important, and it differs from the relationship between the two NPs in a ditransitive sentence. In Sentence (15a), the second NP in the predicate phrase—the predicate complement—serves in a sense to identify the first, such that (15c) would express the relationship between them:

15c. That brilliant sequence of cultural peaks <u>is</u> *The Ascent of Man.*

In essence, there is an understood *be* between the two NPs in the predicate phrase—one that you can mentally insert in order to test for the complex transitive construction.

Because of the implicit *be* hidden in the complex transitive construction investigated in this chapter, we will find that just as an AP can complement a copular VP, it may also serve in the slot following a direct object as a predicate complement. As an example, consider the following sentence from Richard Rodriguez's *Hunger of Memory:*

16a. [My parents] made success possible.

In Sentence (16a), the adjective *possible* serves as the predicate complement of the sentence (*success* is the direct object). As evidence, consider (16b), which explicitly provides the implicit *be:*

16b. Success is possible.

The use of the verb *make* (and, as we shall see in Chapter Four, of verbs closely related to it in meaning, such as *force* and *cause*) in complex transitive sentences such as (16a) is a very important and frequently occurring construction in English. It forms the basis of a structure called the English **causative construction,** which has counterparts in most languages although their syntax will differ considerably. The notion underlying the construction is that the subject of the sentence causes or brings about the relationship between the direct object and the predicate complement. That is, the causative construction in Sentence (16a) can be given as follows, with the italicized elements understood as parts of meaning and not directly parts of syntax:

16c. My parents *caused* {success *be* possible}

What (16c) means is that the subject (a causal agent), *my parents,* brought about the situation presented in the brackets in Sentence (16c), with the result that *success (is) possible.* The grammatically permissible way to express this idea in English is through (16a).

There are many such constructions in English, as demonstrated in the following sentences describing everyday events at my house:

Elizabeth made her room a mess. (NP as predicate complement) →
Elizabeth *caused* {her room *be* a mess}

Elizabeth made her room messy. (AP as predicate complement) →
Elizabeth *caused* {her room *be* messy}

Elizabeth made her mother's hair gray. (AP as predicate complement) →
Elizabeth *caused* {her mother's hair *be* gray}

This last sentence suggests another causative complex transitive construction using a different verb:

Elizabeth turned her mother's hair gray.

Here, *Elizabeth* is the causal agent in the circumstance of the graying of mother's hair. The list of possible verbs could, of course, continue. We will meet causative verbs again in Chapter Four, where we will find predicate complements other than NPs or adjectives following the direct object of complex transitive constructions.

Pattern 5b: The Complex Transitive VP, Part II

The second subtype of complex transitivity primarily involves a particular subset of transitive verbs, a subtype we shall call "causative verbs of motion." These verbs "move" the direct object so that the direct object ends up in the location specified in the predicate complement, which in this case is an obligatory adverbial of space. Another way of describing the causative nature of this subtype is to say that the subject of the sentence causes the direct object to be moved to a location given in an adverbial phrase, frequently a prepositional one. As an example, consider (17a), excerpted from Leslie Marmon Silko's *Ceremony:*

17a. The old man put his sack on his lap. . . .

In (17a), the action *(put)* of the subject *(the old man)* upon the direct object *(his sack)* causes the direct object to be located at the predicate complement *(on his lap).* Notice that the implicit *be* occurs between object and predicate complement in Sentence (17b):

17b. His sack is on his lap.

Put is a particularly good example of a causative verb of motion that is complex transitive, and the reason I present it here is that *put* absolutely *must* have a location following the direct object. To prove this assertion, try formulating sentences with *put* without an adverbial and see what occurs (don't add particles!). This deformation of Sentence (17a) results in:

17c. *The old man put his sack

Clearly, Sentence (17c) and any others like it that you may have constructed are ungrammatical and unacceptable.

The class constituted by such causative verbs of motion is necessarily quite large since many verbs can be used in a causative sense. You will find a good number of them in the upcoming exercises. Here is a preview from Silko's *Ceremony:* The complex transitive verbs are underlined, with the direct object and predicate complement appearing in brackets:

18. Old Grandma pulled [the chair] [from the foot of the bed].

19. He pulled [the blue wool cap] [over his ears].

20. He pressed [his face] [into the pillow] and pushed [his head] hard [against the bed frame].

21. He laid [his head] back [on the dusty seat]. . . .

22. Harley pushed [a bottle of beer] [in front of him].

23. The Army recruiter had taped [posters of tanks and marching soldiers] [around the edge of a folding table].

In most cases, eliminating the adverbial either makes the sentence ungrammatical or changes its meaning somewhat.

You will find from time to time, however, that a sentence may not seem significantly different without its adverbial (cf. Sentence 21 above). This seems to occur only in those cases in which the direction or path of the action is given in the verb itself, instead of leaving this duty to an adverbial. English is a language that typically does not include direction in the meaning of the verb itself, as some other languages do (e.g., Spanish). Instead, English often includes the manner of the action in the core meaning of the verb (think of the verbs *twist, wiggle,* etc.), but rarely direction or location. However, when verbs do include directionality in their core meaning, the adverbial of direction is usually optional. Examine Sentence (24) as a good example:

24. She lowered the box into the ground.

Eliminating the prepositional phrase in (24) not only does not result in an ungrammatical string, it does not even seriously distort the meaning. Thus, calling such an adverbial "obligatory" may seem an overstatement in such circumstances, though it does provide the ending location of the direct object (*The box is in/*into the ground*).

In addition to causative verbs of motion, there is a smaller class of verbs— verbs of perception—that also can be complemented by such obligatory adverbials. Consider Sentence (25), taken from Anne Rice's *The Witching Hour:*

25. I feel the darkness near me.

Notice that the prepositional phrase *near me* does not indicate the location of the VP; rather it locates the direct object, and thus perception verbs behave much like causative verbs with respect to how they are complemented.

The pattern of complex transitivity may be given as follows:

TV-DO-PC where **PC** means "predicate complement," and the predicate complement could be an NP, an AP, or a locational adverbial.

Complex transitive complementation may be represented by one of the following tree diagrams:

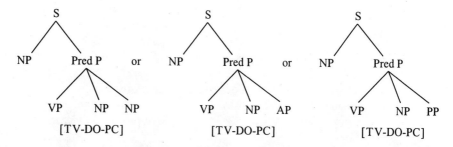

Complex transitive VPs also have passive forms. Just as with all transitive constructions, there is a systematic relationship between the active and passive versions of complex transitive sentences. Let us revisit sentence (23), repeated below as (23a):

23a. The Army recruiter <u>had taped</u> [posters of tanks and marching soldiers] [around the edge of a folding table].

The pattern of the predicate phrase of (23a) is TV-DO-PC. If this sentence were rendered in the passive voice, its direct object *(posters of tanks and marching soldiers)* would be promoted to subject position, though the predicate complement would be unaffected:

23b. Posters of tanks and marching soldiers <u>had been taped</u> [around the edge of a folding table].

Thus, although (23b) now lacks a direct object, it retains its predicate complement.

When we recall what happens in passive versions of the other two types of transitive sentences, we find that only *objects* may be promoted to subject status. As we continue in our investigation of grammar, this feature will acquire increasing significance. At present, it is important in two ways. First, we now understand that intransitive and copular sentences lack passive versions *because they have no objects.* Second, we find that since ditransitive sentences have two objects, passive versions of them typically retain an object, despite the passive character of the verb. It is crucial therefore not to mistake passive VPs for intransitive ones.

Marginal Cases

Assigning words or structures to categories is always problematic because categories actually constitute approximate rather than absolute groupings. Some members of a given category tend to be more central to the category than others. This fact holds in all spheres of human knowledge. For example, if you ask a group of people to name the first vegetable that comes into their minds, more than half of them will typically respond "Carrot." Few, if any, will come up with zucchini or rutabaga, even though these last two also are vegetables. What their response means is that for English-speaking Americans, *carrot* provides a better—or more central—member of the category "vegetable" than do the other two.

This phenomenon exists because categories are artifacts of human intelligence and not something inherent in the nature of things. Things are things, and categories are ideas about things. Therefore, as much as we would like every instance of English VPs to fall discretely into one category or another, many VPs refuse to do so. We have seen a couple of problematic cases. Let's examine a few more:

26a. Someone slept in the bed.

27a. Someone was staring at John.

Following the usual decision procedure by searching for free NPs in the predicate phrase, we find that the NPs are objects of prepositions and therefore not free. We can prove this by checking to see whether the words we think are prepositions are actually particles. Since they lack the mobility of moving to the right of the following NP, we can be certain that the words *in* and *at* are indeed prepositions (review Chapter One if this procedure is unclear to you):

26b. *Someone slept the bed in

27b. *Someone was staring John at

Moreover, the VPs *slept* and *was staring* clearly are not passive, lacking in the first case any auxiliary at all, and in the second case, the required past participle. Our decision procedure (see Chapter Two) tells us that the VPs are intransitive, and indeed this analysis is one widely accepted.

However, when using informal style, a number of speakers and writers routinely treat the objects of the prepositions in these sentences as free NPs and the prepositions as "belonging to" the verb in some sense. Thus, it is fairly common for speakers and writers to treat the VP and the accompanying preposition as transitive "prepositional" verbs (N.B. *not* "particle" verbs) by applying the passive rule, which, of course, never can be applied to truly intransitive verbs:

26c. The bed was slept in.

27c. John was being stared at.

Even though many prescriptive (the "tsk-tsk-don't-do-that") grammarians frown upon them, these passive structures are frequent and stubborn to eradicate. Such persistence points to a particularly entrenched rule of grammar, and so we must deal with it. Thus, although the intransitive analysis is not incorrect, there exists side-by-side with it a competing transitive analysis. What is interesting about Sentences (26a) and (27a) is that the subject NPs behave in semantic terms more as agents ("agent," or doer, is the usual semantic role of the subject in transitive sentences) than as experiencers ("experiencer" is a common role for the subject in intransitive sentences: e.g., *John slept,* where *John* experiences sleep, but doesn't *do* anything to anyone or anything), and this phenomenon may lead to the transitive analysis, in spite of the structural description of the sentence. I suspect that the agent status of the subject, which is the norm for transitive—but not intransitive—sentences, leads to the permissible application of the passive rule. Sometimes, then, the semantics and the syntax of a sentence do not converge, and competing—and equally correct—analyses result.

Moreover, already we have seen examples of sentences with intransitive VPs that seem to require an adverbial prepositional phrase, and we are uncertain about how to describe them, outside of being intransitive verbs. Let us investigate another such sentence, this time from Richard Rodriguez's *Hunger of Memory:*

28a. On Halloween night, all over Sacramento, children dressed up as ghosts or Frankensteins or dime-store skeletons with phosphorescent bones.

The VP of (28a) is *dressed up,* and no free NP follows it; the structure with *as* is a prepositional phrase with coordinated NPs serving as objects of the preposition. Nevertheless, there is a sense in which the sentence would be incomplete without this PP, and yet there is no way to treat *as* as part of a prepositional verb. We simply cannot passivize the sentence:

28b. *Ghosts or Frankensteins or dime-store skeletons with phosphorescent bones were dressed up as by children

The unacceptability of (28b) results from the fact that the NP *children* simply is not an agent. Sentence (28a) is intransitive both syntactically (on the level of structure) and semantically (on the level of meaning). While Sentence (28a) does not represent a central member of the category of intransitivity, the VP is intransitive nonetheless.

Noun Phrases as Adverbials

Prior to this point all NPs—other than appositives—have functioned as subjects, as objects of verbs or prepositions, or as complements. There is, however, one other function that an NP may serve, that of adverbial.

Adverbial NPs generally are not too difficult to recognize, primarily because they seem to be objects of missing (or implicit) prepositions. For example, in Sentence (29), the free NP in the predicate phrase is an adverbial:

29. We met for lunch last Thursday.

You may notice that the NP *last Thursday* might occur as an object of a preposition *(on)* if the adjective *last* were omitted:

30. We met for lunch on Thursday.

This feature leads us to suspect that there really is a hidden preposition in Sentence (29) as well, even though the addition of such a preposition yields at best an awkward sentence:

31. ?We met for lunch on last Thursday.

But perhaps the most convincing evidence that the NP *last Thursday* is an adverbial rests on the fact that it cannot be "promoted" to subject via the passive rule:

32. *Last Thursday was met for lunch by us.

Moreover, the NP gives us the time of the event, which generally is a semantic notion supplied by adverbials in English sentences, as are the notions of duration or location/direction. Thus, the following sentences all contain adverbial NPs, underlined to help you find them:

33. We returned <u>home</u>.
34. We stayed in Europe <u>three months</u>.
35. I studied French <u>last summer</u>.

Be careful not to mistake such NPs for direct objects or other major constituents.

A Note on *There*

English sentences sometimes begin with the word *there,* which does not serve as the subject of the sentence, despite its placement to the left of the VP. In some sentences, *there* is simply an adverb meaning "in that place." In Sentence (36), for example, *there* simply points to a location or direction away from the speaker/writer:

36. There goes the last of the dodoes.

More frequently, *there* is not an adverb at all, but a unique function word whose sole purpose is to announce the inversion of subject and verb. Sentence (37) demonstrates this usage:

37. There are twenty-five sentences in the next exercise.

In (37) *twenty-five sentences* is the subject and *in the next exercise* is the copular complement. Yet *there*-sentences sometimes occur with no complement at all; these sentences serve to posit the existence (or nonexistence in negative sentences) of the subject NP, as illustrated in (38):

38. There must be an answer.

Exercise 3.1

For each of the sentences below, underline the VP (i.e., the verb, all its auxiliaries, and any particles or VP-internal adverbs). Then put brackets around each companion to the VP given in the list of patterns below. In the space below each sentence, write one of the following patterns:

IV
CV-CC
TV-DO
TV-IO-DO
TV-DO-PC

If you find a VP in the *passive* voice, simply underline the verb, and unless it is complex transitive or ditransitive, mark nothing else, but *do* write the word *passive* in the space below the sentence. Then indicate other constituents that occur, if any (remember all passive verbs are inherently transitive). If more than one VP occurs in a sentence, follow the procedure for each. (A summary of the tests for the ditransitive and complex transitive patterns is provided in Appendix A.) All of the sentences come from Gus Lee's novel, *China Boy*.

1. With grand self-recognition, [San Francisco] calls itself "the City."

2. Panhandler boys did not beg.

3. Fighting was a metaphor.

4. The family called the trip to America *Bob-la,* the Run.

5. Even today, this journey would be a hardship.

6. A million extremely hostile enemy soldiers blocked the thousand miles of twisting river road from Shanghai to Chungking.

7. Mother had wanted sons.

8. A first daughter, with some good fortune, could be endured.

9. In 1943 my mother and sisters were alone in a world at war.

10. He was being sought by their gestapo in retribution for his warlike acts.

11. Mother turned to Paternal Grandmother, her mother-in-law.

12. They were leaving the people of their blood and the home and hearth of their ancestors.

13. He gave my sisters their Western names on their last night at home.

14. My mother wept for him.

15. Even today, the name *Chiing chun bao* sends a shiver up my spine.

16. My sister Janie Ming-li also enjoyed the benefits of deep-seated superstition.

17. The herbalist adjusted his wide, white medical headband.

18. Women were expendable birthing organisms for the glory of the family.

19. Mother resisted this status.

20. She was an expert in nonverbal communication.

21. Unlike most of the known world, Mother did not like American cigarettes.

22. Jennifer and Megan made the special Mother's Chicken soup.

23. Dozens of eggs were boiled in bright red dye.

24. Uncle Shim laid lavish praise on my parents for the quality of the food, the effort in preparation.

25. Mother looked out the cracked window of our secretive second-story walk-up apartment.

Answers to Exercise 3.1

1. With grand self-recognition, San Francisco <u>calls</u> [itself] ["the City"].
   TV-DO-PC

2. Panhandler boys <u>did not beg</u>.

    IV

3. Fighting <u>was</u> [a metaphor].

    CV-CC

4. The family <u>called</u> [the trip to America] [*Bob-la,* the Run].

    TV-DO-PC

5. Even today, this journey <u>would be</u> [a hardship].

    CV-CC

6. A million extremely hostile enemy soldiers <u>blocked</u> [the thousand miles of twisting river road from Shanghai to Chungking].

    TV-DO

7. Mother <u>had wanted</u> [sons].

    TV-DO

8. A first daughter, with some good fortune, <u>could be endured</u>.

    passive

9. In 1943 my mother and sisters <u>were</u> [alone] in a world at war.

    CV-CC

10. He <u>was being sought</u> by their gestapo in retribution for his warlike acts.

    passive

11. Mother <u>turned</u> to Paternal Grandmother, her mother-in-law.

    IV

12. They <u>were leaving</u> [the people of their blood and the home and hearth of their ancestors].

    TV-DO

13. He <u>gave</u> [my sisters] [their Western names] on their last night at home.

    TV-IO-DO

14. My mother <u>wept</u> for him.

    IV

15. Even today, the name *Chiing chun bao* <u>sends</u> [a shiver] [up my spine].

    TV-DO-PC

16. My sister Janie Ming-li also <u>enjoyed</u> [the benefits of deep-seated superstition].

    TV-DO

17. The herbalist <u>adjusted</u> [his wide, white medical headband].

    TV-DO

18. Women <u>were</u> [expendable birthing organisms for the glory of the family].

    CV-CC

19. Mother <u>resisted</u> [this status].

    TV-DO

20. She <u>was</u> [an expert in nonverbal communication].

    CV-CC

21. Unlike most of the known world, Mother <u>did not like</u> [American cigarettes].

    TV-DO

22. Jennifer and Megan <u>made</u> [the special Mother's Chicken soup].

    TV-DO

23. Dozens of eggs <u>were boiled</u> in bright red dye.

    passive

24. Uncle Shim <u>laid</u> [lavish praise] [on my parents] for the quality of the food, the effort in preparation.

    TV-DO-PC

25. Mother <u>looked</u> out the cracked window of our secretive second-story walk-up apartment.

    IV

Exercise 3.2

For each of the sentences below, underline the VP (i.e., the verb, all its auxiliaries, and any VP-internal adverbs). Then put brackets around each of the other elements in the predicate phrase listed in the patterns below. In the space below each sentence, write one of the following patterns:

> **IV**
> **CV-CC**
> **TV-DO**
> **TV-IO-DO**
> **TV-DO-PC**

If you find a verb in the passive voice, simply underline the verb, and unless it is complex transitive or ditransitive, mark nothing else, but *do* write the word *passive* in the space below the sentence (remember all passive verbs are inherently transitive). All of the sentences are taken from Anne Rice's *The Witching Hour*.

1. The doctor woke up afraid.

2. He had been dreaming of the old house in New Orleans again.

3. He had seen the woman in the rocker.

4. He'd seen the man with the brown eyes.

5. The doctor sat up in bed.

6. For a moment he couldn't shake the feeling of the old house.

7. He could almost hear the hum of the insects against the screens of the old porch.

8. Gradually his head cleared.

9. He thought of the Englishman at the bar in the lobby again.

10. But the Englishman had been respectfully curious.

11. For a moment the doctor had been tempted.

12. There was a lull in the convention . . . .

13. Alone now in the shadowy hotel room, the doctor felt fear again.

14. The clock ticked in the long dusty hallway in New Orleans.

15. Greek Revival style they called it . . . .

16. The sun came in thin dusty shafts through the twisting branches.

17. Bees sang in the tangle of brilliant green leaves beneath the peeling cornices.

18. Even the approach through the deserted streets seduced him.

19. He could not have gotten his arms around the trunk of it.

20. But the decay here troubled him nevertheless.

21. Spiders wove their tiny intricate webs over the iron lace roses.

22. The smell alone was frightful.

23. Viola would lift her out of the chair and push her patiently step by step.

24. And the patient's eyes, for all their listless stare, were a clear blue.

25. The thorny bougainvillea burst in clumps from beneath the wild cherry laurel.

Answers to Exercise 3.2

1. The doctor <u>woke up</u> [afraid].

    CV-CC (Notice that the VP *woke up,* ordinarily intransitive, is here used copularly to link the adjective *afraid* to the subject NP.)

2. He <u>had been dreaming</u> of the old house in New Orleans again.

    IV (Some grammarians consider *dream of* a prepositional verb; thus there is a competing and equally correct analysis in which *had been dreaming of* is transitive.)

3. He <u>had seen</u> [the woman in the rocker]. *or:* He <u>had seen</u> [the woman] [in the rocker].

    TV-DO, or possibly **TV-DO-PC.** (This one is ambiguous between the two readings. The first reading is that *in the rocker* identifies the N *woman;* the second reading is that *in the rocker* is a prior location of the woman. That is, a possible interpretation is the situation in which the current sentence is followed by *but now she wasn't in it.*)

4. He<u>'d seen</u> [the man with the brown eyes].

    TV-DO

5. The doctor <u>sat up</u> in bed.

    IV

6. For a moment he <u>couldn't shake</u> [the feeling of the old house].

    TV-DO

7. He <u>could almost hear</u> [the hum of the insects] [against the screens of the old porch].

    TV-DO-PC

8. Gradually his head <u>cleared</u>.

    IV

9. He <u>thought</u> of the Englishman at the bar in the lobby again.

    IV (Again, some grammarians consider *thought of* to be a transitive prepositional verb; to simplify analysis, we shall treat it, as we did (2) above, as an intransitive.)

10. But the Englishman <u>had been</u> [respectfully curious].
    CV-CC

11. For a moment the doctor <u>had been tempted</u>.
    passive

12. There <u>was</u> a lull [in the convention] . . . .

    CV-CC (*There* is never a subject; the subject of this sentence actually follows the VP: *a lull* is the subject NP. The copular complement is the obligatory adverbial *in the convention.*)

13. Alone now in the shadowy hotel room, the doctor <u>felt</u> [fear] again.

    TV-DO (*Felt* is here a transitive verb; the direct object, *fear,* is treated as something tangible. If instead of this NP the VP had been followed by the adjective *fearful,* then the VP would have indeed been copular.)

14. The clock <u>ticked</u> in the long dusty hallway in New Orleans.
    IV

15. [Greek Revival style] they <u>called</u> [it] . . . .

    TV-DO-PC (An inversion occurs here; the uninverted form of the sentence is: They called it Greek Revival style.)

16. The sun <u>came</u> in thin dusty shafts through the twisting branches.
    IV

17. Bees <u>sang</u> in the tangle of brilliant green leaves beneath the peeling cornices.
    IV

18. Even the approach through the deserted streets <u>seduced</u> [him].
    TV-DO

19. He <u>could not have gotten</u> [his arms] [around the trunk of it].

    TV-DO-PC (Here, the predicate complement is an obligatory adverbial of location, the PP *around the trunk of it.* In general, the verbs fitting this pattern are causative verbs of motion, i.e., those verbs whose meaning implies that some change of location of the object is caused by the agent-subject. Notice that the obligatory adverbial does not locate the action, but the final location of the object.)

20. But the decay here <u>troubled</u> [him] nevertheless.
    TV-DO

21. Spiders <u>wove</u> [their tiny intricate webs] [over the iron lace roses].
    TV-DO-PC (cf. 19, above)

22. The smell alone <u>was</u> [frightful].
    CV-CC

23. Viola <u>would lift</u> [her] [out of the chair] and <u>push</u> [her] patiently step by step.

   TV-DO-PC (cf. 19, above); **TV-DO** (Notice that in this second part of the sentence, the adverbials are manner adverbials and not locational ones. They are in fact optional, unlike the adverbials of location occurring with causative verbs of motion. *Push* could be complex transitive in another situation; in this sentence, however, it is not.)

24. And the patient's eyes, for all their listless stare, <u>were</u> [a clear blue].

   CV-CC

25. The thorny bougainvillea <u>burst</u> in clumps from beneath the wild cherry laurel.

   IV

Exercise 3.3

For each of the sentences below, underline the VP (i.e., the verb, all its auxiliaries, and any VP-internal adverbs). Then put brackets around each of the other elements in the predicate phrase. In the space below each sentence, write one of the following patterns:

   IV
   CV-CC
   TV-DO
   TV-IO-DO
   TV-DO-PC

If you find a verb in the passive voice, simply underline the verb, and unless it is complex transitive or ditransitive, mark nothing else, but *do* write the word *passive* in the space below the sentence (remember all passive verbs are inherently transitive). All of the sentences are taken from Leslie Marmon Silko's *Ceremony.*

1. The room was almost dark.

2. The old man put his sack on his lap . . . .

3. Auntie woke him up and gave him a cup of Indian tea . . . .

4. Old Grandma was dozing beside her stove.

5. She brought him a bowl of blue cornmeal mush.

6. The cornmeal mush tasted sweet . . . .

7. She took the empty bowl and cup away.

8. He could eat regular food.

9. He seldom vomited any more.

10. Some nights he even slept all night without the dreams.

11. He went with them in the old Ford coupe.

12. The sky was empty.

13. The sun was too hot and it made the color of the sky too pale blue.

14. He was the last one through the screen door at Dixie Tavern.

15. Emo was getting drunk on whiskey.

16. The Army recruiter had taped posters of tanks and marching soldiers around the edge of a folding table.

17. He handed them color pamphlets with a man in a khaki uniform and gold braid on the cover.

18. Rocky read each page of the pamphlet carefully.

19. He looked up at Tayo and his face was serious and proud.

20. The wind blew harder; a gust caught the pamphlets and swirled them off the card table.

Answers to Exercise 3.3

1. The room <u>was</u> [almost dark].
   CV-CC
2. The old man <u>put</u> [his sack] [on his lap] . . . .
   TV-DO-PC
3. Auntie <u>woke</u> [him] <u>up</u> and <u>gave</u> [him] [a cup of Indian tea] . . . .
   TV-DO; TV-IO-DO
4. Old Grandma <u>was dozing</u> beside her stove.
   IV

5. She <u>brought</u> [him] [a bowl of blue cornmeal mush].
   TV-IO-DO

6. The cornmeal mush <u>tasted</u> [sweet] . . . .
   CV-CC

7. She <u>took</u> [the empty bowl and cup] <u>away</u>.
   TV-DO

8. He <u>could eat</u> [regular food].
   TV-DO

9. He <u>seldom vomited</u> any more.
   IV

10. Some nights he even <u>slept</u> all night without the dreams.
    IV (*all night* is an adverbial NP: *all night was slept without the dreams.*)

11. He <u>went</u> with them in the old Ford coupe.
    IV

12. The sky <u>was</u> [empty].
    CV-CC

13. The sun <u>was</u> [too hot] and it <u>made</u> [the color of the sky] [too pale blue].
    CV-CC; TV-DO-PC

14. He <u>was</u> [the last one through the screen door at Dixie Tavern].
    CV-CC

15. Emo <u>was getting</u> [drunk on whiskey].
    CV-CC

16. The Army recruiter <u>had taped</u> [posters of tanks and marching soldiers] [around the edge of a folding table].
    TV-DO-PC

17. He <u>handed</u> [them] [color pamphlets with a man in a khaki uniform and gold braid on the cover].
    TV-IO-DO

18. Rocky <u>read</u> [each page of the pamphlet] carefully.
    TV-DO

19. He <u>looked up</u> at Tayo and his face <u>was</u> [serious and proud].
    IV; CV-CC

20. The wind <u>blew</u> harder; a gust <u>caught</u> [the pamphlets] and <u>swirled</u> [them] [off the card table].
    IV; TV-DO; TV-DO-PC

Terms Used in Chapter Three

adverbial: a PP, NP, or adverb phrase that serves to modify the VP of a sentence.

affected participant: the usual semantic role of the direct object—i.e., the entity acted upon.

causative construction: a construction that indicates that the subject brings about a state of affairs causing the object to experience something or to be located somewhere other than its starting position. *Make* is the best example of a causative verb—e.g., *Chocolate makes my tummy happy.*

complement: a structure that serves as a companion to the VP in the predicate phrase of a sentence and "completes" the predicate phrase. It is often required by the VP, but is not an object.

free NP: an NP that is not caught up in a prepositional phrase or some other structure, making it available to interact directly with the VP of a sentence as a subject, object, or complement.

function: the use to which any given structure is put in a particular sentence, e.g., *subject.*

object: the companion to a transitive verb in the predicate phrase, typically an NP. If the object is affected by the action in the VP, it is a *direct object.* If the object is the recipient in a transaction, it is an *indirect object.*

obligatory element: a sentence element that must be present to ensure the grammatical acceptability of a sentence.

optional element: a sentence element that can be omitted without affecting grammatical acceptability, even though it may contain information important to communication.

passive: the voice of the VP in a sentence in which the subject is not the instigator of the action but the affected participant. The auxiliary *be* occurs in the VP with the past participle of the lexical verb.

semantic: pertaining to meaning.

speech act verb: a verb whose action involves speaking, e.g., *ask, say, tell, promise, urge,* etc.

structure: a particular coherent grouping of elements in a sentence that can be described in terms of the components that comprise it, e.g., NP.

subject: a free NP—or something else that behaves like one—that occurs before the verb, making it the first element in a declarative sentence. Typically, the subject NP is the element that performs the action in an active transitive sentence or experiences the action or state in an intransitive one.

Chapter Quiz

For each of the sentences below, underline the VP (i.e., the verb, all its auxiliaries, and any VP-internal adverbs). Then put brackets around each of the other elements in the predicate phrase that are given in the patterns below. In the space below each sentence, write one of the following patterns:

IV
CV-CC
TV-DO
TV-IO-DO
TV-DO-PC

If you find a verb in the passive voice, simply underline the verb, and unless it is complex transitive or ditransitive, mark nothing else, but *do* write the word *passive* in the space below the sentence. All of the sentences are taken from Iris Murdoch's *A Word Child*.

1. I sat down at the table in the third chair.

2. Crystal had cleared the table.

3. Arthur poured me out a glass of wine.

4. [Crystal] rarely took any exercise.

5. Crystal often appeared stupid.

6. I had not even taken off my coat.

7. He wore oval steel-rimmed glasses.

8. He was an honest man devoid of malice.

9. His soupy eyes could express feelings.

10. I never lingered long on Thursday evenings.

11. Arthur was wearing a sensible absurd woolen cap.

12. I walked abruptly away.

13. There was silence in the flat.

14. I glanced quickly through Tommy's letter.

15. I went to bed in my underclothes.

16. I had never had any sleep problems since the orphanage.

17. A talent for oblivion is a talent for survival.

18. I was not bullied by other children.

19. Probably no adult misery can be compared with a child's despair.

20. Mr. Osmand taught me German in his spare time.

21. I taught myself Latin.

22. I was not a philological prodigy.

23. I never became concerned with the metaphysical aspects of language.

24. We went into the country on bicycles.

25. Mr. Osmand visited me once during my first year.

Chapter Four

Infinitive Clauses

Introduction

Thus far we have learned about the structure of the basic sentence, including the parts of verbs and the ways they combine with particular auxiliaries to signal tense, aspect, voice, and so on. We also have learned about the nature of verbs and the various elements that may occur with them in predicate phrases, such as objects and complements and adverbials. Most of the sentences we examined have been single *clause* sentences, with a few coordinated structures included here and there. Since a **clause** can be defined as a construction containing a subject and a predicate phrase, it is essentially identical in many respects to the basic English sentence, which, in fact, constitutes one clause.

More complex types of sentences, however, may actually comprise several clauses—a main, or **matrix clause,** and one or more *subordinate* clauses serving particular sentence functions such as subject, object, complement, or modifier. In this chapter, we will continue our investigation of the English sentence, concentrating on a particular kind of subordinate clause called the *infinitive clause,* a structure whose chief element—its VP—is the *nonfinite* verb form known as the infinitive (review Chapter Two, if necessary). We will learn to recognize a new structure—the subordinate infinitive clause—and to determine the specific functions it serves within English sentences, none of which are new to you because we studied these functions in Chapter Three. In order to be successful in working through this chapter, then, you must thoroughly understand the nature of the sentence elements we studied in the last chapter, and you must be able to distinguish among mono-, di-, and complex transitivity. Because Chapter Four is particularly challenging, I suggest you allot twice as much study time to it as you would ordinarily.

If you have studied grammar previously, you may have encountered the infinitive clause, but under another name—the *infinitive phrase.* Following the trends in recent scholarly treatments of English grammar, we shall use in this book the term *infinitive clause.* The change in terminology is due to two features of English grammar. First, unlike a phrase, a clause has both a subject and a predicate phrase. The infinitive clause structure, though sometimes lacking an *overt* subject (i.e., one physically present in the sequence of words), always has at least an *implicit* subject (understood, though not physically present); it thus qualifies as a clause. Second, strong structural parallels exist between infinitive clauses and other types of subordinate constructions traditionally considered clauses. You will study these other types of subordinate clauses in Chapters Eight, Nine, and Ten.

Recognizing the Infinitive Clause Structure

Previously, the VPs of the clauses we investigated were *finite.* That is, the VP either contained a modal auxiliary or was inflected for tense and probably for person and number. An **infinitive clause** is a word or word group with a verb in the infinitive form (a nonfinite form) at its head. Typically, it is introduced by *to* (a *complementizer* which, in this case, does *not* function as a preposition) and may contain a direct object, an indirect object, a complement, and/or adverbials, depending upon the nature of the verb with respect to transitivity or copularity. In short, an infinitive clause is a clause whose VP is an infinitive. The following are some examples: *to run, to be happy, to bake bread, to give Ann a present, to elect him chairman.* The variety of these examples demonstrates that intransitive, copular, and mono-, di-, and complex transitive verbs may occur as heads of infinitive clauses.

As the examples listed in the previous paragraph demonstrate, infinitive clauses typically are subjectless. That fact may lead you to wonder how one could ever identify such a structure as a clause, but there is a trick: Although such a subjectless clause can never stand alone as a sentence in its own right, its implied but absent subject is typically identical to something elsewhere in the sentence. In other words, you will be able to recognize that implied subject because there will be an NP somewhere in the sentence that logically services as the instigator of the nonfinite action. You can ask yourself who or what is performing the action or experiencing the state of the nonfinite verb.

In Chapter Two we learned that there are four principal parts to English verbs: the *infinitive,* the *past,* the *present participle,* and the *past participle.* Only one of these forms—the past—is *finite* in character. This means that the lexical verb itself is inflected for tense. The other three forms are either uninflected (the infinitive, for example, has no inflectional endings), or are inflected for aspect (*-ing, -en),* but not for person, number, or tense. These nonfinite forms require auxiliaries to carry the burden of person, number, and tense inflections if they are to serve as part of the principal VP of the sentence.

What makes nonfinite verb forms interesting in their own right is that, together with their obligatory objects and complements and optional modifiers, they can occur without auxiliaries to form structures within sentences called **nonfinite clauses,** which can serve just about any sentence function except principal VP of the sentence. Thus, infinitive clauses, for example, can be subjects, direct objects, copular complements, or predicate complements (i.e., they can serve as NP equivalents in some NP functions), or adverbials, adjectivals, or appositives. Such nonfinite clauses are *subordinate* clauses, serving a subsidiary function in another clause that constitutes the "higher" clause. (To clarify, think of phrase structures trees; a subordinate clause would occur *within* a sentence tree, for example in a position where an NP could appear).

Despite their clearly identifiable and largely consistent structure, infinitive clauses serve many different sentence functions, though these functions will be familiar to you from your previous work in this book. It will be your task in this chapter to identify both the *structure* known as the infinitive clause and the *grammatical function* it serves within the particular matrix clause containing it. In Chapter Three we learned about the constituents—NPs, APs, and PPs—that co-occur with the VP as objects and complements in the predicate phrase. To a great measure, we found that the grammatical functions of these constituents could be determined by the nature of the VP and by the position of the constituent with respect to that VP. In this chapter we will see that infinitive clauses quite readily can take over the functions served by the NPs, APs, and PPs we studied in Chapter Three. However, we will discover that whereas the VP of the matrix clause continues to assign grammatical functions to the elements that co-occur with it, the *position* of an element that happens to be an infinitive clause yields only limited information. Therefore, we must be very careful to understand the nature of the matrix VP and its requirements.

Infinitive Clause Functions—Subject

In Chapter One you were asked to divide sentences into two parts, and you found that the first part generally was the subject of the sentence. Frequently, the "first part" was the first free NP you met that preceded the VP of the sentence. Similar to NPs, infinitive clauses can serve as subjects, but their physical position relative to the VP of the sentence will not always serve as an indicator of that grammatical function. As an example, consider the following pair of sentences from Jacob Bronowski's *The Ascent of Man.* The infinitive clauses are underlined:

1a. <u>To put into the same packet an industrial revolution and two political revolutions</u> may seem strange.

1b. It may seem strange <u>to put into the same packet an industrial revolution and two political revolutions</u>.

In (1a), the infinitive clause appears in the usual subject position, in front of the finite verb. In (1b), which is the way the sentence appeared in the actual text of the book and is the more usual form of sentences with infinitive clause subjects, the infinitive clause serving as subject has been moved to the end of the sentence ("extraposed"), leaving the pronoun *it* to hold the usual slot for the subject. This process of movement is known as **extraposition,** and the pronoun *it* that serves as the placeholder for the moved structure sometimes is called an **anticipatory pronoun** because it anticipates the clause and does not have an **antecedent** (an NP that precedes it and that it replaces). The extraposed infinitive clause, like its counterpart in (1a), is the subject.

Infinitive Clause Functions—Direct Object of a Monotransitive Verb

Like an NP, an infinitive clause may serve as a direct object. And like an NP, the infinitive clause serving as a direct object of a monotransitive VP will occur in the position we have come to expect for this element. The following sentence from *Wild Swans,* whose matrix VP is the monotransitive *learned,* illustrates this property:

2a. She also learned <u>to play Chinese chess, mah-jongg, and *go.*</u>

We have previously used the passive to test for objects in transitive sentences. Unfortunately, the passive test won't work if the presumed object happens to be an infinitive clause. You see, there is a general constraint in English grammar against the process of passivization in just those cases where infinitive clauses serve as direct objects. So, try as we might to use the passive rule to "promote" an infinitive clause from direct object to subject, the result will always be ungrammatical:

2b. *<u>To play Chinese chess, mah-jongg, and *go*</u> was learned by her.

Even extraposition, which frequently improves the acceptability of sentences with infinitive clause subjects, won't help. Sentence (2c) shows that extraposition doesn't do much for (2b):

2c. *It was learned by her <u>to play Chinese chess, mah-jongg, and *go.*</u>

For now, it is enough to recognize that the verb *learn* clearly requires a direct object (cf. *She learned French*).

Several matrix verbs regularly take infinitive clauses as direct objects: *begin, start, continue, attempt, try.* In general, sentences with these verbs indicate the starting point or the difficulty of the infinitive clause event. *(John began to read the book; John attempted to read the book).* Verbs like *begin* and *try* may also take NP objects *(John began the project; John tried the door),* but when they do, the NP typically identifies an event rather than a thing.

Infinitive Clause Functions—Direct Object of a Ditransitive Verb

In addition, an infinitive clause may serve as a direct object of a ditransitive verb. Another sentence from *Wild Swans* illustrates this possibility:

3a. My grandmother . . . begged her <u>to stop</u>.

Sentence (3a) provides an example of an infinitive clause as the direct object of the ditransitive speech act verb *beg*. *Her* in this sentence is the indirect object. Though the passive test cannot give us information about the function of the infinitive clause in (3a), it will confirm that *her* is an object since it can be made the subject of the corresponding passive (3b):

3b. She was begged to stop [*her* changes case because it is now the subject].

Beg is a transaction verb requiring a speaker (the subject), an addressee (the indirect object), and the spoken message (the direct object). Many "speech act" verbs are similarly ditransitive (cf. *Mary <u>told</u> [Jane] [a secret]; Mary <u>told</u> [Jane] [to wash the dishes])*. We shall consider ditransitive matrix VPs in more detail later in this chapter.

Infinitive Clause Functions—Direct Object in Complex Transitive Predicate Phrases

Just as an infinitive clause can serve as a direct object of a ditransitive verb, an infinitive clause also may serve as the direct object of a complex transitive verb taking a predicate complement. Such a clause occurs in the second half of (4a), a sentence taken from Poe's "The Fall of the House of Usher":

4a. I regarded her with an utter astonishment not unmingled with dread, and yet I found it impossible <u>to account for such feelings</u>.

What is interesting about the infinitive clause in this sentence is that it is a direct object that follows—rather than precedes—the predicate complement AP *impossible*. This seeming violation of basic English word order comes about by extraposition of the infinitive clause out of its usual position after the VP. Notice the anticipatory pronoun *it* functioning as a placeholder for the moved object. When a complex transitive verb has an infinitive clause direct object, it is obligatorily extraposed, as the ungrammaticality of (4b) demonstrates:

4b. *I found <u>to account for such feelings</u> impossible.

Nevertheless, (4b) represents the logical form of (4a), and we can use this logical form to help us understand how (4a) is grammatical. First, recall from Chapter Three that there is an implicit *be* between the direct object and the predicate complement, as in (4c):

4c. <u>To account for such feelings</u> *was* impossible.

Sentence (4c) has an infinitive clause subject. As you already know, such subjects can be extraposed, as (4d) demonstrates:

4d. It *was* impossible <u>to account for such feelings</u>.

If we remove the implicit *was* from (4d), we recognize it as the string of elements found in (4a), repeated below as (4e):

4e. I found <u>it impossible to account for such feelings</u>.

Thus, we can interpret the extraposition as coming from the implicit copular sentence relating the direct object and the predicate complement. Remember that an extraposed element retains its logical function, in spite of its "changed" position; *it* is merely a "dummy" direct object of (4a).

In addition to the extraposition of the direct object, there is another way to avoid the ungrammaticality of strings such as (4b), in which an infinitive clause serves as the direct object of a complex transitive verb. Examine (4f):

4f. I found such feelings impossible to account for.

What is interesting about (4f) is that only part of the infinitive clause is extraposed. You see, *to account for such feelings* still is the direct object of the sentence. However, instead of being entirely extraposed, the infinitive clause leaves its own object, *such feelings* (here the object of the preposition *for*), in the direct object slot of the matrix clause. The rest of the infinitive clause moves to the end.

Infinitive Clause Functions—Predicate Complement in Complex Transitive Predicate Phrases

Infinitive clauses may also serve as predicate complements in the complex transitive pattern. (Infinitive clauses serving this function sometimes are called "predication adjuncts.") But before we examine such predicate complements, let us review the complex transitive pattern as we know it thus far. In (5a) we find the verb *make* in its complex transitive usage, followed by a direct object and predicate complement:

5a. The mayor <u>made</u> [the City Council] [angry].
TV-DO-PC

In (5a), the adjective phrase (AP) *angry* serves as the predicate complement. This analysis would result from inserting *be* between the NP *the City Council* and the following AP *angry:*

5b. The City Council *was* angry.

But consider the result if we change (5a) only slightly, resulting in (5c):

5c. The mayor made the City Council get angry.

The only difference between (5c) and (5a) is the presence of the V *get* in (5c). In (5d), I suggest a bracketing of the constituents of (5c), which will show its similarity to (5a):

5d. The mayor <u>made</u> [the City Council] [get angry].
   TV-DO-PC

That is, in (5d) *get angry* (an infinitive clause lacking a *to* because of a special property of *make*) is the predicate complement. Yet we would not be able to figure this out by using the *be* test because the test would not yield grammatical results:

5e. *The City Council *was* get angry.

Actually, there is a very good reason for the failure of the *be* test in (5e). You see, the *be* test works only when there is an implicit *be* tied to the predicate complement, that is, when *be* is logically—but not physically—present. In (5d) there is no *be* because the predicate complement <u>already has another verb</u>, *get*. In fact, we could say that all predicate complements—even those we encountered in Chapter Three—really are infinitive clauses, and if the V of the infinitive clause is *be* (cf. *The mayor made the City Council be angry*), the *be* usually is omitted. But whenever the V of the predicate complement is any other verb, the full infinitive clause will be expressed.

Below, in a sentence from Richard Rodriguez's *Hunger of Memory,* is an example of such a fully expressed infinitive clause (the underlined structure) serving as the predicate complement:

6. Reading also enabled me <u>to sense something of the shape, the major concerns, of Western thought</u>.

You should keep in mind that all of the material on predicate complements you have just read is meant to serve as an introduction only. We will take up the problem of PC clauses in more detail later in the chapter.

Infinitive Clause Functions—Copular Complement

Another function that infinitive clauses may serve is that of copular complement, as the following example from *Wild Swans* illustrates:

7. One of [the police's] main jobs was <u>to check people's registration</u>.

Infinitive clauses serving the copular complement function can be recognized by the presence of the copular verb—here *be*—which clearly requires a complement.

Modifier Functions of Infinitive Clauses—The Adverbial

When an infinitive clause is not serving as an obligatory sentence constituent, it may serve as a modifier. One of the important modifier functions that an infinitive clause may have is that of adverbial (often of purpose or result), demonstrated by (8a) from *Wild Swans:*

8a. <u>To show her reverence for the Buddha</u>, she took perfumed baths and spent long hours meditating in front of burning incense at a little shrine.

Generally, we can recognize adverbial infinitive clauses in two ways. First, they are movable, and often occur at the front of the sentence—in front of the subject, in fact—as in (8a). In addition, we can substitute the complementizer *in order to* for *to.* Sentence (8b) shows what would happen if such an emendation were made to (8a):

8b. <u>In order to show her reverence for the Buddha</u>, she took perfumed baths . . . .

And Sentence (9), from Jamake Highwater's *The Primal Mind,* illustrates that writers sometimes deliberately use this unequivocal sign of adverbial function:

9. <u>In order to penetrate the "perennial springs of change,"</u> Vico began his investigations with "remote and obscure periods of history."

Modifier Functions of Infinitive Clauses—The Appositive

In Chapter One we learned that NPs sometimes modify other NPs, and we learned to call such modificational NPs *appositives.* If you look back to Chapter One, you will see that all the NPs we encountered that were modified by appositive NPs were "concrete" in nature. In other words, the modified NP designated something tangible—a person, place, or thing. There are, however, other kinds of NPs that designate an abstract entity or a mental object (think of nouns such as *invitation, commitment, promise, decision, advice,* etc.). Like their concrete counterparts, abstract NPs can be modified by appositives. In contrast to their concrete sisters, however, these NPs will not be modified by NP appositives, but by appositives that are clauses. These clauses will indicate the content of the abstraction; in fact, because they tell what the abstraction *is,* we can insert *be* between an abstract NP and its infinitive clause appositive. Thus, while the *be* test will not identify predicate complements when the PC is an infinitive clause, it will help us discover infinitive clauses that are appositives. Sentence (10a) from *Wild Swans* is a case in point:

10a. By 11 November, the Soviet Red Army had left the Jinzhou area and pulled back to Northern Manchuria, as part of a commitment by Stalin <u>to withdraw from the area within three months of victory</u>.

The underlined infinitive clause in (10a) is an appositive to *commitment,* as (10b), by passing the *be* test, clearly demonstrates (if the resulting sentence with *be* means "is supposed to" rather than "equals," the infinitive fails the *be* test and is not an appositive):

10b. Stalin's commitment *was* <u>to withdraw from the area within three months of victory</u>.

Nouns taking infinitive clauses as appositives usually are those indicating mental experience or speech acts (*commitment* in the above sentence can be seen as a kind of speech act). Many of these abstract nouns taking infinitive clause appositives have verb counterparts:

Our *attempt* to change his opinion failed.	[noun form: infinitive clause is an appositive]
We *attempted* to change his opinion.	[verb form: infinitive clause is a direct object]
Our *desire* to graduate motivated our studies.	[noun form: infinitive clause is an appositive]
We *desired* to graduate.	[verb form: infinitive clause is a direct object]

In the examples above in which the abstraction occurs as a verb, the infinitive phrase "goes with" the verb as object. When the abstraction is expressed as a noun, the infinitive phrase continues to "go with" it, but as an appositive, giving substance to the abstraction. Do not make the mistake of thinking of the appositive as a direct object of the noun. Such a function is impossible, given our definitions of these constituents.

Modifier Functions of Infinitive Clauses—The Adjectival

Finally, in what may be its rarest function, the infinitive clause can serve as a noun modifier in the function of adjectival. Sentence (11) from *The Primal Mind* provides an example of the adjectival use of an infinitive clause. Notice that the modified noun *thinkers* is not abstract at all:

11. Taking into account the scant and very dubious ethnographic literature of his day, he was among the first thinkers <u>to regard primal peoples as full members of the human race and of social tradition</u>.

Preliminary Summary

The data we have considered thus far clearly show that there are various levels involved in grammar. For example, there is the structural level in which an infinitive clause is an infinitive clause, regardless of its function in the sentence. It consists of a verb in the infinitive form, generally preceded by *to,* and may include a direct or indirect object of the infinitive if the verb is transitive, or a complement if the verb is linking. It also may include adverbials. And there is the functional level, as well, in which an infinitive clause is a clause that has been utilized by a sentence as an obligatory or optional constituent, such as subject, object, complement, or modifier.

Exercise 4.1

The following sentences come from Amy Tan's *The Joy Luck Club*. Underline every infinitive clause, and in the space following each sentence, identify the function that the infinitive clause serves in the sentence. These functions include:

subject
direct object
copular complement
adverbial
appositive

Be careful in underlining; an infinitive clause includes whatever serves as an object or complement to the infinitive VP as well as any modifiers of the infinitive VP or of its objects and complements. Some sentences have more than one infinitive clause.

1. And because of [the missionary ladies'] gifts, my parents could not refuse their invitation to join the church.

2. Nor could they ignore the old ladies' practical advice to improve their English through Bible study class on Wednesday nights.

3. My idea was to have a gathering of four women, one for each corner of my mah jong table.

4. Each week one of us would host a party to raise money and to raise our spirits.

5. But to despair was to wish back for something already lost.

6. And each week, we could hope to be lucky.

7. She promised to warn our other friends.

8. I came hurrying back from the other world to find my mother.

9. I learned to be polite to the Huangs and especially to Huang Taitai.

10. It was not polite not to come.

Answers to Exercise 4.1

1. And because of [the missionary ladies'] gifts, my parents could not refuse their invitation <u>to join the church</u>.

   appositive

2. Nor could they ignore the old ladies' practical advice <u>to improve their English through Bible study class on Wednesday nights</u>.

   appositive

3. My idea was <u>to have a gathering of four women, one for each corner of my mah jong table</u>.

   copular complement

4. Each week one of us would host a party <u>to raise money</u> and <u>to raise our spirits</u>.

   1. adverbial; 2. adverbial

5. But <u>to despair</u> was <u>to wish back for something already lost</u>.

   1. subject; 2. copular complement

6. And each week, we could hope <u>to be lucky</u>.

   direct object

7. She promised <u>to warn our other friends</u>.

   direct object

8. I came hurrying back from the other world <u>to find my mother</u>.

   adverbial

9. I learned <u>to be polite to the Huangs and especially to Huang Taitai</u>.

   direct object

10. It was not polite <u>not to come</u>.

    subject

Problematic Infinitive Clauses

In the grammar of any language there always are examples that are difficult to analyze, and English is no exception. The English infinitive clause may be one of the most troublesome areas of English syntax in this respect. To deal with the complexity of analysis, we can begin with the straightforward cases and move on from there.

In general, if an infinitive clause directly follows a VP, and the sentence would be ungrammatical without the infinitive clause appended to that verb phrase, then we consider the infinitive clause to be the direct object of that verb. Below are some examples:

12a. John decided to leave.

12b. John wanted to leave.

12c. John began to leave.

Notice that the subject/verb combination for each of the above examples would be ungrammatical for a sentence out of the blue if the infinitive clause was omitted:

13a. *John decided.

13b. *John wanted.

13c. *John began.

Thus, although (13a) and (13c) might suffice as, say, responses to questions, unless we knew *what* John decided or began, these strings would not be acceptable.

There are cases, of course, where the verb actually is intransitive, and is followed by an *adverbial* infinitive clause:

14a. John left to catch a bus.

Notice that the corresponding string with the infinitive clause omitted is perfectly grammatical, so the infinitive clause in (14) is an adverbial of purpose:

14b. John left.

It is important to keep in mind that, when considering the NP-infinitive clause strings we will investigate in the next sections, sometimes a monotransitive verb will have an adverbial infinitive clause (generally one of purpose) following its direct object:

15. John left Mary to catch a bus.

In (15), the direct object of *left* is *Mary;* the infinitive clause provides the purpose for the action (notice that *in order* can be inserted in front of *to*). It is therefore an adverbial. Often, the mental insertion of *in order* in front of the complementizer can help us to identify adverbial infinitive clauses.

In previous chapters, if we were uncertain about the transitivity of a VP we were able to use the passive test, which allowed us to tinker with a sentence so that the NP following the VP would be promoted into subject position. If this tinkering had a grammatical result, we decided that the VP was transitive. In addition, if we found that the VP was transitive, we knew by default that the promoted NP was the direct object of the active version of the sentence. In essence, the passive test worked equally well to determine whether a particular NP was a direct object. Unfortunately, because of the constraint in English grammar against promoting an infinitive clause direct object to subject position by applying the passive rule, all attempts to test for direct object status using the passive test will fail when the suspected direct object is an infinitive clause, *regardless of the actual status of that clause.* The *in order to* test thus assumes an important role in differentiating between direct objects and adverbials.

To witness the workings of this test, consider a pair of sentences that are superficially similar:

16a. John wanted to lose weight.

17a. John dieted to lose weight.

Applying the *in order to* test yields the results below:

16b. *John wanted *in order* to lose weight.

17b. John dieted *in order* to lose weight.

Obviously, the infinitive clause in (17b) passes the test, and is therefore an adverbial. The infinitive clause in (16b) clearly fails, and so is not. This test should help you come to a decision regarding the function of certain infinitive clauses.

The Dilemma, Part I—The NP-Infinitive Clause (Ditransitive Cases)

The functional analysis of infinitive clauses becomes a little less clear-cut, however, when an NP intervenes between the VP and the infinitive clause and we can rule out the adverbial of purpose function for the clause. Let's examine a pair of sentences.

18a. John asked Mary a question.

19a. John asked Mary to leave.

Sentence (18a), a simple sentence with no subordinate clauses, clearly exhibits the **TV-IO-DO** sentence pattern, even though the *to* test works only imperfectly here. Notice that the passive test shows that both predicate phrase NPs are objects since either NP can become the subject of the passive counterparts of (18a):

18b. Mary was asked a question (by John).

18c. A question was asked (of) Mary (by John).

Sentence (19a) is analogous to (18a). In (19a), the direct object is the infinitive clause *to leave,* which is, in fact, an abbreviated form of the request that John made.

However, recall that even though the infinitive clause is the direct object of the sentence, it cannot be made the subject via the passive rule because of the general constraint on converting infinitive clause direct objects to subjects through passivization; only the indirect object *Mary* can do so:

19b. *To leave was asked (of) Mary by John.

19c. Mary was asked to leave (by John).

In general, the ditransitive analysis is appropriate when the finite VP is a speech act (i.e., the verb indicates a use of language) and *the NP preceding the infinitive clause is the person addressed by the subject during this speech act. The infinitive clause is a truncated form of the contents of that speech act.* (In Example 19a, we could imagine that what John said was, "Would you please leave?") *Verbs taking an indirect object* NP *followed by a direct object infinitive clause include:* advise, beg, command, instruct, invite, order, persuade, remind, request, teach, tell, *and* urge.

The Dilemma, Part II—A Monotransitive Analysis of NP-Infinitive Clause Constructions

There are cases for which a ditransitive analysis of the VP of the matrix clause will not work. Let us examine some examples:

20a. Peter wanted Paul to pay the rent.

21a. Peter expected Paul to pay the rent.

Neither (20a) nor (21a) has a matrix VP that is a speech act or indeed any other kind of transaction, so these sentences are not ditransitive. However, both require the infinitive structure *to pay the rent,* because without it, the sentences' meanings are radically changed:

20b. Peter wanted Paul.

21b. Peter expected Paul.

In fact, sentences (20a) and (21a) assert not that Peter wanted or expected Paul, but that Peter wanted/expected a certain event to occur, namely that *Paul pay the rent.* We can repeat (20a) and (21a) with this information shown in brackets:

20c. Peter wanted [Paul to pay the rent].

21c. Peter expected [Paul to pay the rent].

That is, *Paul* apparently is the subject of the infinitive clause in both sentences, and the entire subject-bearing infinitive clause (called thus in contrast to the more common subjectless infinitive clause) apparently is the direct object of the matrix VP.

It is here that the similarity ends, however, because the two sentences behave differently when the passive rule is applied to them. Recall that an infinitive clause serving as direct object cannot be promoted to subject. Nonetheless, it is sometimes—though not always—possible to promote to subject of the matrix VP the explicit NP subject of a direct object infinitive clause by applying the passive. The application of the passive to (20c) and (21c) results in the following:

20d. *Paul was wanted to pay the rent.

21d. Paul was expected to pay the rent.

The failure of the passive test in (20d) and its success in (21d) indicates that the verbs *want* and *expect* have different properties. Since only an object of an active VP can be promoted to subject of the passive form of the same verb, the acceptability of (21d) means that, unlike *wanted,* the VP *expected* in the sentences of (21) has extracted the NP *Paul* out of the infinitive clause and claimed it as its direct object, leaving the remainder of the infinitive clause *(to pay the rent)* as predicate complement, an obligatory element. Consequently, we must revise the bracketing shown in (21c) to that shown in (21e), but retain the bracketing in (20c), repeated here as (20e):

20e. Peter wanted [Paul to pay the rent].

21e. Peter expected [Paul] [to pay the rent].

The bracketing provided in (20e) indicates that the DO of *wanted* is the subject-bearing infinitive clause *Paul to pay the rent,* whereas that in (21e) indicates that the DO of *expected* is *Paul* and the predicate complement is the infinitive clause *to pay the rent. Want* is therefore monotransitive, taking only a direct object; *expect* is complex transitive, taking both a direct object and a predicate complement.

Most of the verbs that behave like *want* in taking direct objects that can be subject-bearing infinitive clauses are verbs expressing volition or emotional stance: *want, not want, like, not like, dislike, can't bear, desire, hate, love, prefer, wish,* and so on. Verbs such as *mean* and *intend* in contexts in which they express "wanting" also can take subject-bearing infinitive clauses as direct objects.

Before we conclude this section, let us examine some other sentences with monotransitive matrix VPs. Notice what happens when the subject of the infinitive clause is a pronoun:

22a. John likes students to write publishable papers.

22b. John likes <u>them</u> to write publishable papers.

23a. John hates people to flatter him.

23b. John hates <u>them</u> to flatter him.

In (22b) and (23b), the pronoun subject of the infinitive clause is in the objective case, despite its status as subject of the infinitive. Subjects of nonfinite verbs never appear in the subjective case. Furthermore, many speakers can insert *for* before the subject of subject-bearing infinitive clauses serving as direct objects:

22c. John likes <u>for</u> them to write publishable papers.

23c. John hates <u>for</u> them to flatter him.

The presence of *for* is an additional indication that the NP-infinitive combination operates as a unit: *The entire chunk* constitutes a single construction, an infinitive clause with a subject consisting of the NP that immediately precedes the infinitive complementizer *to.* Moreover, many speakers and writers can insert the pronoun *it* immediately before *for,* and thus "extrapose" the entire clause out of object position. The possibility that the entire string can essentially be replaced with *it* means that the string functions as though it were an NP; it is, in effect, a single element in the sentence:

22d. John likes <u>it</u> for them to write publishable papers.

23d. John hates <u>it</u> for them to flatter him.

In the cases of subject-bearing infinitive clauses we have examined thus far, the infinitive clauses have served the grammatical function of direct object. Sometimes, however, subject-bearing infinitive clauses occur as subjects:

24a. <u>*For* students to write publishable papers</u> is desirable.

When serving the grammatical function of subject, subject-bearing infinitive clauses *must* begin with *for* (which shares the complementizer function) and may be extraposed:

24b. *It* is desirable <u>for students to write publishable papers</u>.

It is also possible to retain the object of the infinitive clause *(publishable papers)* as subject of the matrix VP and move the remainder of the clause to the end of the sentence:

24c. <u>Publishable papers</u> are desirable <u>for students to write</u>.

Notice that in Sentence (24c) the NP *publishable papers* has pretensions to subject status, since the VP of the higher clause *(are)* now shows **agreement** with the NP *publishable papers* (both are plural).

The Dilemma, Part III—Complex Transitive Cases

Just about every remaining case of predicate NP-infinitive clause is like sentence (21a) with *expect,* an instance of complex transitive complementation. The best example of such a complex transitive verb followed by an NP-infinitive clause string is the verb *make,* which will take an infinitive clause without any introductory complementizer when the sentence is active:

25a. They made the children work.

The unmarked infinitive clause *work* in the above example is separate from the preceding NP. Because the NP *the children* can be promoted to subject via the passive rule, it is the direct object of the matrix VP. The complementizer *to* will surface in the passive version:

25b. The children were made to work.

Therefore, a monotransitive analysis of *made* would be inaccurate. And since *make* is not a speech act verb, the relationship of the infinitive clause to the rest of the predicate phrase is that of predicate complement; it completes the meaning of the verb itself as a kind of "predication adjunct," e.g., *made to work.*

The vast number of NP-infinitive clause combinations in the predicate phrase are instances of complex transitive complementation. Most of these verbs are causative verbs. That is, the subject of the matrix verb causes the direct object to do something specified in the infinitive clause and thus to behave as another actor. Causative verbs of this nature include *make, help, cause, force, allow,* etc.

Syntax and semantics do not always converge, however. For example, the verbs, *let, allow, have,* and *force* all have causative senses:

26a. They let the children work.

27a. They allowed the children to work.

28a. They had the children work.

29a. They forced the children to work.

But they do not exhibit the same syntactic behavior; that is, the application of the passive test yields different results for *let* and *allow,* and also for *have* and *force:*

26b. *The children were let [to] work.

27b. The children were allowed to work.

28b. *The children were had [to] work.

29b. The children were forced to work.

Despite their causative status and their resemblance to *make* in not allowing the *to*-complementizer, *let* and *have* are monotransitive matrix verbs, demonstrated by the ungrammaticality of (26b) and (28b). Their synonyms *allow* and *have* are complex transitive (see 27b and 29b) because they can extract subject NPs out of complement infinitive clauses and make those NPs their own direct objects. The appropriate bracketing of object and complements, then, is as follows:

26c. They <u>let</u> [the children work]. (TV-DO)

27c. They <u>allowed</u> [the children] [to work]. (TV-DO-PC)

28c. They <u>had</u> [the children work]. (TV-DO)

29c. They <u>forced</u> [the children] [to work]. (TV-DO-PC)

Do not mistake the absence of *to* as a sign of monotransitivity: Remember that *make* requires no *to,* yet is complex transitive. The same can be said for *help:*

30a. Peter helped Paul complete the assignment.

30b. Paul was helped to complete the assignment.

In (30a), then, the NP *Paul* is the direct object of *helped,* and *complete the assignment* is the predicate complement; the matrix VP *helped* is complex transitive.

Perception Verbs

Verbs that express acts of perception, such as *see* and *hear,* typically are transitive, and are sometimes complex transitive. We first encountered them in complex transitive patterns in Chapter Three. I will repeat two examples from Exercise 3.2 here, with the bracketing provided in the answers:

31a. He <u>had seen</u> [the woman] [in the rocker]. (TV-DO-PC)

32a. He <u>could almost hear</u> [the hum of the insects] [against the screens of the old porch]. (TV-DO-PC)

The application of the passive test confirms the complex transitive analysis:

31b. The woman had been seen in the rocker.

32b. The hum of the insects could almost be heard against the screens of the old porch.

In addition, both *see* and *hear* can occur as matrix verbs followed by an infinitive clause with no *to*-complementizer:

33a. He saw the woman sit in the rocker.

34a. He heard the woman shut the door.

Given the analysis of (31a) and (32a), we would expect that (33a) and (34a) would also exhibit the complex transitive pattern, but the passive test produces ambiguous results:

33b. ?The woman was seen to sit in the rocker.

34b. ?The woman was heard to shut the door.

That is, although native speakers of English are unwilling to reject sentences (33b) and (34b) outright, they generally think they would not use them.

What's a grammarian to do? I suggest we be conservative at this point in our analysis and assume that when perception verbs take an infinitive clause as a direct object, they are not powerful enough to extract the subject of that clause. That is, we shall analyze perception verbs as taking subject-bearing infinitive clauses as direct objects. In the context of infinitive clauses, then, they are monotransitive. The direct objects of (33a) and (34a), subject-bearing infinitive clauses, are underlined as follows:

33c. He saw <u>the woman sit in the rocker</u>.

34c. He heard <u>the woman shut the door</u>.

In Chapter Five, we shall reexamine this issue.

The Infinitive Clause Conspiracy

You may have noticed that the general tendency in grammar is for most infinitive clauses to occur at the end of the sentence:

a) Infinitive clause subjects may be extraposed, and so show up at the end;

b) Infinitive clause direct objects of complex transitive verbs *must* be extraposed, and so show up at the end;

c) Infinitive clause direct objects of monotransitive verbs occur at the end because direct objects follow VPs;

d) Infinitive clause predicate complements of complex transitive verbs occur at the end because the usual position for PCs is the end of the clause;

e) Infinitive clause copular complements generally occur at the end of a clause, because that is the regular position of those constituents;

f) Infinitive clause adverbials often occur at the end of a sentence because in basic declarative word order, adverbials occur last.

The net result of this "conspiracy" of apparently independently motivated rules of English grammar is that, because all infinitive clauses typically occur in sentence-final position, *we cannot rely on positional information to determine the grammatical functions of infinitive clauses,* even though examining the position of a constituent with respect to other sentence elements was a great boon to us in Chapter Three, when we had to investigate only NPs, APs, and PPs. We must therefore rely on tests such as *be, in order to,* and passive to determine the functions of infinitive clauses.

Decision Procedure

When you encounter an infinitive clause, you can approach the analysis by the systematic decision procedure shown in Figure 4–1. First, find what you believe to be the infinitive clause, underline it, and then follow the procedures schematized below. If the VP of the main clause is passive, put the sentence back into the active voice. The function of the infinitive clause in an NP-infinitive clause string in the predicate phrase does not change in the conversion from passive to active and vice versa because of the general constraint against promoting object infinitive clauses to subject. Remember, however, that the decision procedure is no substitute for having read and understood the preceding discussion.

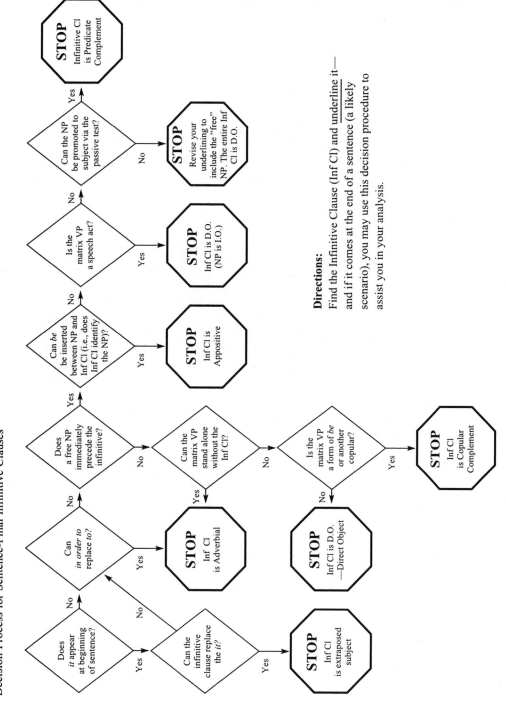

Figure 4–1
Decision Process for Sentence-Final Infinitive Clauses

Directions:
Find the Infinitive Clause (Inf Cl) and underline it—and if it comes at the end of a sentence (a likely scenario), you may use this decision procedure to assist you in your analysis.

STOP
Infinitive Cl is Predicate Complement

Can the NP be promoted to subject via the passive test?

STOP
Revise your underlining to include the "free" NP. The entire Inf Cl is D.O.

Is the matrix VP a speech act?

STOP
Inf Cl is D.O. (NP is I.O.)

Can *be* be inserted between NP and Inf Cl (i.e., does Inf Cl identify the NP)?

STOP
Inf Cl is Appositive

Does a free NP immediately precede the infinitive?

Can the matrix VP stand alone without the Inf Cl?

Is the matrix VP a form of *be* or another copular?

STOP
Inf Cl is Copular Complement

Can *in order to* replace *to?*

STOP
Inf Cl is Adverbial

STOP
Inf Cl is D.O. —Direct Object

Does *it* appear at beginning of sentence?

Can the infinitive clause replace the *it?*

STOP
Inf Cl is extraposed subject

Exercise 4.2

Underline the infinitive clause in each of the following sentences. Then decide what grammatical function the infinitive clause serves in the sentence (i.e., *subject, direct object, copular complement, predicate complement, adverbial, adjectival, appositive*). In the case of predicate phrases containing infinitive clauses, determine the character of the finite verb: copular, transitive, or intransitive? If transitive: monotransitive, ditransitive, or complex transitive? These sentences are taken from Jacob Bronowski's *The Ascent of Man*.

1. One aim of the physical sciences has been to give an exact picture of the material world.

2. [Szilard] wanted to keep the patent secret.

3. He tried to get Fermi not to publish.

4. And Mendel had failed to qualify as a teacher.

5. And Mendel decided to devote his life to practical experiments in biology, here in the monastery.

6. His imagination, his reason, his emotional subtlety and toughness, make it possible for him not to accept the environment but to change it.

7. I, at over forty, having spent a lifetime in doing abstract mathematics about the shapes of things, suddenly saw my knowledge reach back two million years and shine a searchlight into the history of man.

8. The eyesockets are still rather sideways in the skull, on either side of the snout; but compared with the eyes of earlier insect eaters, the lemur's eyes have begun to move to the front and to give some stereoscopic vision.

9. The runner is like a child at play; his actions are an adventure in freedom, and the only purpose of his breathless chemistry was to explore the limits of his own strength.

10. Here by eleven months, [the reflex] urges the baby to crawl.

Answers to Exercise 4.2

1. One aim of the physical sciences has been <u>to give an exact picture of the material world</u>.

   copular complement; the finite verb *has been* is copular

2. [Szilard] wanted <u>to keep the patent secret</u>.

   direct object; the finite verb *wanted* is monotransitive

3. He tried <u>to get Fermi <u>not to publish</u></u>.

   There are two infinitive clauses in this sentence, one embedded within the other. The underlined construction beginning with *to* and ending with *publish* is the direct object of the finite monotransitive verb *tried;* the construction underlined a second time is the direct object of the monotransitive causative verb *get*. Note, however, that *get* is nonfinite in this case.

4. And Mendel had failed <u>to qualify as a teacher</u>.

   direct object of monotransitive VP *had failed*

5. And Mendel decided <u>to devote his life to practical experiments in biology, here in the monastery</u>.

   direct object of monotransitive *decided*

6. His imagination, his reason, his emotional subtlety and toughness, make it possible <u>for him not to accept the environment but to change it</u>.

   direct object of complex transitive VP *make*

7. I, at over forty, having spent a lifetime in doing abstract mathematics about the shapes of things, suddenly saw <u>my knowledge reach back two million years and shine a searchlight into the history of man</u>.

   direct object of *saw*

8. The eyesockets are still rather sideways in the skull, on either side of the snout; but compared with the eyes of earlier insect eaters, the lemur's eyes have begun <u>to move to the front and to give some stereoscopic vision</u>.

   direct object of the monotransitive VP *have begun*. There are two separate infinitive clauses here, serving the single direct object function.

9. The runner is like a child at play; his actions are an adventure in freedom, and the only purpose of his breathless chemistry was <u>to explore the limits of his own strength</u>.

   copular complement of *was*

10. Here by eleven months, [the reflex] urges the baby <u>to crawl</u>.

    direct object of ditransitive VP *urges;* the NP *the baby* is indirect object.

Exercise 4.3

The following sentences come from Jamake Highwater's *The Primal Mind*. Underline every infinitive clause, and in the space following each sentence indicate the function that the infinitive clause serves in the sentence. Be careful, as some are nested inside of others. Keep in mind the following facts:

a. nouns *do not* take objects;

b. an element *cannot* simultaneously be a subject or an object and a modifier (i.e., adverbial or adjectival);

c. a subordinate clause *includes* whatever modifies something within its boundaries;

d. the preposition *to* can be distinguished from the complementizer *to* by observing the kind of element that follows it; prepositions are followed by NPs, not by verbs;

e. the matrix verbs *make, have, let,* and *help* and the perception verbs require their infinitive clauses to omit the complementizer.

1. Political idealists have overemphasized the uniformity of people in their efforts to destroy intolerance.

2. It is no longer realistic for dominant cultures to send out missionaries to convert everyone to their singular ideas of the "truth."

3. Today we are beginning to look into the ideas of groups outside the dominant culture.

4. In order to penetrate the "perennial springs of change," Vico began his investigations with "remote and obscure periods of history."

5. Christian bias required him to give full credence to the biblical Genesis . . . .

6. It isn't easy to overcome this indoctrination.

7. We are asked to grasp the conception of event horizons and clones and other precepts . . . .

8. Most of the great artists of our century have built a mysterious self through their art to fill the vacuum left by the lack of public ceremonial life.

9. In this rather curious fashion [Westerners] have opened the way and made it possible for people to transcend their cultural isolation.

10. [Pollock] sought to avoid fragmentation for its own sake or for the sake of decoration.

Answers to Exercise 4.3

1. Political idealists have overemphasized the uniformity of people in their efforts <u>to destroy intolerance</u>.

   Appositive

2. It is no longer realistic <u>for dominant cultures to send out missionaries to convert everyone to their singular ideas of the "truth."</u>

   There are two infinitive clauses in this sentence, one nested inside the other. The first begins with *for* and goes to the end of the sentence. This one is a subject-bearing infinitive clause, functioning as an extraposed sentence subject. The second begins with *to convert* and goes to the end of the sentence. It is an adverbial within the subject clause.

3. Today we are beginning <u>to look into the ideas of groups outside the dominant culture</u>.

   Direct object of *are beginning*

4. <u>In order to penetrate the "perennial springs of change,"</u> Vico began his investigations with "remote and obscure periods of history."

   Adverbial

5. Christian bias required him <u>to give full credence to the biblical Genesis</u> . . . .

   Predicate complement

6. It isn't easy <u>to overcome this indoctrination</u>.

   Extraposed subject

7. We are asked <u>to grasp the conception of event horizons and clones and other precepts</u> . . . .

   Direct object. When the matrix VP is passive, as this one is, it is often useful to convert the sentence to active voice before using the decision procedure. Infinitive clauses do not change grammatical function in the shift from passive to active or vice versa.

8. Most of the great artists of our century have built a mysterious self through their art <u>to fill the vacuum left by the lack of public ceremonial life</u>.

   Adverbial

9. In this rather curious fashion [Westerners] have opened the way and made it possible <u>for people to transcend their cultural isolation</u>.

   Subject-bearing infinitive clause; direct object of complex transitive *made*. Notice its extraposition out of direct object slot.

10. [Pollock] sought <u>to avoid fragmentation for its own sake or for the sake of decoration</u>.

    Direct object

Terms Used in Chapter Four

agreement: the grammatical process by which a verb phrase carries a plural inflection if its subject is plural, and a singular inflection if its subject is singular. For example, in the sentence *The girls are riding their bikes,* both the subject NP *the girls* and the VP *are riding* indicate plurality.

antecedent: the NP that a pronoun replaces in subsequent mentions of the NP. For example, in the sentence given above, *the girls* is the antecedent of *their.*

anticipatory pronoun: the pronoun *it* that holds the place for a subordinate clause moved to the end of the sentence. An anticipatory pronoun has no antecedent.

complementizer: an essentially meaningless function word serving to signal that the clause it introduces is subordinate. In infinitive clauses, the complementizer *to* generally appears.

clause: a construction containing a subject (though sometimes implied rather than overt) and a predicate phrase. The very basic sentences studied in Chapter One were single clauses.

extraposition: the movement to the end of the sentence of certain subject or object subordinate clauses from the position typical of these functions.

finite VP: a VP that is inflected for tense or contains a modal auxiliary—e.g., *were riding, may leave, jumped.*

infinitive clause: a clause whose VP is the infinitive form of the verb.

inflections: suffixes indicating grammatical information such as person, number, and tense.

matrix clause: the sentence into which a subordinate clause is inserted.

nonfinite verb: any verb form that is not inflected for tense—infinitives and participles.

subordinate clause: a clause that cannot stand as an independent sentence in its own right, but rather serves a particular grammatical function (e.g., subject, object, complement, or modifier) in another "matrix" clause.

Chapter Quiz

The following sentences come from Sue Miller's *The Good Mother*. Underline every infinitive clause and, in the space following each sentence, indicate the function that the infinitive clause serves. If more than one infinitive clause occurs in any sentence, number the clauses and assign the same numbers to your written responses. The point value in parentheses indicates the number of infinitive clauses you should find.

1. It was the cousin's job, though, to distribute the mail after the long trip back to camp down the dirt road, across the lake. (1)

2. She didn't really know; she wanted me to tell her. (1)

3. But then she stood up to look at the young couple in the booth behind her. (1)

4. I wanted . . . to make myself remember everything about it. (2)

5. I leaned forward and began to splash water on her soap-slicked body. (1)

6. I started to brush my hair again. (1)

7. I let Brian . . . comfort me. (1)

8. Sometimes in those weeks alone with her, I had felt overwhelmed by her need to use me as playmate. (1)

9. Then we went to her room to get her clothes. (1)

10. She began to whine. (1)

11. I shut my door quietly in order not to wake her. (1)

12. I had been planning . . . to strike a note of camaraderie, but at the last moment I couldn't bring myself to do it. (2)

13. She pilfered cigarettes and taught us all to smoke. (1)

14. Occasionally he would force her to stay home in the evening. (1)

15. They want me to go to Europe next year. (1)

16. Tears began to slide down her face. (1)

17. I hadn't been at the family picnic, but I had made it a point to come to the service. (1)

18. He invited us to join them for Thanksgiving. (1)

19. I would go as a divorcee, to defiantly represent failure in that nest of accomplishment. (1)

20. I felt shaken with rage, with the impulse to throw something, a paper weight, at him. (1)

21. I arranged to meet Leo at eight. (1)

22. It took me nearly an hour to get to Ursula's. (1)

23. I had turned down an invitation from my parents to come to Chicago. (1)

Chapter Five

Participle Clauses

Introduction

In Chapter Four we learned that sentences typically contain more than one clause. That is, many English sentences comprise a matrix clause (sometimes called a "main" clause) and one or more subordinate clauses. Thus far we have studied one kind of nonfinite clause, the infinitive clause, and the functions it may serve within a sentence. In this chapter we will investigate a second type of nonfinite clause—the **participle clause**—and we will learn to identify the grammatical functions it may serve.

Like infinitive clauses, participle clauses are frequently called participle *phrases* in more traditional treatments of grammar. However, because participle constructions—like infinitive clauses—have a predicate phrase (though nonfinite) and an implicit or overt subject, scholars working within a more modern framework typically call them *clauses* rather than phrases. We shall follow this trend. Before we begin our investigation of participle clauses, we will review what participles are. Recall that English verbs have four principal parts: the infinitive, the past, the present participle, and the past participle.

The present participle for all verbs—both weak and strong—is the form bearing the -*ing* **inflection.** In a very important sense, the word *present* in the term *present participle* is inaccurate since the form itself is nonfinite, signaling no tense whatsoever. As you will remember, the present participle, together with the *be* auxiliary, signals the progressive aspect in English. In the following examples, the auxiliary *be*—not the participle—is inflected for tense. The participle simply indicates that the event continues over a period of time:

1a. I was <u>frowning</u>.

1b. I was <u>crying</u>.

1c. He was <u>lying</u> on a blanket on the floor.

The past participle for all weak verbs is indistinguishable from the past, and for strong verbs sometimes is indistinguishable. The past participle (which, like the present participle, does not indicate tense), together with the *have* auxiliary, signals perfective **aspect,** as the following example from Richard Nixon's *In the Arena* demonstrates:

2. [Tricia's husband Ed Cox] had <u>known</u> several of Jaworski's staff at Harvard Law School and had <u>served</u> with some in the U.S. Attorney's office in New York City.

You will also recall that the past participle, together with the *be* auxiliary, indicates passive **voice** in English, as the following sentences from *Wild Swans* illustrate:

3a. She was <u>invaded</u> by a wave of panic.

3b. At first [Pu Yi] was <u>called</u> Chief Executive; later, in 1934, he was <u>made</u> emperor of Manchukuo.

Participles, both present and past, have other functions as well. Most simply, they can occur between determiner and noun and behave like simple adjectives:

4a. I listened, as if in a dream, to the wild improvisations of his <u>speaking</u> guitar (Edgar Allan Poe, "The Fall of the House of Usher"; present participle as adjective).

4b. I developed my plan in a <u>hurried</u> whisper (Joseph Conrad, "The Secret Sharer"; past participle as adjective).

Present participles also may be used as simple nouns sometimes called *gerunds*. This use is often signaled by the presence of a determiner (*the* in 5a; *an* in 5b):

5a. And then the <u>talking</u> stopped (Amy Tan, *The Joy Luck Club*).

5b. I had always assumed we had an unspoken <u>understanding</u> about these things *(The Joy Luck Club)*.

In addition, like infinitives, participles may form a chunk—a **participle clause**—with elements such as NPs, APs, and adverbials. The resulting construction, now a nonfinite clause, may function as a major constituent or a modifier. In traditional grammars of English, a present participle clause used for a function typically served by an NP, such as subject, direct object, or object of preposition, has been called a **gerund phrase,** with the VP of that "phrase" called a **gerund.** Traditional grammars have also had a special term—**gerundive**—for a present participle clause used as a modifier. Because these terms conflate structure with function yet do not distinguish among particular functions, we will opt in this book for calling all clauses headed by participles, whether present or past, **participle clauses.** Once we have so identified the structure of the clause, we will identify the function of the clause: subject, direct object, object of preposition, adjectival, etc. The following is an example of a present participle clause serving as a major constituent, here a subject:

6. <u>Expressing ideas clearly</u> is necessary for good communication.

The underlined constituent in Sentence (6) functions as the subject of the sentence. Like the subject infinitive clauses we encountered in Chapter Four, it substitutes for an NP. However, unlike a noun, the participle *expressing* retains its verb character: it takes a direct object [*ideas*] and an adverb [*clearly*]. *Expressing ideas clearly* is a partial predicate phrase, a nonfinite participle clause.

Not all occurrences of participles in the subject slot are nonfinite clauses, though, as you will recognize after considering the following sentences:

7a. Writing the book was a laborious task.

7b. The writing of the book was tedious work.

Sentence (7a) clearly includes a participle clause functioning as its subject, whereas (7b) has a true NP as its subject. That is, even though *writing the book* is the subject of (7a), *writing* remains verb-like in that it takes a direct object, *the book.* Sentence (7b) conveys a message similar to that of (7a), but the subject of (7b) clearly is a true NP. Note that the participle *writing* is modified by a prepositional phrase *of the book,* so that the NP *the book* is properly the object of the preposition *of,* not the direct object of the participle. Moreover, and this point is crucial, *writing* is preceded by a determiner—an unequivocal signal of a noun phrase.

Exercise 5.1

In the following sentences from Anne Rice's *Interview with the Vampire,* underline every participle <u>form</u> you encounter and, in the space below each sentence, indicate how it is used: as part of the VP, as an adjective, as a bona fide noun (e.g., *the <u>building</u>*), or as the **head** (chief element) of a participle clause.

1. For a long time he stood there against the dim light from Divisadero Street and the passing beams of traffic.

2. And quickly he removed the small tape recorder from his brief case, making a check of the cassette and the batteries.

3. At once the room was flooded with a harsh yellow light.

4. And the boy, staring up at the vampire, could not repress a gasp.

5. The boy was startled by the preciseness of the date.

6. We were living in Louisiana then.

7. He only hinted at this at first, and he stopped taking his meals altogether.

8. Both St. Dominic and the Blessed Virgin Mary had come to him in the oratory.

9. But I remember the feeling.

10. I loved my brother, . . . and at times I believed him to be a living saint.

11. The main thought was this: I had laughed at him; I had not believed him; I had not been kind to him.

12. He had fallen because of me.

13. I could think of nothing but his body rotting in the ground.

14. He was buried in the St. Louis cemetery in New Orleans, and I did everything to avoid passing those gates; but still I thought of him constantly.

15. Meantime, the slaves on Pointe du Lac (that was my plantation) had begun to talk of seeing his ghost on the gallery, and the overseer couldn't keep order.

16. And then I was attacked.

17. Perhaps I'd seen [my own egotism] reflected in the priest.

18. Living in New Orleans had become too difficult for him, considering his needs and the necessity to care for his father.

19. Handling the dead body with such a purpose caused me nausea.

20. I became almost hypnotized by the quivering of his lip.

21. Now I was not destroying myself but someone else.

22. He sneered with the impatience of people listening to the obvious lies of others.

23. The blood flowed down upon my shirt and coat, and he watched it with a narrow, gleaming eye.

24. And now I saw him filled with his own life and own blood.

25. He appeared frail and stupid to me, a man made of dried twigs with a thin, carping voice.

Answers to Exercise 5.1

1. For a long time he stood there against the dim light from Divisadero Street and the <u>passing</u> beams of traffic.

   adjective

2. And quickly he removed the small tape recorder from his brief case, <u>making</u> a check of the cassette and the batteries.

   head of a clause

3. At once the room was <u>flooded</u> with a harsh yellow light.

   part of a VP (passive)

4. And the boy, <u>staring</u> up at the vampire, could not repress a gasp.

   head of a clause

5. The boy was <u>startled</u> by the preciseness of the date.

   part of a VP (passive)

6. We were <u>living</u> in Louisiana then.

   part of a VP (progressive)

7. He only hinted at this at first, and he stopped <u>taking</u> his meals altogether.

   head of a clause

8. Both St. Dominic and the Blessed Virgin Mary had <u>come</u> to him in the oratory.

   part of a VP (perfective)

9. But I remember the <u>feeling</u>.

   noun

10. I loved my brother, . . . and at times I believed him to be a <u>living</u> saint.

    adjective

11. The main thought was this: I had <u>laughed</u> at him; I had not <u>believed</u> him; I had not <u>been</u> kind to him.

    all three are parts of VPs (all perfective)

12. He had <u>fallen</u> because of me.

    part of a VP (perfect)

13. I could think of nothing but his body <u>rotting</u> in the ground.

    head of a clause

14. He was <u>buried</u> in the St. Louis cemetery in New Orleans, and I did everything to avoid <u>passing</u> those gates; but still I thought of him constantly.

    1. part of a VP (passive); 2. head of a clause

15. Meantime, the slaves on Pointe du Lac (that was my plantation) had <u>begun</u> to talk of <u>seeing</u> his ghost on the gallery, and the overseer couldn't keep order.

    1. part of a VP (perfective); 2. head of a clause

16. And then I was <u>attacked</u>.

    part of a VP (passive)

17. Perhaps I'd <u>seen</u> [my own egotism] <u>reflected</u> in the priest.

    1. part of a VP (perfective); 2. head of a clause

18. <u>Living</u> in New Orleans had <u>become</u> too difficult for him, <u>considering</u> his needs and the necessity to care for his father.

    1. head of a clause; 2. part of a VP (perfective); 3. head of a clause

19. <u>Handling</u> the dead body with such a purpose caused me nausea.

    head of a clause

20. I became almost <u>hypnotized</u> by the <u>quivering</u> of his lip.

    1. head of a clause; 2. noun

21. Now I was not <u>destroying</u> myself but someone else.

    part of a VP (progressive)

22. He sneered with the impatience of people <u>listening</u> to the obvious lies of others.

    head of a clause

23. The blood flowed down upon my shirt and coat, and he watched it with a narrow, <u>gleaming</u> eye.

    adjective

24. And now I saw him <u>filled</u> with his own life and own blood.

    head of a clause

25. He appeared frail and stupid to me, a man <u>made</u> of <u>dried</u> twigs with a thin, <u>carping</u> voice.

    1. head of a clause; 2. adjective; 3. adjective

Grammatical Functions of Participle Clauses—Major Constituents

Recall that participle clauses function as major constituents or as modifiers within matrix clauses. Sentences (6) and (7a) have provided clear examples of participle clauses functioning as *subjects* of sentences. In the previous exercise we encountered two additional instances of participle clauses having the grammatical function of sentence subject:

8a. <u>Living in New Orleans</u> had become too difficult for him . . . .

9a. <u>Handling the dead body with such a purpose</u> caused me nausea.

You will notice that these participle clauses, unlike infinitive clauses, cannot be extraposed in Standard Written English:

8b. ?It had become too difficult for him <u>living in New Orleans</u>.

9b. ?It caused me nausea <u>handling the dead body with such a purpose</u>.

The lack of acceptability of (8b) and (9b) contrasts sharply with the extraposed versions of similar sentences with infinitive clause subjects:

8c. It had become too difficult for him <u>to live in New Orleans</u>.

9c. It caused me nausea <u>to handle the dead body with such a purpose</u>.

You may notice that when we read the sentences aloud, a pause inserted just before the moved clauses in (8b) and (9b) improves acceptability. Rather than extraposition, such pauses suggest a phenomenon I would call *afterthought*. In fact, spoken English often allows a speaker to use a pronoun in a subject slot, postponing until the end the specific NP, which may be momentarily forgotten; for example, "He's a really fine student, that John Doe." When we examine (8c) and (9c), we find in contrast to (8b) and (9b) that no pauses are necessary for the sentences to be acceptable.

In addition to subject, participle clauses serve a number of other grammatical functions. In Exercise 5.1, for example, we found a participle clause functioning as direct object of the infinitive *avoid:*

10a. I did everything to avoid <u>passing those gates</u>.

and another functioning as direct object of the finite VP *stopped:*

10b. He stopped <u>taking his meals altogether</u>.

Participle clauses also serve as objects of prepositions, and once again Exercise 5.1 provides an example:

11. Meantime, the slaves on Pointe du Lac . . . had begun to talk of <u>seeing his ghost on the gallery</u>.

Another example of a participle clause functioning as object of a preposition also comes from *Interview with the vampire,* but was not included in the exercise:

12. Then came only my mild alarm at <u>having to share a coffin with Lestat</u>.

Like infinitive clauses, participle clauses may occur as the complement of a copular verb. However, a participle clause generally will not occur as the copular complement of *be* since grammarians consider {*be* + present participle} to constitute the progressive aspect of the verb. An exception occurs if the participle clause expresses some activity that identifies the subject (e.g., *His occupation is training horses*). However, other copular verbs may take a participle clause as a complement more readily:

13. The old woman remained <u>kneeling at the altar</u>.

The final major constituent function a participle clause is likely to serve is that of predicate complement, particularly with verbs of perception. These include *see, hear, feel,* and even *find, imagine,* and *discover.* In Chapter Four, we first encountered the interesting problem presented by perception verbs. There, we learned that although perception verbs are complex transitive when a PP of location serves as predicate complement:

14. He had seen the woman in the rocker.

they are monotransitive if an infinitive clause appears in the predicate phrase:

15a. George heard the woman shut the door.

The justification for the monotransitive analysis lies in the questionable result obtained if we try to promote to subject the NP following the matrix VP by applying the passive test:

15b. ?The woman was heard to shut the door.

We therefore decided that the matrix perception verb is not powerful enough to claim as its direct object the NP that is the subject of the infinitive clause; the entire subject-bearing infinitive clause serves as the direct object of the matrix VP.

However, a curious predicament faces us when, instead of an infinitive clause, we find a participle clause in the predicate phrase of a perception VP:

15c. George heard the woman leaving the house.

Notice that in (15c), the logical object of *heard* is *the woman leaving the house* because what George hears is not merely the woman, but the action of the woman. This object is therefore a subject-bearing participle clause. Nevertheless, the matrix VP *heard* is powerful enough in this case to claim the subject of the participle clause as its direct object, as the passive test clearly demonstrates:

15d. The woman was heard leaving the house.

Since only an object of an active VP can be promoted to subject of its passive form, (15d) demonstrates that *heard* is able to extract the NP *the woman* out of the participle clause, with the result that the subjectless clause *leaving the house* remains in the predicate phrase as the predicate complement. In (15c), the matrix VP is complex transitive, due more, it would seem, to the nature of participle clauses than to the strength of the matrix. You will notice too that the *be* test for predicate complements works again now that the complement is a participle rather than an infinitive clause, though here the inserted *be* serves as an auxiliary rather than a copula. The following sentences from *Interview with the Vampire* demonstrate the operation of the *be* test with both present and past participle clauses serving the predicate complement function:

16a. Drunk or sober, I saw his body <u>rotting in the coffin</u>, and I couldn't bear it.

16b. His body was <u>rotting in the coffin</u>.

17a. Perhaps I'd seen [my own egotism] <u>reflected in the priest</u>.

17b. My own egotism was <u>reflected in the priest</u>.

18a. And now I saw him <u>filled with his own life and own blood</u>.

18b. He was <u>filled with his own life and own blood</u>.

Grammatical Functions of Participle Clauses—Modifiers

The most common modificational function of the participle clause is that of adjectival modifier, which, like prepositional phrases and appositives, may be either restrictive or nonrestrictive (review Chapter One if you do not remember these terms). You have encountered restrictive adjectival participle clauses already in Exercise 5.1. They are repeated here in (19), which has a present participle clause, and in (20), which has a past participle clause:

19. He sneered with the impatience of people <u>listening to the obvious lies of others</u>.

20. He appeared frail and stupid to me, a man <u>made of dried twigs</u> with a thin, carping voice.

These participle clauses limit the meaning of the general Ns *people* and *man* to more specific reference. Participle clauses following nouns and not separated from those nouns by commas serve to limit (i.e., restrict) the meaning of those nouns. These kinds of modifiers are called *restrictive modifiers.*

Very frequently, however, participle clauses serve as nonrestrictive adjectival modifiers. As you will recall, such modifiers are set off from the head of the NP by commas:

21. And the boy, <u>staring up at the vampire</u>, could not repress a gasp.

22a. And quickly he removed the small tape recorder from his brief case,
<u>making a check of the cassette and the batteries</u>.

Sentence (22a) is a particularly important example because it demonstrates a peculiar property of nonrestrictive adjectivals that happen to be participle clauses: There is no requirement for them to appear adjacent to the noun they modify. In fact, they have a movability that resembles that for adverbials, yet we shall take the position in this book that they are adjectivals. Notice that in (22a), the implicit subject of the participle clause is the pronoun *he* of the matrix clause. Note that this subject is simultaneously involved in two actions, one of which *(making)* grows out of or serves as background to the other.

Students often are puzzled by such nonrestrictive modifiers. In (22a), *making a check of the cassette and the batteries* seems to be adverbial in that it tells us the manner of the action *removed.* However, traditional grammars of English nearly unanimously deem such modifiers adjectivals. One very old grammar a student once showed me held that this type of modifier is adjectival in form, but adverbial in force. That position seems to me correct.

Here's how we can tell. Let us put this sentence in the passive voice:

22b. ?Quickly the small tape recorder was removed from his brief case by him, making a check of the cassette and the batteries.

This result is marginal at best. Let us further delete the *by* phrase, a common omission in passive sentences:

22c. *Quickly the small tape recorder was removed from his brief case, making a check of the cassette and the batteries.

This sentence is unacceptable, for it seems that an inanimate object—the tape recorder—is engaging in purposeful action. *Making a check of the cassette and the batteries* seems to be tied to the NP *he,* although in a nonrestrictive way; because of its affiliation with an NP, it is an adjectival modifier. Notice that *quickly*—a true, unequivocal adverb—can appear in both the active and passive versions without affecting acceptability (I have removed the participle clause so as not to confuse the issue):

22d. Quickly he removed the small tape recorder from his brief case.

22e. Quickly the small tape recorder was removed from his brief case.

The acceptability of both the active and the passive versions results from the fact that the adverb *quickly* modifies the verb *removed,* and so the subject of the sentence may be changed without introducing a distortion. However, if the implicit subject of the participle is removed, as it is in the passive versions of the above examples, then there is no NP with which the participle clause is affiliated. The result (cf. 22c) is the syntactic infelicity known in English handbooks everywhere as the **dangling participle.**

The adverbial feel of the participle clauses in the examples given in (21) and (22a) results from the fact that these modifiers are nonrestrictive. A nonrestrictive modifier does not narrow the meaning of the noun, but instead adds information that is not absolutely necessary for the correct identification of the noun phrase. A nonrestrictive modifier is typically set off from the element it modifies by a comma or commas. And perhaps most adverb-like of all, a nonrestrictive modifier is movable.

Adjectival vs. Adverbial

Most instances of participle clauses serving as modifiers are adjectival rather than adverbial. In general, although the participle is a nonfinite, often subjectless form, it has a logical (though not explicit) subject that must appear in the sentence in some other capacity. It is the logical subject that the participle clause modifies, even if it does not immediately follow (or precede) that logical subject. However, even though modifier participle clauses are most frequently adjectival, there are some adverbial uses as well. Examine the following pair of sentences:

23a. The woman sat reading a book.

23b. The woman reading a book sat.

Reading a book in sentence (23b) is clearly adjectival in character, and restrictive as well. But sentence (23a) is analogous to (23c),

23c. The woman was reading a book.

which undoubtedly we would analyze as having a progressive VP followed by a direct object. However, trying to add *sat* to the auxiliary category in English on the basis of this usage is clearly *ad hoc*. We shall consider *reading a book* to be an adverbial participle clause complementing the verb in cases such as this.

Past Participle Clauses

Past participles of verbs, as we have seen, also may serve as heads of nonfinite clauses. Like present participle clauses, past participle clauses may function as predicate complements, and when they function as modifiers, typically they are adjectival. They are tricky to identify because the form of the past participle frequently is indistinguishable from the past tense of the verb. Thus, one might think a modifier is actually the verb of a sentence:

24. Catherine and Heathcliff, dressed in their warmest clothing, roamed through the moors.

It is critical, then, to locate the VP of the sentence, in this case *roamed*.

Past participle clauses can be adverbial in exactly those same contexts as present participle clauses:

25. He sat dressed in his warmest clothing.

Compare (25) to our example of the adverbial present participle clause:

23a. The woman sat reading a book.

Exercise 5.2

The following sentences come from Jamake Highwater's *The Primal Mind.* Underline every participle clause, and in the space following each sentence, identify the function that the clause serves in the sentence. These functions include: *subject, direct object, object of preposition, predicate complement, restrictive adjectival, nonrestrictive adjectival,* and *adverbial.*

When working on this exercise, keep in mind the following facts:

a. nouns *do not* take objects;

b. the restrictive/nonrestrictive distinction pertains to *modifiers* only;

c. a constituent *cannot* simultaneously be a subject or an object and a modifier (i.e., adverbial or adjectival);

d. a subordinate clause *includes* whatever modifies something within its boundaries.

1. By methodically divesting their children of the capacity for vision they have forfeited the ability to see anybody but themselves.

2. The people of the caves of Altamira built scaffolds in the dark interiors of their rock caverns, and with pigments made from ground roots and bark and minerals they painted an amazing world upon their ceilings by the meager light of oil lamps.

3. Taking into account the scant and very dubious ethnographic literature of his day, he was among the first thinkers to regard primal peoples as full members of the human race and of social tradition.

4. According to Vico, some of Noah's unruly sons wandered away after the Flood and eventually forgot all vestiges of their Judaic culture—losing even the capacity for language and descending "to the level of wild beasts."

5. Startled by great thunderclaps in the first mornings of the world, Vico's "savages" sought shelter in caves, and from there the European conception of the history of cultural evolution began.

6. There are many different ways of making and experiencing images.

7. [Pollock's] pictorial effort was to unify the picture by unifying experience and by seeing all things in the cosmos as part of a vast general order.

8. Making an unannounced and unwelcomed entrance through the widely neglected arts of the West, primal mentality has become the conscious and unconscious focus of the twentieth century.

Answers to Exercise 5.2

1. By <u>methodically divesting their children of the capacity for vision</u> they have forfeited the ability to see anybody but themselves.

   This participle clause functions as the object of the preposition *by*. Notice that the participle that functions as the head of this clause is modified on its left by an adverb.

2. The people of the caves of Altamira built scaffolds in the dark interiors of their rock caverns, and with pigments <u>made from ground roots and bark and minerals</u> they painted an amazing world upon their ceilings by the meager light of oil lamps.

   Past participle clause, restrictive adjectival modifier of *pigments*

3. <u>Taking into account the scant and very dubious ethnographic literature of his day</u>, he was among the first thinkers to regard primal peoples as full members of the human race and of social tradition.

   The participle clause functions as a nonrestrictive adjectival modifier of *he*.

4. According to Vico, some of Noah's unruly sons wandered away after the Flood and eventually forgot all vestiges of their Judaic culture—<u>losing even the capacity for language</u> and <u>descending "to the level of wild beasts</u>."

   These are a pair of coordinated present participle clauses, functioning as nonrestrictive adjectival modifiers of *some of Noah's unruly sons*. N.B.: if you identified *according to Vico* as a clause, I suggest you review the list of prepositions given in Chapter One.

5. <u>Startled by great thunderclaps in the first mornings of the world</u>, Vico's "savages" sought shelter in caves, and from there the European conception of the history of cultural evolution began.

   Past participle clause; nonrestrictive adjectival modifier of *Vico's "savages"*

6. There are many different ways of <u>making and experiencing images</u>.

   Present participle clause; object of the preposition *of*

7. [Pollock's] pictorial effort was to unify the picture by <u>unifying experience</u> and by <u>seeing all things in the cosmos as part of a vast general order.</u>

Each of these participle clauses functions as the object of the preposition *by,* which immediately precedes it.

8. <u>Making an unannounced and unwelcomed entrance through the widely neglected arts of the West,</u> primal mentality has become the conscious and unconscious focus of the twentieth century.

Present participle clause; nonrestrictive adjectival modifier of *primal mentality*

Subject-Bearing Participle Clauses

Like most infinitive clauses, most participle clauses lack explicit subjects. However, like some infinitive clauses, some participle clauses *do* have explicit subjects, though these subjects never are in the subjective case. Let me give you an example I encountered one morning while listening to *Sesame Street* with my then two-year-old daughter:

26. I hear the sound of Sully hammering.

One might be inclined to interpret *hammering* as a predicate complement; however, we have no precedent for such an analysis within a prepositional phrase. Another guess might be that *hammering* is a restrictive modifier of *Sully;* however, a proper noun such as *Sully* cannot ordinarily be modified restrictively in English (unless it is taken in a common sense: e.g., *the New York I left behind*). Looking at (26) with an eye to meaning yields a reading something like: "I hear something, and what I hear is that Sully is hammering." *Sully hammering* is in fact a **subject-bearing participle clause.** We often find such clauses as nonrestrictive modifiers in sentences that have a subject different from the participle's subject. In (27) and (28), for example, the subjects of the matrix clauses (*Fabio* and *Mary,* respectively) differ from the subjects of the participles *(unbuttoned, gleaming),* yet the entire participle clause in each case nonrestrictively modifies the subject of the matrix verb. Such modifiers are sometimes called **absolute phrases:**

27. <u>His shirt unbuttoned,</u> Fabio strutted onto the stage.

28. <u>Her teeth gleaming,</u> Mary left the dentist's office.

Sometimes, a subject-bearing participle clause appears as the object of a verb, with many of the same matrix verbs that take subject-bearing infinitive clauses as objects (e.g., *want, like,* etc.):

29. Mary didn't like <u>John going away to college.</u>

If a pronoun were substituted for the NP that serves as the explicit subject in (29), *John,* that pronoun would have to occur in the **objective case,** as shown in (30a):

30a. Mary didn't like him going away to college.

and *not* in the **subjective case,** as the ungrammatically of (30b) clearly demonstrates:

30b. *Mary didn't like he going away to college.

In some circumstances, the explicit subject of a participle clause will occur in the **possessive case:**

31. Mary didn't like <u>John's going away to college</u>.

The possessive form of the subject of the subordinate clause indicates both the unity of the subject with the rest of the participle clause (that is, *John's* obviously cannot be the direct object of *didn't like*), and the NP-like behavior of participle clauses that have such subjects. (Remember that possessive forms are members of the determiner class, and determiners have thus far been shown to belong exclusively to NPs; see Chapter One for review.) Thus, subject-bearing participle clauses with possessive case subjects lurk in the shadowy world at the edges of categories, half NPs and half bona fide clauses. Because they take determiners, these clauses look like NPs; because the participles continue to behave like VPs by taking objects and adverbials, they look like clauses. You will find possessive subjects only for participle clauses that fill NP slots, such as subject and object; they will not occur in modificational clauses, even though these too may be subject bearing, as we saw in (28), repeated here as (32), but with a possessive (and badly ungrammatical) subject:

32. *<u>Their gleaming</u>, Mary left the dentist's office.

It may be helpful to keep in mind that for *any* nonfinite clause bearing an explicit pronoun subject (both infinitive and participle), that subject cannot be in the subjective case. This fact seems to be tied to another fact—that the nonfinite clause is not an independent entity and always is subordinate to elements in a larger clause.

When Is a Subject-Bearing Clause Not a Subject-Bearing Clause?

At this point, you may be somewhat puzzled about subject-bearing clauses, since it is sometimes difficult to distinguish them from subject-*less* participle clauses which, in spite of their subjectless status, happen to have a relationship to a preceding NP. For example, take another look at (26):

26. I hear the sound of Sully hammering.

Now suppose that the sentence were slightly changed so that it read as (33):

33. I hear Sully hammering.

In (33) we find a perception verb, *hear,* followed by an NP, followed in turn by a single item participle clause, *hammering.* If we analyze this sentence along the lines suggested earlier for matrix verbs of perception (cf. 15a), *Sully* is the direct object of *hear* and *hammering* is the predicate complement. But how is *Sully hammering* any different in (33) from *Sully hammering* in (26)? After all, in both sentences Sully is the one doing the hammering, and in both cases the subject *I* is the one hearing this activity. How do I know whether Sentence (33) contains a subject-bearing participle clause or a direct object followed by a predicate complement?

If you have been thinking along these lines, you have hit on an important problem in syntax: that of multiple analyses. That is, *Sully* is in fact the subject of the participle clause in both (26) and (33), but—and this is an important *but*—in Sentence (33) that subject has been essentially promoted to the "higher" or matrix clause as the direct object of the verb.

To help you understand this idea, recall the important syntactic rule that converts active sentences to passive ones. For an active sentence to become passive requires that the predicate phrase of that sentence have an object, or the sentence cannot be made passive at all. Sentence (33) does have a passive counterpart, given in (34a) below:

34a. Sully was heard hammering.

However, the string *Sully hammering* cannot be so promoted:

34b. *Sully hammering was heard.

What these examples demonstrate is that *Sully,* although logically the subject of the participle clause, functions in (33) as the direct object of the matrix VP. We can say, then, that after the subject of a participle clause is promoted to direct object status in the matrix clause, the remainder of the participle clause—the head and its objects and modifiers, should any occur—relates to the matrix VP as predicate complement.

Exercise 5.3

The following sentences come from Robert Fulghum's *All I Really Need to Know I Learned in Kindergarten.* Underline every participle clause and, in the space following each sentence, identify the function that the clause serves in the sentence. These functions include: *subject, direct object, object of preposition, predicate complement, restrictive adjectival, nonrestrictive adjectival,* and *adverbial.*

When working on this exercise, keep in mind the following facts:

a. nouns *do not* take objects;

b. the restrictive/nonrestrictive distinction pertains to *modifiers* only;

c. a constituent *cannot* simultaneously be a subject or an object and a modifier (i.e., adverbial or adjectival);

d. a subordinate clause *includes* whatever modifies something within its boundaries;

e. subjects of subject-bearing clauses not claimed as DO by the matrix VP are part of the subordinate construction.

1. This lady raccoon and her suitor were squared off in a corner, fangs bared, covered with mud and blood, and not looking very sexy at all.

2. I sat there in the rain, my light still shining into the trysting chamber.

3. Pieces of sanity are found washed ashore on all kinds of beaches these days.

4. There must be billions of sheets of paper in every country in the world, in billions of boxes and closets and attics and cupboards, covered with billions of pictures in crayon.

5. I thought about setting the leaves on fire to drive him out.

6. Getting found would have kept him in the game.

7. Medieval theologians even described God in hide-and-seek terms, calling him *Deus Absconditus*.

8. One of my students suggested putting all my money into drugs.

9. I remember riding home on a summer's eve in the back of an ancient Ford pickup truck, with two eight-year-old cousins for company and my uncle Roscoe at the wheel.

10. [Mr. Washington] started fondling his weed-eater and mixing up vile potions in vats in his garage.

11. Sure enough, one morning I caught him over in my yard spraying dandelions.

12. Nobody ever complains about your picking them.

13. Most of the time daily life is a lot like an endless chore of chasing chickens in a large pen.

14. Snow is God's way of telling people to slow down and rest and stay in bed for a day.

15. Being left in charge of about eighty children seven to ten years old, . . . I mustered my troops in the church social hall and explained the game.

16. The following August, I was nesting in the attic, trying to establish some order in the mess, and found stacked in with the holiday decorations a whole box of unopened greeting cards from the previous Christmas.

17. And we had this outrageous Christmas ordeal right there on my deck in the middle of August, singing along with the Mormon Tabernacle Choir to the final mighty strains of "O Holy Night."

18. He belongs to a family settled into the neighborhood by the Quakers last year.

19. Singing about riding in a one-horse open sleigh is ludicrous.

20. Using an ice pick and chopstick, I tried to pry the creature forth.

21. Close inspection revealed a small corpse with a spring around its neck, lying on its side.

22. Well, I still don't have a cuckoo clock of my own. But I have kept something. It is the memory of the Christmas message written on the packing carton.

23. Raking leaves means *all* the leaves.

24. I note his picking up several of the brightest yellow leaves and putting them into the pocket of his sweat shirt.

25. Every person passing through this life will unknowingly leave something and take something away.

Answers to Exercise 5.3

1. This lady raccoon and her suitor were squared off in a corner, <u>fangs bared</u>, <u>covered with mud and blood</u>, and <u>not looking very sexy at all</u>.

   The three participle clauses here are all nonrestrictive adjectival modifiers of the subject of the matrix clause. The first is a subject-bearing past participle clause. The second is a past participle clause, and the third is a present participle clause.

2. I sat there in the rain, <u>my light still shining into the trysting chamber</u>.

   This subject-bearing present participle clause is a nonrestrictive adjectival modifier of the subject of the matrix clause, *I.*

3. Pieces of sanity are found <u>washed ashore on all kinds of beaches these days</u>.

   This past participle clause is the predicate complement of the matrix clause. To see this function more clearly, it is helpful to covert this passive sentence into its active counterpart: [*People*] *find pieces of sanity washed ashore on all kinds of beaches these days.*

4. There must be billions of sheets of paper in every country in the world, in billions of boxes and closets and attics and cupboards, <u>covered with billions of pictures in crayon</u>.

   Past participle clause; nonrestrictive adjectival modifier of *billions of sheets of paper*

5. I thought about <u>setting the leaves on fire to drive him out</u>.

   Present participle clause; object of preposition *about*

6. <u>Getting found</u> would have kept him in the game.

   Present participle clause; subject

7. Medieval theologians even described God in hide-and-seek terms, <u>calling him *Deus Absconditus*</u>.

   Present participle clause; nonrestrictive adjectival modifier of *medieval theologians*

8. One of my students suggested <u>putting all my money into drugs</u>.

   Present participle clause; direct object of matrix verb *suggested*

9. I remember <u>riding home on a summer's eve in the back of an ancient Ford pickup truck, with two eight-year-old cousins for company and my uncle Roscoe at the wheel</u>.

   Present participle clause; direct object of matrix verb *remember*

10. [Mr. Washington] started <u>fondling his weed-eater</u> and <u>mixing up vile potions in vats in his garage</u>.

    Together these two present participle clauses function as the direct object of *started.*

11. Sure enough, one morning I caught him over in my yard <u>spraying dandelions</u>.

    Present participle clause; predicate complement (*caught* here operates as a perception verb)

12. Nobody ever complains about <u>your picking them</u>.

    Subject-bearing present participle clause (notice the possessive subject of the participle, and the fact that it has a direct object, *them*); object of preposition *about*

13. Most of the time daily life is a lot like an endless chore of <u>chasing chickens in a large pen</u>.

    Present participle clause; object of preposition *of*

14. Snow is God's way of <u>telling people to slow down and rest and stay in bed for a day</u>.

    Present participle clause; object of preposition *of*

15. <u>Being left in charge of about eighty children seven to ten years old,</u> . . . I mustered my troops in the church social hall and explained the game.

    Present participle clause; nonrestrictive adjectival modifier of *I*

16. The following August, I was nesting in the attic, <u>trying to establish some order in the mess,</u> and found <u>stacked in with the holiday decorations</u> a whole box of unopened greeting cards from the previous Christmas.

    The first subordinate clause, a present participle clause, is a nonrestrictive adjectival modifier of *I;* the second, a past participle clause, is the predicate complement of *found.* Notice that there is an inversion of the usual DO-PC order, due to the inordinate length of the PC. Such inversions are possible so long as the PC is not an NP.

17. And we had this outrageous Christmas ordeal right there on my deck in the middle of August, <u>singing along with the Mormon Tabernacle Choir to the final mighty strains of "O Holy Night."</u>

    Present participle clause; nonrestrictive adjectival modifier of *we*

18. He belongs to a family <u>settled into the neighborhood by the Quakers last year</u>.

    Past participle clause; restrictive adjectival modifier of *family.*

19. <u>Singing about riding in a one-horse open sleigh</u> is ludicrous.

    1. Present participle clause; subject

    2. Present participle clause; object of preposition

20. <u>Using an ice pick and chopstick,</u> I tried to pry the creature forth.

    Present participle clause; nonrestrictive adjectival modifier

21. Close inspection revealed a small corpse with a spring around its neck, <u>lying on its side.</u>

    Present participle clause; nonrestrictive adjectival modifier of *corpse*

22. Well, I still don't have a cuckoo clock of my own. But I have kept something. It is the memory of the Christmas message <u>written on the packing carton.</u>

    Past participle clause; restrictive adjectival modifier of *message*

23. <u>Raking leaves</u> means *all* the leaves.

    Present participle clause; subject

24. I note <u>his picking up several of the brightest yellow leaves and putting them into the pocket of his sweat shirt.</u>

    Subject-bearing present participle clause (with conjoined VPs sharing a single subject, *his*); direct object

25. Every person <u>passing through this life</u> will unknowingly leave something and take something away.

Present participle clause; restrictive adjectival modifier of *person*

Exercise 5.4

The following sentences come from Jung Chang's *Wild Swans*. Underline every nonfinite subordinate clause (i.e., infinitive clause or participle clause) and, in the space following each sentence, indicate the function that the nonfinite clause serves. If more than one nonfinite clause occurs in any sentence, number the clauses and assign the same numbers to your written responses. The number in parentheses indicates how many nonfinite clauses you should find.

1. Grandmother would always ask my mother to stick some honey on her lips (1).

2. The people living in the next house to the Xias were Japanese, and my grandmother was friendly with them (1).

3. One of [the police's] main jobs was to check people's registration (1).

4. It was socially acceptable for women to get a high school education (1).

5. With a tremendous effort, my mother tried to hide her emotions (1).

6. On 23 August the neighborhood chiefs told residents to go to the railway station the next day to welcome the Russians (2).

7. A friend of my mother's offered to lend them a house inside the city gates, surrounded by high stone walls (2).

8. The family decamped immediately, taking my mother's Japanese teacher with them (1).

9. One day a jeep-load of laughing Russian soldiers skidded to a halt near her and the Russians jumped out and started running in her direction (1).

10. Dr. Xia had seen the Russians chasing my mother into the building (1).

Answers to Exercise 5.4

1. Grandmother would always ask my mother <u>to stick some honey on her lips</u> (1).

infinitive clause; direct object

2. The people <u>living in the next house to the Xias</u> were Japanese, and my grandmother was friendly with them (1).

   participle clause; restrictive adjectival

3. One of [the police's] main jobs was <u>to check people's registration</u> (1).

   infinitive clause; copular complement

4. It was socially acceptable <u>for women to get a high school education</u> (1).

   infinitive clause; extraposed subject

5. With a tremendous effort, my mother tried <u>to hide her emotions</u> (1).

   infinitive clause; direct object

6. On 23 August the neighborhood chiefs told residents <u>to go to the railway station the next day to welcome the Russians</u> (2).

   1. [from *to go* to *Russians*] infinitive clause; direct object

   2. [from *to welcome* to *Russians*] infinitive clause; adverbial

7. A friend of my mother's offered <u>to lend them a house inside the city gates, surrounded by high stone walls</u> (2).

   1. [from *to lend* to the end] infinitive clause; direct object

   2. [from *surrounded* to the end] participle clause; nonrestrictive adjectival

8. The family decamped immediately, <u>taking my mother's Japanese teacher with them</u> (1).

   participle clause; nonrestrictive adjectival

9. One day a jeep-load of laughing Russian soldiers skidded to a halt near her and the Russians jumped out and started <u>running in her direction</u> (1).

   participle clause; direct object

10. Dr. Xia had seen the Russians <u>chasing my mother into the building</u> (1).

    participle clause; predicate complement

Terms Used in Chapter Five

absolute phrases: a term used for subject-bearing participle clauses that modify NPs nonrestrictively.

aspect: a grammatical category, usually associated with verbs in English, that indicates the nature of an event, e.g., whether it is ongoing or whether it occurs at a single point in time.

dangling participle: a participle clause used in a sentence lacking the NP needed to serve as the implicit subject of the participle, e.g., *Riding in the car, the countryside seemed more colorful than ever.*

head: the chief element in a phrase or clause. An N, for example, is the head of an NP.

inflection: a suffix indicating a word's grammatical status in a sentence—e.g., *-ed* indicates past tense in English.

objective case: an inflection now limited to English pronouns, that typically indicates that the pronoun serves as the object of some other sentence element. The pronouns *me, us, her, him,* and *them* all are objective case.

participle clause: a nonfinite subordinate clause headed by a participle verb form and generally lacking an overt subject.

possessive case: an inflection found on English nouns and pronouns indicating that the NP "possesses"—sometimes only in a loose sense—the NP that follows it. On nouns, the possessive inflection is *-'s.*

subject-bearing participle clause: a participle clause that contains an explicit and overt subject.

subjective case: the inflection on a pronoun indicating that the pronoun is the subject of a finite verb. The pronouns *I, we, he, she,* and *they* all are subjective case.

voice: an inflection on a transitive VP that indicates whether the VP is active or passive.

Chapter Quiz

The following sentences come from *A Yellow Raft in Blue Water,* a novel by Michael Dorris. Underline every nonfinite subordinate clause and, in the space following each sentence, identify the kind of nonfinite clause you have underlined (i.e., infinitive clause or participle clause). Also, indicate the grammatical function that the nonfinite clause serves in the sentence. If more than one nonfinite clause occurs in any sentence, number the clauses and assign the corresponding numbers to your written responses. The point value given in parentheses indicates how many nonfinite clauses occur in the sentence.

1. We play solitaire on the sliding desk pulled across the foot of the electric bed (1).

2. The last pass through I have seen a two of clubs and a jack of spades hidden below an early ten of hearts (1).

3. The object of the game is to reduce everything to one stack (1).

4. I start to reach for the white cord with a button on the end, but Mom snatches it first and puts it under the sheet (1).

5. I turn and see my father standing in the doorway (1).

6. He inspects me like a first class package, looking for loose flaps (1).

7. Her eyes are narrow slits buried in the fullness of her flushed cheeks (1).

8. Her lips press together in a tight seal and she tries to drag the pillow out from under her legs (1).

9. He'd smile or send me a postcard or promise to call tomorrow and then weeks would pass (1).

10. He'd invite me to share his lunch under a shade tree, and people passing in cars would smile at us (2).

11. And there, big as life, is a fat candy striper from the hospital trying to jimmy the door (2).

12. In the uniform, two or three sizes too small, Mom looks bursting with strength (2).

13. I'm tired of convincing her to be reasonable (2).

14. Mom sends her a present every Christmas and makes me sign the card, but they aren't close (1).

15. In the distance, on the highway beyond the park, I see the headlights of cars move by, back and forth, out of reach (1).

Chapter Six

Taking Stock—A Midterm Review

By now, you have learned quite a bit about grammar; in fact, you have learned just about all one needs to know to be able to say, "I know something about doing grammar." But, of course, it never hurts to take stock of what you have learned and to test yourself. This chapter will allow you to see just what you have learned and to pinpoint what you need to review.

To get the maximum benefit of this chapter, work through each of the exercises carefully. Remember, never turn to the answers provided before you have completed the work. As with physical exercise, you must exert yourself, because the adage "No pain, no gain" can be applied to improving one's understanding of grammar, as well.

Exercise 6.1

Some of the constituents of each of the following sentences have been isolated and written out below the sentence. On the line next to the constituent, identify the constituent as to both structure and function, being as specific as you can. Determine whether a modifier is adverbial or adjectival and indicate what it modifies; describe objects of the verb as direct or indirect. Be sure to indicate whether a VP is transitive, intransitive, or copular. Watch out for passive constructions. If you find that the VP of a nonfinite clause takes an object, be sure to identify the object specifically as the object of the particular nonfinite verb. The sentences come from *The Ascent of Man.*

Example: From an early time man made tools by working the stone.

From an early time: adverbial prepositional phrase, modifies *made*
man: NP, subject
made: VP, transitive
tools: NP, direct object
by working the stone: adverbial PP, modifies *made*
working the stone: participle clause, object of the preposition *by*
the stone: NP, direct object of *working*

The notion of discovering an underlying order in matter is man's basic concept for exploring nature.

1. The notion of discovering an underlying order in matter _____

2. of discovering an underlying order in matter _____

3. discovering an underlying order in matter _____

4. an underlying order _____

5. in matter _____

6. is _____

7. man's basic concept for exploring nature _____

8. for exploring nature _____

9. exploring nature _____

10. nature _____

A large system of irrigation extending over an empire requires a strong central authority.

11. A large system of irrigation extending over an empire _____

12. of irrigation _____

13. extending over an empire _____

14. over an empire _____

15. an empire _____

16. requires _____

17. a strong central authority _____

The most powerful drive in the ascent of man in his pleasure in his own skill.

18. The most powerful drive in the ascent of man _____

19. in the ascent of man _____

20. of man _____

21. is _____

22. his pleasure in his own skill _____

23. in his own skill _____

24. his own skill _____

Almost ten thousand years ago, not long after the beginning of the settled communities of agriculture, men in the Middle East began to use copper.

25. Almost ten thousand years ago, not long after the beginning of the settled communities of agriculture

_____

26. not long after the beginning of the settled communities of agriculture

_____

27. the beginning of the settled communities of agriculture _____

28. of the settled communities of agriculture _____

29. of agriculture _____

30. men in the Middle East _____

31. in the Middle East _____

32. the Middle East _____

33. began _____

34. to use copper _____

35. copper _____

_____

Answers to Exercise 6.1

1. The notion of discovering an underlying order in matter   NP, subject

2. of discovering an underlying order in matter   PP, adjectival, mod. *notion*

3. discovering an underlying order in matter   participle clause, object of the preposition *of*

4. an underlying order   NP, direct object of *discovering*

5. in matter   PP, adverbial, mod. *discovering*

6. is   VP, copular

7. man's basic concept for exploring nature   NP, copular complement

8. for exploring nature   PP, adjectival, mod. *concept*

9. exploring nature   participle clause, object of the preposition *for*

10. nature   NP, direct object of *exploring*

11. A large system of irrigation extending over an empire   NP, subject

12. of irrigation   PP, adjectival, modifies *system*

13. extending over an empire   participle clause, restrictive adjectival modifier of *system*

14. over an empire   PP, adverbial, modifies *extending*

15. an empire   NP, object of the preposition *over*

16. requires <u>VP, transitive</u>

17. a strong central authority <u>NP, direct object of *requires*</u>

18. The most powerful drive in the ascent of man <u>NP, subject</u>

19. in the ascent of man <u>PP, adjectival, modifies *drive*</u>

20. of man <u>PP, adjectival, modifies *ascent*</u>

21. is <u>VP, copular</u>

22. his pleasure in his own skill <u>NP, copular complement</u>

23. in his own skill <u>PP, adjectival, modifies *pleasure*</u>

24. his own skill <u>NP, object of the preposition *in*</u>

25. Almost ten thousand years ago, not long after the beginning of the settled communities of agriculture <u>adverbial phrase (*not* prepositional), modifies *began*</u>

26. not long after the beginning of the settled communities of agriculture <u>PP, nonrestrictive adverbial modifier of *almost ten thousand years ago* (note that *not long* modifies *after*, a preposition; when a preposition is modified, it is an adverb appearing to its left that does the work)</u>

27. the beginning of the settled communities of agriculture <u>NP, object of the preposition *after*</u>

28. of the settled communities of agriculture <u>PP, adjectival, modifies *beginning*; note that *beginning* is a true noun here because of the presence of the determiner</u>

29. of agriculture <u>PP, adjectival, modifies *communities*</u>

30. men in the Middle East <u>NP, subject</u>

31. in the Middle East <u>PP, adjectival, modifies *men*</u>

32. the Middle East <u>NP, object of the preposition *in*</u>

33. began <u>VP, transitive</u>

34. to use copper   <u>infinitive clause; direct object of *began*</u>

35. copper   <u>NP, direct object of *use*</u>

Exercise 6.2

Fill in the blanks below, following the same procedure you used in Exercise 6.1. These sentences come from Tolkien's *The Hobbit.*

The glade in the ring of trees was evidently a meeting-place of the wolves.

1. The glade in the ring of trees _____

2. in the ring of trees _____

3. the ring of trees _____

4. of trees _____

5. trees _____

6. was _____

7. evidently _____

8. a meeting-place of the wolves _____

9. of the wolves _____

10. the wolves _____

Now they had planned with the goblins' help to come by night upon some of the villages nearest the mountains.

11. they _____

12. had planned _____

13. with the goblins' help _____

14. the goblins' help _____

15. to come by night upon some of the villages nearest the mountains _____

_____

16. by night _____

17. upon some of the villages nearest the mountains _____

18. some of the villages nearest the mountains _____

19. nearest the mountains _____

There for ages his huge bones could be seen in calm weather amid the ruined piles of the old town.

20. There _____

21. for ages _____

22. his huge bones _____

23. could be seen _____

24. in calm weather _____

25. calm weather _____

26. amid the ruined piles of the old town _____

27. the ruined piles of the old town _____

28. of the old town _____

29. the old town _____

Soon the raft was drawn out of the current of the Forest River and towed away round the high shoulder of rock into the little bay of Lake-town.

30. Soon _____

31. the raft _____

32. was drawn _____

33. out of the current of the Forest River _____

34. the current of the Forest River _____

35. of the Forest River _____

36. the Forest River _____

37. towed away _____

38. round the high shoulder of rock _____

39. the high shoulder of rock _____

40. of rock _____

41. rock _____

42. into the little bay of Lake-town _____

43. the little bay of Lake-town _____

44. of Lake-town _____

_____

Answers to Exercise 6.2

1. The glade in the ring of trees   <u>NP, subject</u>

2. in the ring of trees   <u>PP, adjectival, modifies *glade*</u>

3. the ring of trees   <u>NP, object of the preposition *in*</u>

4. of trees   <u>PP, adjectival, modifies *ring*</u>

5. trees   <u>NP, object of the preposition *of*</u>

6. was   <u>VP, copular</u>

7. evidently   <u>adverb, acts as a modifier of the entire sentence; such modifiers are called "sentence adverbials"</u>

8. a meeting-place of the wolves   <u>NP, copular complement</u>

9. of the wolves   PP, adjectival, modifies *meeting-place*

10. the wolves   NP, object of the preposition *of*

11. they   NP, subject

12. had planned   VP, transitive

13. with the goblins' help   PP, adverbial, modifies *had planned*

14. the goblins' help   NP, object of the preposition *with*

15. to come by night upon some of the villages nearest the mountains   infinitive clause; direct object of *had planned*

16. by night   PP, adverbial, modifies *come*

17. upon some of the villages nearest the mountains   PP, adverbial, modifies *come*

18. some of the villages nearest the mountains   NP, object of the preposition *upon*

19. nearest the mountains   PP, adjectival, modifies *villages*

20. There   adverb, adverbial, modifies *could be seen*

21. for ages   PP, adverbial, modifies *could be seen*

22. his huge bones   NP, subject

23. could be seen   VP, passive

24. in calm weather   PP, adverbial, modifies *could be seen*

25. calm weather   NP, object of the preposition *in*

26. amid the ruined piles of the old town   PP, adverbial, modifies *could be seen*

27. the ruined piles of the old town   NP, object of the preposition *amid*

28. of the old town   PP, adjectival, modifies *piles*

29. the old town   NP, object of the preposition *of*

30. Soon   adverb; adverbial, modifies *was drawn out . . . and towed away* etc.

31. the raft   NP, subject

32. was drawn   VP, passive

33. out of the current of the Forest River   PP, adverbial, modifies *was drawn*

34. the current of the Forest River   NP, object of the preposition *out of*

35. of the Forest River   PP, adjectival, modifies *current*

36. the Forest River   NP, object of the preposition *of*

37. towed away   VP, passive (this VP is connected by *and* to *drawn;* it shares the auxiliary *was*)

38. round the high shoulder of rock   PP, adverbial, modifies *towed away*

39. the high shoulder of rock   NP, object of the preposition *round*

40. of rock   PP, adjectival, modifies *shoulder*

41. rock   NP, object of the preposition *of*

42. into the little bay of Lake-town   PP, adverbial, modifies *towed away*

43. the little bay of Lake-town   NP, object of the preposition *into*

44. of Lake-town   PP, adjectival, modifies *bay*

Exercise 6.3

Part I. For each of the sentences below, underline the VP (i.e., the verb, all its auxiliaries, and any particles or VP-internal adverbs). Then put brackets around each of the other obligatory elements in the predicate phrase. In the space below each sentence, write one of the following patterns:

IV
CV-CC
TV-DO
TV-IO-DO
TV-DO-PC

If you find a verb in the *passive* voice, simply underline the verb, and unless it is complex transitive or ditransitive, mark nothing else, but **do** write the word *passive* in the space below the sentence. Then indicate other constituents that occur, if any. (Remember all passive verbs are inherently transitive.) All of the sentences come from Anne Rice's *The Witching Hour*.

1. The wave must have knocked him unconscious.

2. He would have a house with white columns on the front and flagstone walks.

3. The salesgirls behind the counter at the dime store were rude.

4. [The nuns] gave the children a beautiful handwriting.

5. They taught them their arithmetic tables, and they even taught Latin and history and some literature.

6. The visit of Aunt Vivian was brief.

7. His mother's sister came to town on a train.

8. They met her at Union Station.

9. Then he looked up fire fighters and fires in the [library] catalog.

10. His aunt told him the story after his mother's death.

11. By late May, the house on Annunciation Street was sold.

12. And his black curly hair, his large blue eyes, and the light freckles on his cheeks remained his distinctive features.

Part II. Identify each of the isolated portions of the following sentences by both structure and function. If a particular structure is a modifier, indicate what it modifies.

He would have a house with white columns on the front and flagstone walks.

13. with white columns on the front and flagstone walks _____

14. the front _____

The salesgirls behind the counter at the dime store were rude.

15. behind the counter at the dime store _____

16. at the dime store _____

Then he looked up fire fighters and fires in the [library] catalog.

17. in the [library] catalog _____

By late May, the house on Annunciation Street was sold.

18. By late May _____

19. on Annunciation Street _____

And his black curly hair, his large blue eyes, and the light freckles on his cheeks remained his distinctive features.

20. his black curly hair, his large blue eyes, and the light freckles on his cheeks

    _____

21. on his cheeks _____

His mother's sister came to town on a train.

22. to town _____

23. on a train _____

24. a train _____

They met her at Union Station.

25. at Union Station _____

Answers to Exercise 6.3

Part I.

1. The wave <u>must have knocked</u> [him] [unconscious].
   TV-DO-PC

2. He <u>would have</u> [a house with white columns on the front and flagstone walks].
   TV-DO

3. The salesgirls behind the counter at the dime store <u>were</u> [rude].
   CV-CC

4. The nuns <u>gave</u> [the children] [a beautiful handwriting].
   TV-IO-DO

5. They <u>taught</u> [them] [their arithmetic tables], and they even <u>taught</u> [Latin and history and some literature].
   TV-IO-DO; TV-DO

6. The visit of Aunt Vivian <u>was</u> [brief].
   CV-CC

7. His mother's sister <u>came</u> to town on a train.
   IV

8. They <u>met</u> [her] at Union Station.
   TV-DO

9. Then he <u>looked up</u> [fire fighters and fires] in the library catalog.
   TV-DO

10. His aunt <u>told</u> [him] [the story] after his mother's death.
    TV-IO-DO

11. By late May, the house on Annunciation Street <u>was sold</u>.
    passive

12. And his black curly hair, his large blue eyes, and the light freckles on his cheeks <u>remained</u> [his distinctive features].
    CV-CC

Part II.

He would have a house with white columns on the front and flagstone walks.

13. with white columns on the front and flagstone walks   PP, adjectival
    (house)

14. the front   NP, object of preposition *(on)*

The salesgirls behind the counter at the dime store were rude.

15. behind the counter at the dime store   PP, adjectival *(girls)*

16. at the dime store   PP, adjectival *(counter)*

Then he looked up fire fighters and fires in the [library] catalog.

17. in the [library] catalog   PP, adverbial

By late May, the house on Annunciation Street was sold.

18. By late May   PP, adverbial

19. on Annunciation Street   PP, adjectival *(house)*

And his black curly hair, his large blue eyes, and the light freckles on his cheeks remained his distinctive features.

20. his black curly hair, his large blue eyes, and the light freckles on his
    cheeks   NP, subject

21. on his cheeks   PP, adjectival *(freckles)*

His mother's sister came to town on a train.

22. to town   PP, adverbial

23. on a train   PP, adverbial

24. a train   NP, object of preposition *(on)*

They met her at Union Station.

25. at Union Station   PP, adverbial

Exercise 6.4

Examine each of the following sentences carefully. On separate paper, identify every element of each sentence, giving where possible both a structural and functional description. That is, be as specific as you can: Identify constructions as to type (structure), and then identify their function. Describe modifiers as adverbial or adjectival; describe objects as direct or indirect. Be sure to indicate whether a verb is transitive, intransitive, or copular. Identify passive construction. Don't complete this exercise all at once, but analyze a few sentences each time you study grammar. One is done for you. The following sentences come from Louise Erdrich's *The Bingo Palace.*

Example: Lipsha could almost feel Shawnee's smile open in the dark.

Lipsha: NP, subject

could almost feel: VP transitive

Shawnee's smile open in the dark: subject-bearing infinitive clause, DO of *could almost feel*

Shawnee's smile: subject of infinitive clause

open: VP of infinitive clause

in the dark: adverbial PP, modifies *open*

the dark: NP, object of preposition *in*

1. I hate to talk about it in front of you.

2. A cool wind flowed down, reaching from the shadows of the low belt of olive-pale mountains to the north.

3. A deeper part of her was listening.

4. An hour or two of asking around for jobs made Lipsha restless.

5. Passing public phones, he usually slipped his hand into the dark apertures of their coin boxes in the hope of a stray quarter.

The following sentences come from Toni Morrison's *Beloved.*

6. Baby Suggs didn't even raise her head.

7. Walking back through the woods, Sethe put an arm around each girl at her side.

8. Lady Jones gave her some rice, four eggs and some tea.

9. The interview ended with Janey telling her to come back in a few days.

10. He walks to the front door and opens it.

The following sentences come from Richard Rodriguez's *Hunger of Memory*.

11. A woman leaves him her entire library of several hundred books.

12. I consider my book a kind of pastoral.

13. I write in the tradition of that high, courtly genre.

14. Language has been the great subject of my life.

15. In the early years of my boyhood, my parents coped very well in America.

16. I would also hear then the high nasal notes of middle-class American speech.

17. The air stirred with sound.

18. Intimacy is not created by a particular language.

19. In spite of my earnestness, I found reading a pleasurable activity.

20. I became a highly rewarded minority student.

The following sentences come from Gus Lee's *China Boy*.

21. Edna dressed me in Little Lord Fauntleroy outfits to make me look good.

22. Edna stopped buying such clothes for a while.

23. The Chinese eat with the joy of abandonment, the relish of a pride of lions.

24. [The Chinese] permit the child within us all to romp freely with happy little chopsticks at dinnertime.

25. I was caught in the stairway by Edna.

Chapter Quiz

Examine each of the following sentences carefully, and on the lines that follow, identify each of the isolated constructions by both *structure* and *function*. Be as specific as possible; if a construction is a modifier, identify what it modifies; if it is a complement, identify what it complements. An example is provided to help you understand how to proceed. Please study it carefully. The sentences in this exercise have been taken from Edgar Allan Poe's "The Fall of the House of Usher."

Example: Noticing these things, I rode over a short causeway to the house.

a. *noticing these things:* participle clause, nonrestrictive adjectival modifier of *I*

b. *these things:* NP, direct object of *noticing*

c. *rode:* VP, intransitive

d. *over a short causeway:* PP, adverbial, modifies *rode*

e. *to the house:* PP, adverbial, modifies *rode*

f. *the house:* NP, object of the preposition *to*

Minute fungi overspread the whole exterior, hanging in a fine tangled webwork from the eaves.

1. Minute fungi _____

2. overspread _____

3. the whole exterior _____

4. hanging in a fine tangled webwork from the eaves _____

5. in a fine tangled webwork _____

6. from the eaves _____

7. the eaves _____

A letter had lately reached me in a distant part of the country.

8. A letter _____

9. had lately reached _____

10. me _____

11. in a distant part of the country _____

12. a distant part of the country _____

13. of the country _____

14. the country _____

The disease of the lady Madeline had long baffled the skill of her physicians.

15. The disease of the lady Madeline _____

16. of the lady Madeline _____

17. had long baffled _____

18. the skill of her physicians _____

19. of her physicians _____

During this period I was busied in earnest endeavors to alleviate the melancholy of my friend.

20. During this period _____

21. in earnest endeavors to alleviate the melancholy of my friend _____

22. earnest endeavors to alleviate the melancholy of my friend _____

23. to alleviate the melancholy of my friend _____

24. the melancholy of my friend _____

25. of my friend _____

Chapter Seven

Coordination

Introduction

We already have met the process of *coordination* in previous chapters, specifically when we encountered sentences that had at least two elements connected by the coordinator *and.* In the present chapter we will examine coordination in more detail so that we thoroughly understand how the process operates. In particular, we will learn to recognize coordinating conjunctions and to identify the elements they connect. In order to be successful in working through this chapter, however, you must be thoroughly familiar with basic sentence structure.

Generally speaking, two or more sentences, two or more predicate phrases, two or more subjects, or, indeed, two or more of any sentence elements of the same status may be combined through the use of specific English particles called **coordinating conjunctions** *(and, but, or, for, yet, so,* and *nor).* A handy mnemonic device for remembering these particles is the acronym FANBOYS *(for, and, nor, but, or, yet, so).* When a merger of elements occurs through the use of these conjunctions, the result is a single sentence that is a logical combination of more than one basic proposition. The syntactic process that brings about such fusion is called **coordination;** the elements connected through this process are called **conjuncts.**

Sometimes entire independent clauses may be coordinated. For example, the notions inherent in Sentences (1) and (2) may be expressed as conjuncts of a single compound sentence, given (3):

1. John went to the store.
2. Many went to the store.
3. John went to the story and Mary went to the store.

However, the notions conveyed by (1) and (2) may be more economically expressed through (4), in which the differing subjects of (1) and (2) are expressed as conjuncts within a subject NP sharing a single predicate phrase:

4. John and Mary went to the store.

Sentence (3), in which two independent clauses are combined, is an example of **clausal coordination;** Sentence (4), which demonstrates combined sentence subjects sharing a predicate phrase, is an example of **phrasal coordination.**

Although it may seem at first that (4) is equivalent to (3) in terms of meaning and the difference is simply one of economy, the distinction between the two is not trivial. Sentence (4) more nearly conveys the idea that John and Mary went to the store together; (3) would be more likely to occur if John and Mary went separately, perhaps in different vehicles, perhaps at different times. The slight difference in meaning between (3) and (4) sheds light on why both versions of coordination are grammatical. The syntactic difference reflects a semantic distinction.

Which Elements May Be Combined?

It is important to understand that any two or more elements of equal status may undergo the process of coordination. Frequently, only portions of NPs or VPs are coordinated. As an example, consider the following sentence from Stuart Berg Flexner's Preface to the *Dictionary of American Slang:*

5. A dialecticism is a <u>regionalism</u> or <u>localism</u>.

Neither of the underlined nouns in (5) constitutes a complete NP; the article *a* modifies both nouns and is not itself part of the coordinated structure. The coordinator *or* connects just the two nouns, which are only partial NPs themselves. As a result of the coordination, the complete NP is (6):

6. a regionalism or localism

It is not the case, however, that an article or other "left-hand" element preceding the left-most element of a coordinated pair always modifies or governs both elements in the pair. This fact sometimes leads to ambiguity. Sentence (7) is a famous example:

7. old men and women

In (7), which are the coordinated elements? One interpretation has *men* and *women* as the coordinated elements. This reading leads us to think of (7) as being an abbreviated version of (8):

8. old men and old women

That is, *old* in (7) is seen as modifying the coordination of the two nouns, as in the following phrase structure tree:

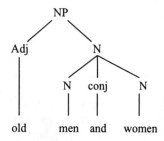

However, there is another possible interpretation—one in which only the first noun is modified by *old*. In this reading, (7) would be paraphrased by (9):

9. men who are old and women of any age

The phrase structure tree for this interpretation is as follows:

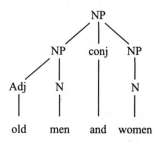

Sometimes, because of the meaning of the modifier and of the conjuncts, a left-hand modifier may unambiguously modify only the first. Here is an example from the November 1987 issue of *Discover* magazine (Michael Ghiglieri, "War Among the Chimps"):

10. Upon reaching adulthood [male primates] <u>abruptly break their early bonds</u> and <u>wander off to seek entry into another established group.</u>

The coordinated elements in (10) are underlined. Now, you may be wondering why the adverb *abruptly* is underlined as part of the first conjunct, and not treated as a modifier of the verb of the second conjunct as well. The answer lies in the aspectual character of the adverb and of the two verbs *break* and *wander*. The adverb *abruptly* must occur with a verb whose action occurs at a single point in time, not over an interval. Such verbs are said to exhibit "punctual" aspect. The verb *break* is just such a verb, whereas *wander* serves as an excellent example of activity occurring over a span of time. Notice the peculiarity of a sentence in which *abruptly* is made to modify the latter verb without the intervening grace of the punctual verb:

11a. ?male primates abruptly wander off.

We clearly sense the need for some intervening punctual predicate to make (11) more acceptable. For example, making *wander off* the head of an infinitive clause serving as the direct object of *start* vastly improves the acceptability of (11a):

11b. male primates abruptly start to wander off.

When modifiers, objects, or complements occur to the right of the first of two coordinated structures, they may only modify or complement the first; if they occur to the right of the second, they may modify or complement the first conjunct as well. The coordination with *and* in example (12) from *The Ascent of Man* illustrates the scope of both left- and right-hand modifiers:

12. Agriculture is one part of the biological revolution; the domestication and harnessing of village animals is the other.

In the second half of (12), only the nouns *domestication* and *harnessing* are coordinated with *and;* the determiner *the*—a left-hand modifier—modifies both nouns, and so does the adjectival prepositional phrase *of village animals*—a right-hand modifier.

Coordination with *And, But,* and *Or*

The conjunctions *and, but,* and *or* are considered to be the best examples of coordinating conjunctions; they are *primary.* Unlike *so* and *yet,* which may be preceded by *and,* no other element may precede a primary conjunction. That is, structures such as *and yet* and *and so* are perfectly acceptable in English, whereas *and but is strictly ungrammatical. Moreover, all three primary conjunctions may be used in either phrasal or clausal coordination, as the examples below illustrate:

13. [The female] tentatively touched him, *and* he tried to rise [from M. Ghiglieri, "War Among the Chimps," *Discover,* November 1987; clausal coordination].

14. She stayed with him until the next day, brushed flies from his wounds, *and* groomed him ["War Among the Chimps"; phrasal coordination: three predicate phrases are coordinated].

15. We painted and read together; *or* I listened, as if in a dream, to the wild improvisations of his speaking guitar [Edgar Allan Poe, "The Fall of the House of Usher"; clausal coordination].

16. I lack words to express the full extent, *or* the earnest *abandon* of his persuasion ["The Fall of the House of Usher"; phrasal coordination: coordination of partial NPs].

17. The pallor of his countenance had assumed, if possible, a more ghastly hue—*but* the luminousness of his eye had utterly gone out ["The Fall of the House of Usher"; clausal coordination].

18. Many books and instruments lay scattered about, *but* failed to give any vitality to the scene ["The Fall of the House of Usher"; phrasal coordination: predicate phrases are coordinated].

It is true that *yet* may also be used in clausal and phrasal coordination, as (19) and (20) demonstrate,

19. No outlet was observed in any portion of its vast extend, and no torch or other artificial source of light was discernible; *yet* a flood of intense rays rolled throughout, and bathed the whole in a ghastly and inappropriate splendor ["The Fall of the House of Usher"; clausal coordination: there are multiple forms of coordination within each of the two large clauses connected with *yet*].

20. It was, indeed, a tempestuous *yet* sternly beautiful night, and one wildly singular in its terror and its beauty ["The Fall of the House of Usher"; phrasal coordination: adjective phrases are coordinated].

However, (21) shows that *and* may precede *yet* in a coordinated structure, and so *yet* differs syntactically from the primary coordinators:

21. I regarded her with an utter astonishment not unmingled with dread, *and yet* I found it impossible to account for such feelings ["The Fall of the House of Usher"; clausal coordination].

How Many Conjuncts May Be Coordinated?

Most conjunctions connect two items, but *and* and *or* may connect indefinitely many, with the understanding that the relation of addition in the case of *and* and the relation of choice in the case of *or* hold between each of the conjuncts. In (22), for example, *and* occurs logically between *music* and *literature,* even though it surfaces as an actual word only between the last two conjuncts:

22. [Vienna] was a famous centre of music, literature, and the arts [from *The Ascent of Man.* Understood: *music and literature and the arts*].

Similarly, in (23) *and* is implied between *food* and *clothing:*

23. Supplies of food, clothing, and other necessities became drastically curtailed [from *Wild Swans;* understood: *food and clothing and other necessities*].

Sometimes, for purposes of emphasis or focus, the logical connection between more than two conjuncts is explicitly marked for each with *and,* as the first two instances of *and* in (24) demonstrate:

24. The theory has turned <u>physicists into mathematicians,</u> *and* <u>mathematicians into physicists,</u> *and* <u>the universe into an entity in which all matter and energy, all forces, all people, planets, stars, cats and dogs, quasars, atoms, automobiles, and everything else, from the instant of the Big Bang to the end of time, are the result of the actions and the interactions of these infinitesimal strings</u> [*Discover,* November 1986].

This same sentence also provides evidence that a large number of conjuncts, some with internal coordination (e.g., *matter and energy; cats and dogs*), may be connected with *and* occurring only between the last two conjuncts:

25. <u>all matter and energy,</u> <u>all forces,</u> <u>all people, planets, stars, cats and dogs, quasars, atoms, automobiles,</u> *and* <u>everything else, from the instant of the Big Bang to the end of time</u>

Or operates similarly. In (26), we find an example where for purposes of shifting the reader's focus the conjunction appears between each of the three conjuncts:

26. Another string, shaking and rolling in a different fashion, might appear as <u>an electron,</u> *or* <u>a photon,</u> *or* <u>one of the many other creatures of the subatomic bestiary</u> [*Discover,* November 1986].

The Clausal Coordinators *For* and *So*

The connectives *for* always and *so* generally connect entire clauses. As a rule, the connective *for* occurs only in written English, and if used in speech, usually appears only in ceremonial contexts. The conjunction *for,* which must be distinguished from the preposition *for* and the subject marker *for* in subject-bearing infinitive clauses, indicates a connection of either *reason* or *evidence* between the conjuncts. The second clause provides the reason for the assertion of the first (e.g., 27), or the evidence that allows the writer to assert the first (e.g., 28), as the following sentences from Poe's "The Fall of the House of Usher" demonstrate:

27. <u>Our glances, however, rested not long upon the dead</u>—*for* <u>we could not regard her unawed</u> (REASON).

28. <u>At times, again, I was obliged to resolve all into the mere inexplicable vagaries of madness,</u> *for* <u>I beheld him gazing upon vacancy for long hours, in an attitude of the profoundest attention, as if listening to some imaginary sound</u> (EVIDENCE).

In colloquial English, clauses such as those introduced by *for* in (27) and (28) are usually introduced by *because,* a subordinating particle.

So typically coordinates only entire clauses, but unlike *for,* is used quite extensively in spoken and casual English. The following sentences from the November 1986 issue of *Discover* demonstrate the use of *so* to indicate that the relation of the second clause to the first is that of RESULT:

29. And nobody knew anything about [string theory] yet, *so* they thought it was all a joke [G. Taubes, "Everything's Now Tied to Strings"].

30. The kitchen's also the busiest room in the house, *so* most of the dust keeps moving along rather than curling up in great balls [P. W. Moser, "All the Real Dirt on Dust"].

Sentence (29) is interesting, not only because it illustrates conjunction with *so*, but also because it reminds us that *yet* can be used as an adverb meaning "to this point," and because it demonstrates that sentences may acceptably begin with a particle that ordinarily serves as a coordinating conjunction. The *and* in (29) serves to tie all that follows it with what has been mentioned previously in the text, probably the preceding sentence. Because of this function, *and* resembles a sentence adverbial in this context, although it does not share an adverbial's freedom of position (see page 168). *But, so,* and *yet* also may be used in this larger sense, as the following sentences from *The Ascent of Man* demonstrate:

31. *But* war, organised war, is not a human instinct. It is a highly planned and cooperative form of theft.

32. *So* it must seem strange that I choose as my model for science, which is usually thought of as an abstract and cold enterprise, the warm, physical actions of sculpture and architecture.

33. To us, that scheme of cycles and epicycles seems both simple-minded and artificial. *Yet* in fact the system was a beautiful and workable invention, and an article of faith for Arabs and Christians right through the Middle Ages.

For—like *and* and *but*—also may function to bring about discourse cohesion, as (34), taken from a magazine subscription solicitation letter, demonstrates. As you would expect, such uses are relatively rare in informal letters and in casual speech:

34. While there is a provision in the Acceptance Form's wording for a 52-week *Science News* subscription at just $33.95, . . . this does not obligate you in any way at all! *For* if you choose not to take advantage of this special discount opportunity after receiving your twelve trial issues—you have only to write the word "cancel" across the invoice we'll send you and return it.

Thus, although you have probably learned that it is not acceptable to begin a sentence with a conjunction, many writers, some of them excellent, do so with good effect. The fact of the matter is that starting a sentence with a conjunction is not in the least ungrammatical. When your elementary school teachers told you to avoid doing it, they were trying to get you to vary sentence structure; you see, if left to their own proclivities, children tend to chain ideas together by using *and then . . . and then . . . and then,* a tactic that obviously does not lead to effective writing. One way to encourage the development of writing skills is to discourage overused techniques, but this pedagogical strategy does not necessarily render the technique ungrammatical.

Exercise 7.1

Circle the coordinators and then underline the coordinated elements in the following passages from *The Ascent of Man*. If more than one coordinator occurs in a given sentence, follow the procedure for each. The result may be that some words are underlined more than once. Indicate whether the coordination is phrasal or clausal.

1. The humming-bird beats the air and dips its needle-fine beak into hanging blossoms.

2. The stonework of Machu Picchu in the Andes and the geometry of the Alhambra in Moorish Spain seem to us, five centuries later, exquisite works of decorative art.

3. Splitting and fusing the atom both derive, conceptually, from a discovery made in prehistory.

4. In following the turning-points and the continuities of culture, I shall follow a general but not a strict chronological order.

5. The serval cat is still powerful in pursuit, and the oryx is still swift in flight.

6. In a parched African landscape like Omo, man first put his foot to the ground. That seems a pedestrian way to begin the Ascent of Man, and yet it is crucial.

7. He has a shorter snout than the lemur, his teeth are ape-like, and he is larger—yet still lives in the trees.

8. The combination is several thousand years old, but I saw it used by gipsies making chair-legs in a wood in England in 1945.

9. Agriculture is one part of the biological revolution; the domestication and harnessing of village animals is the other.

10. Genghis Khan was a nomad and the inventor of a powerful war machine—and that conjunction says something important about the origins of war in human history.

11. But war, organised war, is not a human instinct. It is a highly planned and cooperative form of theft.

12. [The nomad] gathered from the four corners of the world the cultures, mixed them together, and sent them out again to fertilise the earth.

13. The hidden forces within the earth have buckled the strata, and lifted and shifted the land masses.

14. Man has also become an architect of his environment, but he does not command forces as powerful as those of nature.

15. [The school of the Perspectivi] was a school of thought, for its aim was not simply to make the figures lifelike, but to create the sense of their movement in space.

16. Franklin and his friends lived science; it was constantly in their thoughts and just as constantly in their hands.

17. The link between Göttingen and the outside world was the railway.

18. The world is not a fixed, solid array of objects, out there, for it cannot be fully separated from our perception of it.

19. That idea would not have occurred to Newton or to Galileo.

20. Every judgement in science stands on the edge of error, and is personal.

Answers to Exercise 7.1

1. The humming-bird <u>beats the air</u> *and* <u>dips its needle-fine beak into hanging blossoms</u>.

   phrasal coordination

2. <u>The stonework of Machu Picchu in the Andes</u> *and* <u>the geometry of the Alhambra in Moorish Spain</u> seem to us, five centuries later, exquisite works of decorative art.

   phrasal coordination

3. <u>Splitting</u> *and* <u>fusing</u> the atom both derive, conceptually, from a discovery made in prehistory.

   phrasal coordination

4. In following <u>the turning-points</u> *and* <u>the continuities</u> of culture, I shall follow <u>a general</u> *but* <u>not a strict</u> chronological order.

   both instances of coordination are phrasal

5. <u>The serval cat is still powerful in pursuit</u>, *and* <u>the oryx is still swift in flight</u>.

   clausal coordination

6. In a parched African landscape like Omo, man first put his foot to the ground. <u>That seems a pedestrian way to begin the Ascent of Man</u>, *and yet* <u>it is crucial</u>.

   clausal coordination; *it* serves as the subject of the second conjunct

7. <u>He has a shorter snout than the lemur</u>, <u>his teeth are ape-like</u>, *and* <u>he is larger</u>—*yet* <u>still lives in the trees</u>.

   yet brings about phrasal coordination *(is larger, still lives in the trees);* and brings about the coordination of three independent clauses.

8. <u>The combination is several thousand years old</u>, *but* <u>I saw it used by gipsies making chair-legs in a wood in England in 1945</u>.

   clausal coordination

9. Agriculture is one part of the biological revolution; the <u>domestication</u> *and* <u>harnessing</u> of village animals is the other.

   phrasal coordination; the semicolon functions to implicitly connect two independent clauses (more on this later)

10. <u>Genghis Khan was a nomad</u> *and* <u>the inventor of a powerful war machine</u>—*and* <u>that conjunction says something important about the origins of war in human history</u>.

    the first *and* is a phrasal coordinator of the doubly underlined elements; the second brings about clausal coordination

11. But war, organised war, is not a human instinct. It is a highly <u>planned</u> *and* <u>cooperative</u> form of theft.

    phrasal coordination; *highly* is used ambiguously, so it may be possible to underline it as part of the first conjunct

12. [The nomad] <u>gathered from the four corners of the world the cultures</u>, <u>mixed them together</u>, *and* <u>sent them out again to fertilise the earth</u>.

    phrasal coordination; notice the unusual word order of the first predicate phrase conjunct: the direct object and adverbial are in inverted order

13. The hidden forces within the earth have <u>buckled the strata</u>, *and* <u>lifted *and* shifted the land masses</u>.

    the second *and* phrasally connects *lifted* with *shifted;* the first *and* phrasally connects *buckled the strata* with *lifted and shifted the land masses;* these two partial predicate phrases share the auxiliary *have.*

14. <u>Man has also become an architect of his environment</u>, *but* <u>he does not command forces as powerful as those of nature</u>.

    clausal coordination

15. [The school of the Perspectivi] was a school of thought, *for* its aim was not simply to make the figures lifelike, *but* to create the sense of their movement in space.

    but phrasally connects the doubly underlined items; *for* connects the underlined independent clauses

16. Franklin *and* his friends lived science; it was constantly in their thoughts *and* just as constantly in their hands.

    both cases of coordination are phrasal

17. The link between Göttingen *and* the outside world was the railway.

    phrasal coordination

18. The world is not a fixed, solid array of objects, out there, *for* it cannot be fully separated from our perception of it.

    clausal coordination

19. That idea would not have occurred to Newton *or* to Galileo.

    phrasal coordination

20. Every judgement in science stands on the edge of error, *and* is personal.

    phrasal coordination

Coordination as a Particular Syntactic Process

Coordination is a particular syntactic process with specific constraints that make it different from other methods of combining elements. By way of illustration, let us examine the following group of sentences, which are paraphrases of one another:

35. He wanted to pay back the loan, but he had no money.

36. Although he wanted to pay back the loan, he had no money.

37. He wanted to pay back the loan; however, he had no money.

Sentence (35) consists of independent clauses linked by the coordinator *but*. The coordinator *but* cannot be moved to a position inside the clause that it introduces (see, for example, 38 and 39), nor can the second clause introduced by *but* be moved to a position in front of what is now the first clause (see 40):

38. *He wanted to pay back the loan, he had no money but.

39. *He wanted to pay back the loan, he but had no money.

40. *But he had no money, he wanted to pay back the loan.

Unlike the clauses of (35), those of (36) have more freedom of movement. Sentence (41) demonstrates that their position can be interchanged with no change in the status of the resulting sentence's grammaticality:

41. He had no money, although he wanted to pay back the loan.

However, the **subordinating conjunction** *although* is similar to *but* in that it has no freedom of movement within its own clause; it is restricted to clause-initial position:

42. *He wanted to pay back the loan although, he had no money.

43. *He although wanted to pay back the loan, he had no money.

44. *He wanted although to pay back the loan, he had no money.

The clauses of (37) are merely juxtaposed, with no conjunction. The semicolon serves to delineate the boundaries of the independent clauses, and *however* is not a conjunction at all. It is a sentence adverbial serving to contrast the contents of its clause to that of the preceding clause. As an adverbial, it may be freely positioned between the constituents of its clause. Thus, (45), (46), and (47) all are grammatical:

45. He wanted to pay back the loan; he, however, had no money.

46. He wanted to pay back the loan; he had no money, however.

47. He wanted to pay back the loan; he had, however, no money.

Other sentence connectives function like *however*, including *thus, therefore, of course, hence,* etc.

Exercise 7.2

Circle the coordinators and then underline the coordinated elements in the following passages from Bill Cosby's *Fatherhood.* If more than one coordinator occurs in a given sentence, follow the procedure for each. The result may be that some words are underlined more than once. Are there some sentences that seem indeterminate as to whether the coordination is phrasal or clausal? Why?

1. In spite of the six thousand manuals on child raising in the bookstores, child raising is still a dark continent and no one really knows anything.

2. A baseball manager has learned a lot about his job from having played the game, but a parent has not learned a thing from having once been a child.

3. A baby, however, sells itself and needs no advertising copy; few people can resist it.

4. A baby turtle has to be the ugliest baby around, with sand all over the eggwhite sauce and arms bent in the wrong direction.

5. There will be sudden flashes of anger and tears, and from time to time she will blame you for everything from her backaches to the balance of trade.

6. So he got the salad spoons, the baby came out, and my wife and I were suddenly sharing the greatest moment in our lives.

7. The new father also loses privacy for taking naps and for working at home.

8. Sometimes, at three or four in the morning, I open the door to one of the children's bedrooms and watch the light softly fall across their little faces.

9. The new American father has more responsibilities than ever, but the children seem to have fewer.

10. In any stressful situation, fathering is always a roll of the dice. The game may be messy, but I have never found one with more rewards and joys.

11. Well, she almost succeeds in giving the change to you, but instead she decides to roll the quarter down the aisle.

12. Girls at eleven and even twelve are physiologically like boys. And these boys are not ready for them yet; they are still involved with lower species. They are wandering around with frogs, sleeping with lizards, and cutting the heads off flies.

13. At once, you turn from the dripping victim and call in the older sister, that dastardly girl.

14. And she underscores her point by starting to cry again and flinging herself on the bed.

15. In the entire history of civilization, no little boy or girl ever wished on a star for soap-on-a-rope.

16. We could also do without a ninety-seventh tie or another pair of socks, and we do not want a sweater in June.

17. A mother, however, will refuse to accept such a bottle [of cologne] or a little tin trophy and will send the children back to the store to get it right.

18. From time to time my father would come by, kick the door open, and then stand there under the assault of the music. He had the look of a sailor standing on a deck in a typhoon. And then his lips would start to move. I couldn't hear him, but I didn't have to, for he was sending an ancient message: *Turn that crap down.*

19. Only two hours later, the unit was assembled and I was issuing wise paternal advice.

20. She simply flew [her clothes] home every few weeks and put ten thousand dollars' worth of laundry into our washing machine.

Answers to Exercise 7.2

1. In spite of the six thousand manuals on child raising in the bookstores, <u>child raising is still a dark continent</u> *and* <u>no one really knows anything</u>.

2. <u>A baseball manager has learned a lot about his job from having played the game</u>, *but* <u>a parent has not learned a thing from having once been a child</u>.

3. A baby, however, <u>sells itself</u> *and* <u>needs no advertising copy</u>; few people can resist it.

4. A baby turtle has to be the ugliest baby around, <u>with sand all over the eggwhite sauce</u> *and* arms <u>bent in the wrong direction</u>.

5. <u>There will be sudden <u>flashes of anger</u> *and* tears</u>, *and* <u>from time to time she will blame you for everything from her backaches to the balance of trade</u>.

   The first coordination allows several interpretations in addition to the one given here, in particular, *anger* may be coordinated with *tears;* or *sudden flashes* of *anger* may be coordinated with *tears.*

6. So <u>he got the salad spoons</u>, <u>the baby came out</u>, *and* <u>my wife *and* I were suddenly sharing the greatest moment in our lives</u>.

7. The new father also loses privacy <u>for taking naps</u> *and* <u>for working at home</u>.

8. Sometimes, at <u>three</u> *or* <u>four</u> in the morning, I <u>open the door to one of the children's bedrooms</u> *and* <u>watch the light softly fall across their little faces</u>.

9. <u>The new American father has more responsibilities than ever</u>, *but* <u>the children seem to have fewer</u>.

   Fewer seems to be operating as a headless NP in this sentence; I would hesitate to claim that *responsibilities than ever* is not part of the coordination.

10. In any stressful situation, fathering is always a roll of the dice. <u>The game may be messy</u>, *but* <u>I have never found one with more rewards *and* joys</u>.

11. Well, <u>she almost succeeds in giving the change to you</u>, *but* <u>instead she decides to roll the quarter down the aisle</u>.

12. Girls at <u>eleven</u> *and* <u>even twelve</u> are physiologically like boys. And these boys are not ready for them yet; they are still involved with lower species. They are <u>wandering around with frogs</u>, <u>sleeping with lizards</u>, *and* <u>cutting the heads off flies</u>.

13. At once, you <u>turn from the dripping victim</u> *and* <u>call in the older sister, that dastardly girl</u>.

    Since *that dastardly girl* modifies *the older sister*, it is included in the coordination.

14. And she underscores her point by <u>starting to cry again</u> *and* <u>flinging herself on the bed</u>.

15. In the entire history of civilization, no little <u>boy</u> *or* <u>girl</u> ever wished on a star for soap-on-a-rope.

16. <u>We could also do without a ninety-seventh tie</u> *or* <u>another pair of socks</u>, *and* <u>we do not want a sweater in June</u>.

17. A mother, however, <u>will refuse to accept such a bottle [of cologne]</u> *or* <u>a little tin trophy</u> *and* <u>will send the children back to the store to get it right</u>.

18. From time to time my father would <u>come by</u>, <u>kick the door open</u>, *and* <u>then stand there under the assault of the music</u>. He had the look of a sailor standing on a deck in a typhoon. And then his lips would start to move. <u>I couldn't hear him</u>, *but* <u>I didn't have to</u>, *for* <u>he was sending an ancient message: *Turn that crap down*</u>.

    There is more than one possibility for the last sentence, including a reading in which the three conjuncts are chained together through the use of successive conjunctions.

19. Only two hours later, <u>the unit was assembled</u> *and* <u>I was issuing wise paternal advice</u>.

20. She simply <u>flew [her clothes] home every few weeks</u> *and* <u>put ten thousand dollars' worth of laundry into our washing machine</u>.

When Is Clausal Coordination Not Really Clausal Coordination?

If you were careful in doing the preceding exercise, undoubtedly you were puzzled by a couple of sentences in which the coordination seems at first to be clausal and then on closer inspection seems to be phrasal. In fact the "distinction" between phrasal and clausal coordination really is more of a continuum than an opposition, as the following sentences, taken from the last exercise, will amply demonstrate:

48. In spite of the six thousand manuals on child raising in the bookstores, child raising is still a dark continent and no one really knows anything.

49. Only two hours later, the unit was assembled and I was issuing wise paternal advice.

In (48), the coordination is between two clauses, given in (50) and (51):

50. child raising is still a dark continent

51. no one really knows anything

However, the coordination of these two clauses together is embedded in the adverbial phrase given in (52):

52. In spite of the six thousand manuals on child raising in the bookstores

That is, (52) does not merely modify (50); it modifies the *coordination* of (50) and (51). In effect, the coordination lies in some middle ground between phrasal and clausal. In fact, only partial clauses are coordinated, yet each of these clauses could conceivably stand on its own as a complete independent clause. The same phenomenon is apparent in (49). The coordinated elements are:

53. the unit was assembled

54. I was issuing wise paternal advice

The coordination of the seemingly independent clauses given in (53) and (54) is modified by the temporal adverbial phrase *only two hours later*.

Exercise 7.3

The following passages are taken from "Everything's Now Tied to Strings," an article by Gary Taubes that appeared in the November 1986 issue of *Discover*. Circle the coordinating conjunctions and underline the conjuncts. If a sentence contains more than one coordinator, follow the procedure for each. Pay particular attention to sentences in which an adverbial or other element applies to a coordination of clauses. Are there any ambiguous cases? Be able to defend your analyses.

1. Superstring theory is the product of an unprecedented alliance between theoretical physics and mainline mathematics.

2. This theory had only ten dimensions. And it did account for fermions. But it still included the tachyon, it was still a theory of the strong force, and it still had all those dimensions.

3. Physicists have concocted quantum theories to explain the strong, weak, and electromagnetic forces.

4. [Supersymmetry] was an offshoot of the early string work, and was yet another unification concept touted as a potential Theory of Everything.

5. Their concentration on string theory wasn't doing much for Green's and Schwarz's careers.

6. In 1979, 13 years after getting his Ph.D., Schwarz was still only a research associate at Caltech, and Green had finally gotten a permanent job, albeit the lowest possible one, at Queen Mary after nine years of floating.

7. Now the two were speaking weekly and at great length, even at East Coast institutions like Harvard and Princeton.

8. For Green, the serendipitousness of his and Schwarz's discovery precludes any comparison between Einstein and Schwarz and himself.

9. [Quantum physics] began at the turn of the century and blossomed around 1913 with the development of the Bohr atom.

10. In 1927, Heisenberg created the uncertainty principle, and quantum mechanics was really born.

Answers to Exercise 7.3

1. Superstring theory is the product of an unprecedented alliance between theoretical physics *and* mainline mathematics.

2. This theory had only ten dimensions. And it did account for fermions. But it still included the tachyon, it was still a theory of the strong force, *and* it still had all those dimensions.

   Remember that conjunctions at the beginning of sentences are not true conjunctions. However, the use of *but* at the beginning of the third sentence serves to contrast the coordination of the three clauses connected by *and* to everything in the prior two sentences.

3. Physicists have concocted quantum theories to explain the strong, weak, *and* electromagnetic forces.

4. [Supersymmetry] was an offshoot of the early string work, *and* was yet another unification concept touted as a potential Theory of Everything.

   Yet does not function as a conjunction in this sentence. It serves to add a bit of irony to the meaning of *another*.

5. Their concentration on string theory wasn't doing much for <u>Green's</u> *and* <u>Schwarz's</u> careers.

6. <u>In 1979, 13 years after getting his Ph.D., Schwarz was still only a research associate at Caltech,</u> *and* <u>Green had finally gotten a permanent job, albeit the lowest possible one, at Queen Mary after nine years of floating</u>.

   This one is tricky. Although it is true that the events of both clauses seem to have taken place in 1979, the nonrestrictive modifier of *in 1979,* namely, *13 years after getting his Ph.D.,* is clearly tied by the pronoun *his* to *Schwarz,* which occurs in the first clause only. There is thus a pull-along effect, and so the initial adverbial syntactically modifies only the first clause. The relevance of the date to the second clause is given logically through a discourse phenomenon called **implicature,** but is implicit and not explicit.

7. Now the two were speaking <u>weekly</u> *and* <u>at great length</u>, even at East Coast institutions like <u>Harvard</u> *and* <u>Princeton</u>.

   The first coordination demonstrates that although the conjuncts are structurally dissimilar (one is an adverb; the other is a prepositional phrase), they have the same function: they both are adverbials.

8. For Green, the serendipitousness of <u>his</u> *and* <u>Schwarz's</u> discovery precludes any comparison between <u>Einstein</u> *and* <u>Schwarz *and* himself</u>.

   The result of the coordination of *Schwarz* with *himself* is then coordinated with *Einstein.* Students often have difficulty here. The best way to begin is to ask yourself what the antecedent of the pronouns *his* and *himself* is. The antecedent of *his* is *Green,* and the fact that the *discovery* is one shared by *Green* and *Schwarz* should tell you that they are working as a team. *Between* is a preposition with a very special property: The NP serving as its object must either be plural, or a coordination of *two* conjuncts, *but not more than two.* Thus, since Schwarz and Green constitute a team, the comparison is between Einstein on the one hand, and the team of Schwarz and Green on the other.

9. [Quantum physics] <u>began at the turn of the century</u> *and* <u>blossomed around 1913 with the development of the Bohr atom</u>.

   Each predicate phrase has its own temporal adverbial. The result is that the second conjunct implies that the development of the Bohr atom occurred in 1913, and *not* at the turn of the century.

10. In 1927, Heisenberg created the uncertainty principle, and quantum mechanics was really born.

    As you can see, I've indicated no answer for this one. It seems to me that the comma between the two clauses indicates a break that in turn indicates something like: *in 1927, Heisenberg created the uncertainty principle, and as a result quantum mechanics was born.* In this reading, the introductory temporal adverbial modifies the first clause only and would be underlined with the first clause. However, it seems also possible to regard the adverbial as modifying the coordination of the two clauses. If so, then *in 1927* would not be underlined.

Implicit Coordination

Sometimes clauses or clause elements are coordinated without the presence of an actual conjunction. When entire clauses are simply juxtaposed in this manner, they are separated by a semicolon. Example (55), which we have previously encountered in (12), provides an illustration of such **implicit** clausal **coordination:**

55. Agriculture is one part of the biological revolution; the domestication and harnessing of village animals is the other.

In (55), the clauses are connected by a common topic, with the second clause providing the second part of the "biological revolution" given in the first. Thus there is an *additive* relation between the clauses, a relation that could be expressed with *and.*

Sometimes the second of two such clauses provides a contrast, a relation that could be captured by *but:*

56. During the late 1950s and early 1960s the lab pioneered solar heating and cooling; in the '70s it focused on solar desalinization and controlled-environment agriculture [*Discover,* May 1987].

And sometimes the second clause provides the evidence for the assertion made in the first, a notion that could be signaled by *for:*

57. Franklin and his friends lived science; it was constantly in their thoughts and just as constantly in their hands [*The Ascent of Man*].

58. To a young person, naps don't mean much; he casually takes them in English class [*Fatherhood*].

59. A baby, however, sells itself and needs no advertising copy; few people can resist it [*Fatherhood*].

Elements less than entire clauses also may be implicitly linked, as (60), from Louise Erdrich's *The Beet Queen,* amply demonstrates; commas separate the implicitly linked predicate phrases:

60. She threw her head back and forth, would not speak, shuddered like a broken doll.

In (61), from *Dracula,* commas separate implicitly linked NPs, all subjects:

61. But there was no sign of movement, no pulse, no breath, no beating of the heart.

More Explicit Coordination—Correlative Conjunction

Sometimes the force of coordination is heightened by the addition of a particle in front of the first conjunct; this particle then co-occurs with the coordinating conjunction, which appears in its usual place in front of the second conjunct. Together, these two particles constitute a subclass of coordinating conjunctions called **correlative conjunctions.** Included in this class are the following correlative pairs:

>*both . . . and, either . . . or, neither . . . nor, not (only) . . . but*

The following sentences illustrate the operation of these correlative pairs:

62. Call it just another part of being a father: trying to catch up to *both* misery *and* joy [*Fatherhood*].

63. [The Count] was *either* dead *or* asleep, I could not say which—for the eyes were open and stony, but without the glassiness of death—and the cheeks had the warmth of life through all their pallor, and the lips were as red as ever [*Dracula*].

64. *Not only* is her figure changing, *but* her personality is too [*Fatherhood*].

Neither . . . Nor, and *Nor*

If you have been observant, you have noticed that we have not seen any examples of the "negative" coordinators, *nor,* and *neither . . . nor.* In fact, these connective devices are used only rarely in modern writing, and so appropriate genuine examples are difficult to come by. However, here are some examples I've created for the occasion:

65. Jasper did not lend Maximillian any money, nor did he intend to.

66. Jasper has neither friends nor fortune.

67. Neither Jasper nor Maximillian will ever get rich.

Neither . . . nor, like *both . . . and,* ordinarily is not used to connect clauses. When *nor* connects two clauses, two syntactic changes of note occur. The second clause will omit material that is identical to what occurs in the first clause. For (65), that material is (68):

68. lend Maximillian any money.

Secondly, the second clause will evidence a subject/auxiliary inversion, as is seen in the second half of (65). (Inversions are common when a negative element begins a clause. See (74) below.)

Gapping

Sometimes coordinated elements do not occur side-by-side, but are separated by intervening material. This phenomenon typically occurs when the common—repeated—element is a VP or a partial predicate phrase (e.g., VP + NP). In such cases, the second occurrence of the element is omitted, leaving a "gap" in the second clause. The following sentence from *The Bingo Palace* by Louise Erdrich exemplifies this process of **gapping:**

69a. His beard was pure white, long and patchy, and his big eyes frozen blue.

In (69a) the omitted common material is the VP *were.* What is understood, then, is (69b):

69b. His beard was pure white, long and patchy, and his big eyes *were* frozen blue.

In the light of this knowledge, we may be able to reanalyze (64) as another instance of gapping:

64. *Not only* <u>is her figure changing,</u> *but* <u>her personality is too</u>.

Notice that *changing* is the understood element omitted from the second clause.

Although gapping remains grammatical in English, it does not occur frequently, and tends to be a literary and not a conversational process. It seems to involve a kind of condensation of information that does not lend itself well to conversation.

Function Shift Is Alive and Well and Living in Transylvania—and Elsewhere

Sometimes the conjunctions *and* and particularly *but* do not connect two elements of equal status at all, but serve to connect what follows them to an implication drawn from the previous assertion. Here are two examples from *Dracula:*

70. There lay the Count, *but* looking as if his youth had been half renewed, for the white hair and moustache were changed to dark iron grey; the cheeks were fuller, and the white skin seemed ruby-red underneath . . . .

71. I bent over him, and tried to find any sign of life, *but* in vain.

And here is another from *A Word Child,* by Iris Murdoch:

72. They pursued and cultivated all sorts of "grandees" and had them to dinner, *but* of course not on the days when I was there.

As you can see, there is no structural or functional equivalent preceding *looking as if his youth had been half renewed* in (70), nor any equivalent prepositional phrase or adverbial preceding *in vain* in (71). In both cases, *but* serves to mark the denial of the expectation to which the previous portion of the sentence gives rise. This semantic function is exactly equivalent to what goes on elsewhere when *but* apparently connects elements of equal status, as these examples from *Dracula* illustrate:

73. He might kill me, but death now seemed the happier choice of evils.
74. I felt all over the body, but no sign could I find of the key.

In (73), *but* connects two clauses. The first clause, however, leads to an inference that the narrator might not be too happy about this turn of events; the second clause, introduced by *but, denies* this expectation. Similarly, in (74) the narrator is searching for something, and hopes to find it, but the second clause denies the expectation set up by the first.

The uses of *but* demonstrated in (70), (71), and (72), then, are not true coordinative uses, but reveal that the semantics of a word sometimes outweighs its syntax. The word then *shifts* its function, in this case from a coordinator to something else similar, but not quite the same.

Exercise 7.4

In each of the following sentences from Louise Erdrich's novel *Love Medicine,* circle the coordinating conjunction and underline the equal parts that it connects. If a sentence contains more than one coordinator, follow the procedure for each.

1. The wind was mild and wet.

2. She made a right turn off the road, walked up a drift frozen over a snow fence, and began to pick her way through the swirls of dead grass and icy crust of open ranchland.

3. I opened the envelope and read the words.

4. Her clothes were full of safety pins and hidden tears.

5. She puffed her cheeks out in concentration, patting and crimping the edges of the pies.

6. They were beautiful pies—rhubarb, wild Juneberry, apple, and gooseberry, all fruits preserved by Grandma Kashpaw or my mother or Aurelia.

7. King Junior was bundled in the front seat and both Grandma and Grandpa Kashpaw were stuffed, incredibly, into the tiny backseat.

8. The older children left, but the brothers still lived on opposite ends of Rushes Bear's land.

9. King's lip curled down in some imitation of soap-opera bravado, but his chin trembled.

10. Lynette shrugged brightly and brushed away King's remark.

11. His voice was ripped and swollen.

12. I tipped the bottle, looked up at the sky, and nearly fell over, in amazement and too much beer, at the drenching beauty.

13. The mix of beer and rosé made my head whirl.

14. He read books about computers and volcanoes and the life cycles of salamanders.

15. I was cold, damp, and sick.

16. She struggled powerfully, but he had her.

17. I grabbed a block of birch out of the woodbox and hit King on the back of the neck.

18. He reeled backward, bucking me off, and I flew across the room, hit the refrigerator solidly, and got back on my feet.

19. For a while we worked in silence, mixing up the dough and pounding it out on stone slabs.

20. Words came from nowhere and flooded my mind.

21. But the outstretched poker hit the back wall first, so she rebounded.

22. Her voice box evidently did not work, for her mouth opened, shut, opened, but no sound came out.

23. She banged the side of the house, ordered me off, and wedged her cane behind the door as a lock.

24. He watched without moving, so finally I got up and stood over Moses.

25. The ground is cluttered with car parts, oil pans, pieces of cement block, and other useful junk.

Answers to Exercise 7.4

1. The wind was <u>mild</u> *and* <u>wet</u>.
2. She <u>made a right turn off the road</u>, <u>walked up a drift frozen over a snow fence</u>, *and* <u>began to pick her way through</u> the swirls of dead grass *and* icy crust of open ranchland.
3. I <u>opened the envelope</u> *and* <u>read the words</u>.
4. Her clothes were full of <u>safety pins</u> *and* <u>hidden tears</u>.
5. She puffed her cheeks out in concentration, <u>patting</u> *and* <u>crimping</u> the edges of the pies.
6. They were beautiful pies—<u>rhubarb</u>, <u>wild Juneberry</u>, <u>apple</u>, *and* <u>gooseberry</u>, all fruits preserved by <u>Grandma Kashpaw</u> *or* <u>my mother</u> *or* <u>Aurelia</u>.
7. <u>King Junior was bundled in the front seat</u> *and* *both* <u>Grandma</u> *and* <u>Grandpa Kashpaw were stuffed, incredibly, into the tiny backseat</u>.
8. <u>The older children left</u>, *but* <u>the brothers still lived on opposite ends of Rushes Bear's land</u>.
9. <u>King's lip curled down in some imitation of soap-opera bravado</u>, *but* <u>his chin trembled</u>.
10. Lynette <u>shrugged brightly</u> *and* <u>brushed away King's remark</u>.
11. His voice was <u>ripped</u> *and* <u>swollen</u>.
12. I <u>tipped the bottle</u>, <u>looked up at the sky</u>, *and* <u>nearly fell over, in amazement</u> *and* <u>too much beer, at the drenching beauty</u>.
13. The mix of <u>beer</u> *and* <u>rosé</u> made my head whirl.
14. He read books about <u>computers</u> *and* <u>volcanoes</u> *and* <u>the life cycles of salamanders</u>.
15. I was <u>cold</u>, <u>damp</u>, *and* <u>sick</u>.
16. <u>She struggled powerfully</u>, *but* <u>he had her</u>.
17. I <u>grabbed a block of birch out of the woodbox</u> *and* <u>hit King on the back of the neck</u>.

18. He reeled backward, bucking me off, *and* I flew across the room, hit the refrigerator solidly, *and* got back on my feet.

19. For a while we worked in silence, mixing up the dough *and* pounding it out on stone slabs.

20. Words came from nowhere *and* flooded my mind.

21. But the outstretched poker hit the back wall first, *so* she rebounded.

22. Her voice box evidently did not work, *for* her mouth opened, shut, opened, *but* no sound came out.

23. She banged the side of the house, ordered me off, *and* wedged her cane behind the door as a lock.

24. He watched without moving, *so* finally I got up *and* stood over Moses.

25. The ground is cluttered with car parts, oil pans, pieces of cement block, *and* other useful junk.

Terms Used in Chapter Seven

clausal coordination: the connection of two or more independent clauses through the process of coordination or conjunction.

coordinating conjunctions: members of the small class of function words that bring about coordination in English—*for, and, nor, but, or, yet, so.*

coordination: the fusion of two or more of any sentence elements of the same status through the use of coordinating conjunctions.

conjuncts: the elements connected through the process of coordination.

correlative conjunctions: conjunctions made up of two separate words, each marking the start of a conjunct, e.g., *both . . . and, either . . . or.*

function shift: the use of a word from a particular word class as some other word class. The word thus *shifts* its function from noun to verb.

gapping: the omission of repeated material from within a conjunct.

implicature: a logical assumption derived from the supposition that writers or speakers have some intent to communicate in mind when they use the language.

implicit coordination: the connection of two or more elements of equal status through the process of coordination, but without the use of an expressed coordinating conjunction.

phrasal coordination: the connection of two or more phrasal elements through the process of coordination or conjunction.

primary conjunctions: the most important and frequent coordinators—*and, but, or.*

subordinating conjunction: a function word that introduces a clause that is subordinate to another structure—*because* is a good example.

Chapter Quiz

In each of the following sentences from *The Queen's Physician,* by Edgar Maass, circle the coordinating conjunction and underline the equal parts that it connects. If more than one coordinator occurs in a given sentence, follow the procedure for each. Be careful; some coordinated elements occur inside of elements that are themselves coordinated to other structures.

1. A couple of years at Oxford had taught me little, for I was not attracted by the pedantry of philosophical pursuits.

2. After leaving Oxford I toyed with the idea of selling my English properties and settling in Virginia.

3. The weather, fortunately, was still pleasant, and so I was not too much disconcerted by the delay.

4. The happy prospect of being homeward bound and within fair distance of my goal buoyed up my heart.

5. Her face was round, yet not overly full.

6. She tried to control herself but again pain got the upper hand.

7. Immediately he took me by the shoulders and pushed me away from the weeping lady.

8. Moonlight and shadow filled the narrow streets.

9. Actually I did not understand at all, but I bowed in silent assent.

10. The Queen came in immediately after me and motioned with her hand for me to sit down.

11. She herself took the bench beside the harp, but in deference to her rank I determined to remain standing.

12. The chronic longing for her children and the enforced isolation in this strange castle are disturbing her to the core.

13. The idea, of course, was fascinating, but my strength and my experience still seemed grossly disproportionate to the needs of any such far-reaching plan.

14. A strange power had come into my life, and I was no longer my own master.

15. He turned white as a sheet and for a long time stared at the floor without answering me.

16. He let his snuff box fall and both of us bent at the same time to pick it up.

17. I have nothing written with me, for that would be too dangerous.

18. Over our heads hung the ubiquitous hams and sausages of Hanover.

19. My thoughts were focused on her and her strange fate.

20. I went directly to the garden, and of course arrived too early.

21. The folk at work in the fields pause in their labors, wipe hot sweat from their foreheads with swollen hands, and look up into the cloudless sky.

22. Unwillingly, the hands in the field bow their backs and resume their toil.

23. Their sons served as officer-candidates and lieutenants in the Danish, Prussian and Hanoverian armies, or tried to get a footing for themselves as officials in the various states.

24. The Count, with his iron-gray hair and his tall figure, was something of a ladies' man.

25. But in this current epoch the Count had returned to his wife and child in Holstein, on the way suffering a minor, but fateful, accident.

Chapter Eight

Finite Subordination— Content Clauses and Relative Clauses

Introduction

In Chapters Four and Five we learned about nonfinite subordinate clauses, and we found that such clauses could serve as subjects, objects, and other complements, as well as modifiers. In this chapter we will learn about **finite subordinate clauses,** which are subordinate clauses with tensed VPs. We will focus on two finite subordinate types: *content clauses,* which typically function as subjects, objects, and complements within other clauses, and *relative clauses,* which function as adjectival modifiers within NPs.

Finite Subordinate Clauses

A **finite subordinate clause** is a proposition [think: "subject-predicate"] that has the basic structure of a sentence, but that has been altered in some way so that it functions as a constituent in another clause. This kind of clause is called "finite" because, unlike the nonfinite clause, it always has a VP inflected for tense or containing a modal. Moreover, all finite clauses in English must have explicit subjects, another feature distinguishing them from the nonfinite variety, which typically are subjectless. Like nonfinite clauses, finite subordinate clauses may function as major sentence constituents, such as subjects, objects, or complements, or as modifiers, such as adjectivals or adverbials.

Content Clauses

A variety of names has been applied to finite subordinate clauses serving as major constituents. Sometimes they are called noun clauses or substantive clauses (*substantive* being a more technical name for *noun*), and sometimes they are called complement clauses or content clauses. In this book, we shall use the term **content clause.**

The most common type of content clause is introduced by the subordinate marker *that,* which is not a pronoun or determiner in this usage, but simply an indicator that what follows is a subordinate entity. When *that* is used to introduce a content clause, it is called a **complementizer.** The underlined portions of sentences (1) and (2) are subordinate content clauses:

1. John knew <u>that his brother would be late</u>.

2. <u>That Mary would win the prize</u> seemed obvious to everyone.

In Sentence (1), the subordinate clause functions as the direct object of the verb phrase of the principal clause (sometimes called the **matrix** sentence). In Sentence (2), the subordinate content clause functions as the subject of the VP of the matrix. Sentences such as (2) frequently appear with the subject clause **extraposed,** that is, moved to the end of the sentence. When extraposition occurs, the "anticipatory pronoun" *it* occurs in the subject slot as a placeholder for the true subject, which now, contrary to everything we know about English sentence structure, appears at the end of the sentence. Thus, a sentence such as (2) is likely to be rendered as (3):

3. It seemed obvious to everyone <u>that Mary would win the prize</u>.

The subordinate content clause of (3), in spite of its changed position, remains the subject of the matrix VP.

It is frequently the case that the complementizer *that* may be entirely omitted from a sentence. For example, a sentence such as (1) is likely to be rendered as (4):

4. John knew <u>his brother would be late</u>.

The underlined clause of (4), just like its nearly identical counterpart in (1), is the direct object of *knew.* However, the complementizer is less likely to be omitted in writing than it is in speaking, and it may never be omitted when the subordinate content clause begins the sentence, as the ungrammaticality of (5) clearly demonstrates:

5. *<u>Mary would win the prize</u> seemed obvious to everyone.

It is important to understand that position, and not function, causes (5) to be ungrammatical. That is, the complementizer *that* can quite acceptably be omitted from a subject clause—if that subject clause is extraposed. Thus, (6) is a perfectly acceptable English sentence, even though it seems better as a spoken form than as a written one:

6. It seemed obvious to everyone <u>Mary would win the prize</u>.

Embedded Questions

All of the content clauses described so far are based on the status of the dependent clause as an inherently declarative clause. But sometimes content clauses are inherently interrogative or even exclamatory. When a content clause has missing information, it is generally an "embedded question" and will begin with an interrogative pronoun—or question word—just the way an ordinary question would. Generally, it is one of the *wh-* series: *who, whose, when, where,* and *how.* In the embedded question, however, the subject and the auxiliary verb are not inverted as they are in an ordinary question. Typically, a content clause is introduced by a *wh-* word when the VP of the matrix clause is a **speech act verb,** that is, one involving asking or telling:

7. I told him [*or* asked him, *or* revealed] <u>who gave me the answer</u>.

8. I asked him <u>what time it was</u>.

In (7), the subordinate content clause functions as the direct object of the VP *told.* In (8), the subordinate clause functions as the direct object of the VP *asked.* Sometimes such *wh-* clauses appear as subjects, and in these cases the *wh-* clause is more nearly a content clause with some NP left unspecified than it is a true "embedded question." One such subject clause appears in (9), from Shakespeare:

9. <u>Who steals my purse</u> steals trash.

and another occurs in (10), from Bronowski's *The Ascent of Man:*

10. <u>What makes the Industrial Revolution so peculiarly English</u> is that it is rooted in the countryside.

Sentence (10) also demonstrates that a subordinate clause may occur as a copular complement (i.e., *that it is rooted in the countryside*). In fact, content clauses may occur in nearly every function that may be served by a simple NP, including that of object of a preposition. The underlined portion of the following sentence from *Dracula* exemplifies a *wh-* content clause functioning as object of the preposition *of:*

11. It gave me an idea of <u>what a terrible strain Lucy's system must have undergone</u> that what weakened Arthur only partially restored her. [Note: the *that* clause that ends the sentence is an extraposed subject. In addition, the extraposed subject has a subordinate clause as its own subject. Can you find it?]

Exercise 8.1

The following sentences come from Bram Stoker's *Dracula*. Each contains one or more content clauses. Underline each one that you find, and in the space below each sentence, identify the function that the content clause serves in the sentence. The possibilities for this exercise are: *subject, direct object, copular complement, object of a preposition*. When underlining the content clauses, remember the following considerations:

a. A subordinate clause includes whatever modifies an element within its bounds and whatever serves as object or complement to an element within its bounds.

b. A finite clause has only one finite verb, unless coordination takes place. If you find more than one finite verb and the second is not coordinated to the first, the VPs belong to different clauses, although one clause may be *nested* (i.e., entirely contained) inside the other.

c. A finite clause *must* have an explicit subject. If that subject is a pronoun, it must occur in the subjective case (e.g., *I, we, he, she, they*). If you find more than one subjective case in a sentence, the odds are that the second occurrence belongs to a finite subordinate clause.

1. It so happened that there was no one at the moment on Tate Hill Pier.

2. I thought I would watch for the Count's return, and for a long time sat doggedly at the window.

3. Then I began to notice that there were some little specks floating in the rays of the moonlight.

4. To my intense astonishment, I saw that [the door] was unlocked.

5. At last I felt that subtle change in the air, and knew that the morning had come.

6. I knew I must search the body for the key, so I raised the lid and laid it back against the wall.

7. I thought and thought what should be my next move, but my brain seemed on fire, and I waited with a despairing feeling growing over me.

8. I could not pity her, for I knew now what had become of her child, and she was better dead.

9. I knew then that to struggle at the moment against the Count was useless.

10. Suddenly it struck me that this might be the moment and the means of my doom.

11. Then came the welcome cock-crow, and I felt that I was safe.

12. I do not know how I am writing this even to you.

13. I need not tell you this is a secret.

14. It astonished me how long the drug took to act.

15. Dr. Van Helsing had directed that I should sit up with him.

Answers to Exercise 8.1

1. It so happened <u>that there was no one at the moment on Tate Hill Pier</u>.
   extraposed subject of the sentence

2. I thought <u>I would watch for the Count's return</u>, and for a long time sat doggedly at the window.
   direct object of *thought*

3. Then I began to notice <u>that there were some little specks floating in the rays of the moonlight</u>.
   direct object of *notice*

4. To my intense astonishment, I saw <u>that [the door] was unlocked</u>.
   direct object of *saw*

5. At last I felt that subtle change in the air, and knew <u>that the morning had come</u>.
   direct object of *knew*

6. I knew <u>I must search the body for the key</u>, so I raised the lid and laid it back against the wall.
   direct object of *knew*

7. I thought and thought <u>what should be my next move</u>, but my brain seemed on fire, and I waited with a despairing feeling growing over me.
   direct object of *thought and thought*

8. I could not pity her, for I knew now <u>what had become of her child</u>, and she was better dead.
   direct object of *knew*

9. I knew then <u>that to struggle at the moment against the Count was useless</u>.

    direct object of *knew*

10. Suddenly it struck me <u>that this might be the moment and the means of my doom</u>.

    extraposed subject of the sentence

11. Then came the welcome cock-crow, and I felt <u>that I was safe</u>.

    direct object of *felt*

12. I do not know <u>how I am writing this even to you</u>.

    direct object of *do not know*

13. I need not tell you <u>this is a secret</u>.

    direct object of *need not tell* (*you* is the indirect object)

14. It astonished me <u>how long the drug took to act</u>.

    extraposed subject of the sentence

15. Dr. Van Helsing had directed <u>that I should sit up with him</u>.

    direct object of *had directed*

Kinds of Predicates Accepting Content Clauses

If you have been paying close attention to elements in addition to the subordinate clauses in the preceding exercise, you may have noticed that two semantic categories of verbs admit content clauses as complements. One of these is the **speech act verb.** The other is the **mental experience verb,** a verb that captures a mental activity such as *know, think, perceive, feel,* etc. These verbs should serve as indicators to you that a content clause may be in the vicinity.

Relative Clauses

Some finite subordinate clauses are adjectivals. Adjectival subordinate clauses generally are called **relative clauses** because they "relate" to the head noun of the NP of which they are a part. Relative clauses are post nominal (i.e., following the noun) adjectival elements that have sentence structure of their own. The underlined portions of Sentences (12) and (13) are relative clauses:

12. The man <u>who lives across the street</u> is leaving for Denver tomorrow.

13. The man <u>whom you met at dinner last evening</u> is leaving for Denver tomorrow.

In (12), the word *who* is a **relative pronoun.** It is "relative" because it relates an adjectival clause to an N or NP, and it is a pronoun because it substitutes for the noun *man* in the subordinate clause itself. That is, the underlined portion of (12) is an altered version of the following proposition (14):

14. The man lives across the street.

In (12), the relative pronoun *who* has replaced the NP *the man,* which would be fully specified in an independent clause such as (14). Similarly *whom* in (13) serves as a relative pronoun substituting for the NP *the man* in the analogous independent clause given in (15):

15. You met the man at dinner last evening.

Probably you are wondering why it is that *the man* follows the verb in (15) but precedes it in (14). A general principle regarding the formulation of all relative clauses in English, which applies with few exceptions, is that a relative pronoun, regardless of the position of its NP counterpart in the analogous independent clause, appears at the beginning of the relative clause, and thus serves as a marker—a flag, so to speak—of the subordinate status of the clause. Thus, *the man* is the direct object of *met* in (15), and *whom* is the direct object of *met* in (13), even though it does not appear in canonical direct object position. What seems to be a word order violation for an English structure comes about because of a general "movement" rule in the language: Taking the independent version of the relative clause as basic and therefore the logical form of the structure, we "move" the NP that has become relativized to the front of the clause, with the result that the relative pronoun appears first in the clause. In those cases in which the relative pronoun already is clause initial because of its status as subordinate subject, we can conceive of the movement rule applying vacuously. That is, it applies, but we do not see any tangible result of the movement, because the original string and the final "post-movement" string look exactly the same.

You will notice that the relative pronoun *whom* ends with *-m.* This suffix is ancient in English, and it indicates "objective" case, or the case inflection for elements serving as objects of various types, whether of verbs or prepositions. Although English has lost most case inflections for nouns, the personal and relative pronouns still retain them: the *-m* occurring in *him, them,* and *whom* is a relic from an earlier stage of the language, but now, as then, it indicates the object status of the word to which it is appended.

Relative Pronouns

Who and *whom* are not the only relative pronouns: *whose, which, that,* and sometimes *when* and *where* also may function as relative pronouns. *Whose* replaces a possessive NP:

16. The man whose hat you found was happy to have it back.

Sentence (16) is interesting not only because it shows that the NP that can be replaced by a relative pronoun is any NP whatsoever, but also because it demonstrates something else important about relative pronouns: Relative pronouns do not always operate as isolated elements, capable of moving to the front of their clauses by themselves. If they are part of a complex construction, they may drag that entire construction with them to clause-initial position, sometimes optionally, sometimes obligatorily. The independent clause that is the logical structure of the subordinate clause in (16) is (17):

17. You found the man's hat.

The man's hat becomes *whose hat* in its relative form, and the entire NP moves front. Sentence (18) is an intermediate form of (16):

18. *the man <u>you found whose hat</u> was happy to have it back.

A brief examination of (18) should convince you that the entire relativized NP *whose hat* has shifted from its logical place as direct object of the subordinate VP to clause initial position. Thus, it is not the relative pronoun that appears at the front of the relative clause but the relativized NP. Trying to move the pronoun alone results in an ungrammatical string:

19. *the man <u>whose you found hat</u> was happy to have it back.

The general rule for relative pronouns is that *who* and *whom* replace NPs indicating human beings, whereas *which* replaces nonhuman NPs. *Whose* is generally indifferent to the human status of its antecedent and may replace either human or nonhuman NPs. When *when* serves as a relative pronoun, it must be connected to a time noun:

20. That was the time <u>when my car broke down</u>.

and *where* must be connected to a noun of location:

21. Or am I just on the street <u>where you live</u>?

A brief study of (20) and (21) should convince you that *when* and *where* are adverbials in their own clauses and in canonical sentence position would occur last in the subordinate clause. Like any other relative pronoun, these relative pronouns always move to the front of their clauses.

One final word about relative pronouns is that there is no distinction between singular and plural forms, although relative pronouns may replace both singular and plural NPs. Sentences (22a) and (22b) from *Dracula* demonstrate that *which* may have a singular or plural antecedent, and (23a) and (23b) from *Interview with the Vampire* illustrate the same property for *who*. I have underlined the relative pronouns and italicized their antecedents:

22a. At last I pulled open a heavy *door* <u>which</u> stood ajar. [singular]

22b. She . . . cried the same words in *tones* <u>which</u> wrung my heart. [plural]

23a. He had . . . a blind *father* <u>who</u> did not know his son was a vampire . . . . [singular]

23b. *People* <u>who</u> cease to believe in God or goodness altogether still believe in the devil. [plural]

The result is that the verb of the relative clause agrees with the subordinate subject, and if that subject happens to be a relative pronoun, the antecedent NP that the relative pronoun replaces will determine agreement of the subordinate verb. The VP of the relative clause of (24), *have encouraged,* is plural because the antecedent of *who, bishops and popes,* is plural:

24. Recently, bishops and popes who have encouraged liturgical reforms have seemed surprised at the insistence of so many Catholics to determine for themselves the morality of such matters as divorce, homosexuality, contraception, abortion, and extramarital sex [from *Hunger of Memory*].

Restrictive and Nonrestrictive Relative Clauses

Just like other kinds of modifiers, relative clauses may be either restrictive or nonrestrictive, and just like other restrictive and nonrestrictive modifiers, the distinction between the two kinds is made concrete in writing through the use of commas separating the nonrestrictive clause from the noun it modifies. One straightforward way of identifying a nonrestrictive relative clause is to look for a comma between the head noun of the NP and the relative pronoun. When a comma appears in that spot, the relative clause usually is nonrestrictive. When it does not, the relative clause is restrictive. There is, however, much more to the restrictive/nonrestrictive dichotomy than mere comma placement, for the presence or absence of the comma corresponds to an important distinction in meaning.

The relative clauses you have observed in Examples (12), (13), (16), (20), and (21) above are all **restrictive;** that is, they limit or restrict the meaning of the noun they modify to the case specified in the relative clause. In general, they help to identify the **referent** indicated by the noun. In (12), for example, the referent of the noun *man* is restricted by the relative clause to mean a specific male human being whose identity as someone living across the street is given in the subordinate modifier. The unmodified noun *man* is not narrow enough in meaning to allow such a precise reading of the sentence. In (25), in contrast, the reader or listener has no means of determining the precise identity of the subject NP:

25. The man is leaving for Denver.

Although (25) is not ungrammatical, it is somewhat peculiar because of its lack of specificity. Only if *the man* had been mentioned in a previous reference would such a sentence be acceptable in a conversation, or in an expository text. Fiction, of course, may flout such conventions, but for our purposes we shall take as the norm what people do with language in ordinary circumstances. Fiction can then be partially interpreted in terms of how linguistic style deviates from the norm to achieve a certain effect, such as thrusting the reader into the middle of a conversation, or of the narrator's thoughts.

Other relative clauses are nonrestrictive. These clauses can essentially be omitted without changing the meaning of the sentence, even though from the point of view of style, clarity, or descriptive detail, the sentence may be more elegant with them. In general, a nonrestrictive relative clause provides details about a noun that are not essential to limiting that noun to a particular case. The underlined portion of (26) is an example of just such a nonrestrictive clause:

26. My friend Eleanor, <u>who just moved to Denver</u>, sublet her apartment to me.

The NP *my friend Eleanor* is specific enough not to need restriction by a modifying clause; the nonrestrictive clause does, however, provide descriptive detail. Sentence (26) provides an example of the case in which nonrestrictive modification would be the norm: the case of the proper noun, which by its function of singling out a particular individual, is inherently restrictive in meaning.

Although proper nouns usually are modified nonrestrictively, common nouns also may be nonrestrictively modified. However, restrictive and nonrestrictive modification of a particular common noun will result in different meanings. It helps to examine a pair of sentences which, although they have the same words in the same order, mean very different things if the relative clause is interpreted once as restrictive and once as nonrestrictive:

27a. Ten-year-old boys <u>who are hyperactive</u> are difficult. [restrictive]

27b. Ten-year-old boys, <u>who are hyperactive</u>, are difficult. [nonrestrictive]

Sentence (27a) asserts that not all ten-year-old boys, but only that subset of them that are hyperactive, are difficult. The writer or speaker who would conceive of (27b) is far more cynical; that user of English asserts that *all* ten-year-old boys are difficult. As you can see, the relative clause in (27a) restricts the meaning of *boys,* whereas the relative clause in (27b) does not.

That Revisited—The Relative Pronoun

There is one other relative pronoun we must meet, and it is our old friend *that,* which we have already encountered in its demonstrative and complementizer incarnations. A restrictive relative clause—and a restrictive one only—may have *that* as its relative pronoun, although *who, whom,* and *which* also may serve in restrictive clauses. The advantage of *that* as a relative pronoun is that it is invariant in form, being indifferent to its syntactic function in its clause (i.e., it is caseless), and that it is similarly indifferent to the human or nonhuman status of the NP it replaces, and so it occurs quite frequently.

One other thing to keep in mind about restrictive clauses is that sometimes, when a restrictive relative pronoun serves as an object in its own clause, it is entirely omitted. For example, compare Sentences (28) and (29):

28. The bread <u>that you brought home</u> was stale.

29. The bread <u>you brought home</u> was stale.

Sentence (29) is identical to (28), except that the relative clause in (29) has no relative pronoun. The independent clause that serves as the logical structure of both is (30):

30. you brought the bread home.

As you can see, the NP *the bread* functions as the direct object of the VP, *brought*. Because this NP is a relativized object in a restrictive clause, it may be omitted. Restrictive clauses with or without a relative pronoun object are equally grammatical.

How Real Is the Restrictive/Nonrestrictive Distinction?

Just in case you think that the distinction between restrictive and nonrestrictive clauses is a plot devised by sadistic grammarians to torment overworked university students, an excerpt from a newspaper report on the proceedings of the 1984 Republican National Convention should help to convince you otherwise:

> Tuesday's big fight was over the pledge against higher taxes.
>
> Reagan has said repeatedly that he has "no plans" to raise taxes and is opposed to tax increases as a matter of principle. But he wanted enough ambiguity in the wording of the platform to permit a tax increase at some point in a second Reagan term as a "last resort," as he put it in a statement Sunday.
>
> The White House therefore approved platform language that said: "We oppose any attempts to increase taxes *which would harm the recovery and reverse the trend to restoring control of the economy to individual Americans.*" [italics added]
>
> Written that way, the sentence appeared to say the Republicans opposed not all tax increases but just those that would have bad effects.
>
> Then the conservatives went to work. The economic policy subcommittee voted unanimously to insert the comma between the word "taxes" and the word "which." That appeared to have the effect of opposing all tax increases and was vigorously fought by Lewis and White House supporters.
>
> —*San Jose Mercury News, 8/15/84*

Movement Rules Revisited—The Relative Pronoun and Its Companions

We already know that relative pronouns may function as subjects or various objects in their own clauses, but regardless of where its corresponding NP would appear in an analogous independent clause, the relative pronoun must move to the front of its clause, yielding a particular subordinate word order for English relative clauses. We saw an interesting example in (16),

16. The man whose hat you found was happy to have it back.

which demonstrated that if a relative pronoun is part of a complex construction, it may drag that entire construction with it to clause-initial position, sometimes optionally, sometimes obligatorily. Sentence (16) was an example of an obligatory movement of the entire construction, here an NP, of which the relative pronoun constituted only a part. In this case, the relative pronoun still is in clause-initial position. There are circumstances, however, in which the relative pronoun, because of its status as object of a preposition, will not be the first element in the relative clause, although it will not occur in the canonical position for its function. Take, for example, the following sentence from *The Ascent of Man:*

31. The hall <u>in which Galileo was tried</u> is now part of the Post Office of Rome.

The underlined portion of (31) has (32) as its independent analog:

32. Galileo was tried in the hall.

In the hall is an adverbial prepositional phrase in (32), and the NP *the hall* is, like most objects of prepositions, bound to its preposition in the prepositional phrase construction. When this NP becomes relativized, it may become *in which*. And when this happens, the frontward movement of the relativized NP causes the preposition to which it is attached to move with it, and so we have (31), where the relative clause begins not exactly with a relative pronoun, but with the construction in which the relative pronoun plays a part, in this case the adverbial prepositional phrase.

Relativized objects of prepositions do not always pull along their preposition. Examples (33)–(35) provide possible alternate forms of the relative clause in (31), which are all perfectly grammatical for English, although perhaps not all equally elegant:

33. The hall <u>which Galileo was tried in</u>

34. The hall <u>that Galileo was tried in</u>

35. The hall <u>Galileo was tried in</u>

A preposition may move to the front of the clause only when the relativized NP is replaced by a *wh-* relative pronoun. Observe the unacceptability of having the preposition first if the relative pronoun is *that:*

36. *The hall <u>in that Galileo was tried</u>

and the utter impossibility of having the preposition first if the relative pronoun is omitted altogether because it is an object in a restrictive clause (an acceptable omission in 35):

37. *The hall <u>in Galileo was tried</u>

Keep in mind that both restrictive and nonrestrictive relative clauses may have initial prepositions.

The case of (31) discussed above is similar to that of most relative clauses having **fronted** prepositions. Most relativized NPs that are objects of prepositions are objects of adverbial phrases. But every now and then you will encounter a relativized NP that is an object of an adjectival prepositional phrase, such as that in (38):

38. And [string theory] included one nonsensical particle known as a tachyon—which could exist only by perpetually moving faster than the speed of light—and other massless particles, <u>the purpose of which nobody could really understand</u>. [from Gary Taubes, "Everything's Now Tied to Strings," *Discover,* November 1986]

The clause that serves as the independent analog to the underlined relative clause in (38) is the following:

39. Nobody could really understand the purpose of other massless particles.

The NP *the purpose of other massless particles* is the direct object of the VP of the clause. The structure of the NP is DET-N-PP, with the PP being *of other massless particles*. The phrase structure tree for (39) would be rendered as follows (triangles are used when specific details of the tree are irrelevant):

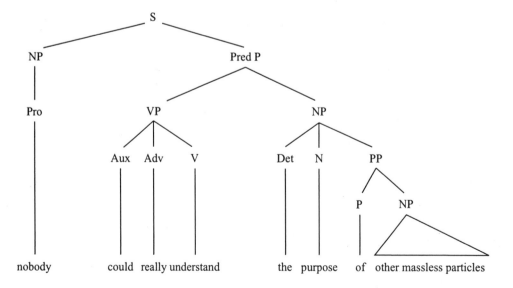

If the NP functioning as the object of this PP *(other massless particles)* becomes relativized, the intermediate form of the relative clause becomes (40):

40. *nobody could really understand the purpose of which

The phrase structure tree for (40) would be rendered as follows:

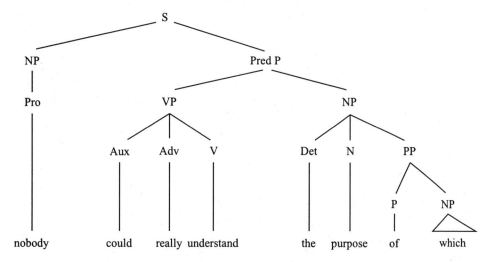

There are three ways (40) could appear in final form when the relative pronoun is fronted. Just the final NP could be fronted, and (41) would be the result:

41. which nobody could really understand the purpose of

The tree for (41) would appear thus (the moved **node** is circled):

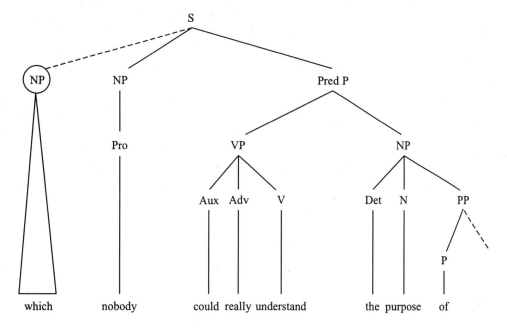

A second possibility is that the PP could be fronted:

42. of which nobody could really understand the purpose

The tree for (42) would appear as follows:

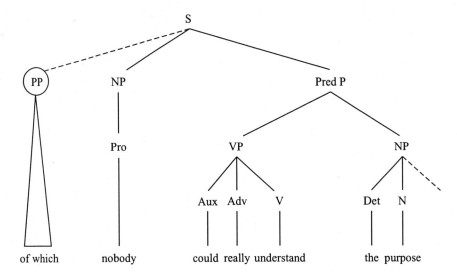

And finally, the higher NP that contains the PP that contains the relativized NP could be fronted, with (43) as the result:

43. the purpose of which nobody could really understand

Here, the tree would be given as:

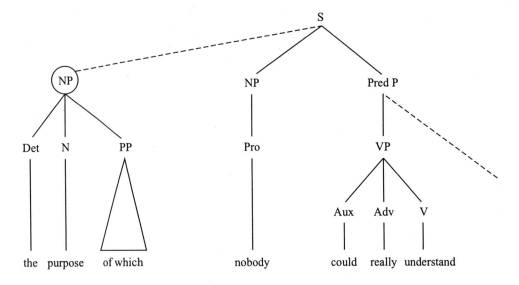

In (41), the NP containing solely the relative pronoun moves unaccompanied to the front of the clause. In (42), because the relativized NP is the object of a preposition, it may be accompanied by that preposition, and so the PP node moves to the front. And finally, in (43), because the relativized NP belongs not merely to a prepositional phrase, but to an *adjectival* prepositional phrase, it is accompanied not only by its preposition, but also by the N *purpose* and its determiner *the*. The relativized NP is so powerful an attractant, it takes with it the entire complex NP in which it serves as part of an adjectival modifier (here a PP) of the NP. Notice that in all of the three cases, a phrasal node moves to the front, not a lexical (or single word) node.

It is interesting to note that just about every case of fronted adjectival PPs containing relativized NPs actually are paraphrases of possessive constructions. That is, it would be possible to render (38) as (44):

44. And [string theory] included one nonsensical particle known as a tachyon—which could exist only by perpetually moving faster than the speed of light—and other massless particles, <u>whose purpose nobody could really understand</u>.

Some English speakers have the intuition that *whose* is the possessive form of *who,* and so they avoid its use to replace nonhuman NPs, particularly in writing. This tendency is part of a more general trend to avoid the possessive inflection altogether on nonhuman nouns. Sentence (39) above, for example, is only awkwardly rendered as (45):

45. Nobody could really understand <u>other massless particles' purpose</u>.

Sentence (44) is interesting in that it shows that *whose,* a determiner, cannot be fronted without its noun. Thus, we see once again that phrasal nodes move to the front of relative clauses, and not lexical (i.e., word) nodes.

Exercise 8.2

Underline the relative clauses in each of the following sentences from *Dracula.* Then, in the space following each sentence, indicate whether the relative clause is restrictive or nonrestrictive. Specify the head noun of the NP in which the relative clause serves as modifier.

1. One of the men who come up here often to look for the boats was followed by his dog.

2. Something made me start up, a low, piteous howling of dogs somewhere far below in the valley, which was hidden from my sight.

3. The phantom shapes, which were becoming gradually materialised from the moonbeams, were those of the three ghostly women to whom I was doomed.

4. She threw herself on her knees, and raising up her hands, cried the same words in tones which wrung my heart.

5. Lucy has not walked much in her sleep the last week, but there is an odd concentration about her which I do not understand.

6. At last I pulled open a heavy door which stood ajar, and found myself in an old ruined chapel, which had evidently been used as a graveyard.

7. With hands that trembled with eagerness, I unhooked the chains and drew back the massive bolts.

8. The mouth was redder than ever, for on the lips were gouts of fresh blood, which trickled from the corners of the mouth and ran over the chin and neck.

9. This was the being I was helping to transfer to London, where, perhaps, for centuries to come he might, amongst its teeming millions, satiate his lust for blood, and create a new and ever-widening circle of semi-demons to batten on the helpless.

10. There was no lethal weapon at hand, but I seized a shovel which the workmen had been using to fill the cases, and lifting it high struck, with the edge downward, at the hateful face.

11. The last glimpse I had was of the bloated face, bloodstained and fixed with a grin of malice which would have held its own in the nethermost hell.

12. Last night one of my post-dated letters went to post, the first of that fatal series which is to blot out the very traces of my existence from the earth.

13. It was barely furnished with odd things, which seemed to have never been used.

14. There, in one pile of the great boxes, of which there were fifty in all, on a pile of newly dug earth, lay the Count.

15. You English have a saying which is close to my heart, for its spirit is that which rules our *boyars.*

16. The last I saw of Count Dracula was his kissing his hand to me, with a red light of triumph in his eyes, and with a smile that Judas in hell might be proud of.

17. Lord, help me, and those to whom I am dear.

18. The Szgany and the Slovaks of whom the Count had spoken were coming.

19. With a last look around and at the box which contained the vile body, I ran from the place and gained the Count's room.

20. Then there came the sound of many feet tramping and dying away in some passage which sent up a clanging echo.

Answers to Exercise 8.2

1. One of the men <u>who come up here often to look for the boats</u> was followed by his dog.

   restrictive relative clause, head noun = *men*

2. Something made me start up, a low, piteous howling of dogs somewhere far below in the valley, <u>which was hidden from my sight</u>.

   nonrestrictive relative clause, head noun = *valley*

3. The phantom shapes, <u>which were becoming gradually materialised from the moonbeams</u>, were those of the three ghostly women <u>to whom I was doomed</u>.

   1. nonrestrictive, *shapes;* 2. restrictive, *women*

4. She threw herself on her knees, and raising up her hands, cried the same words in tones <u>which wrung my heart</u>.

   restrictive, *tones*

5. Lucy has not walked much in her sleep the last week, but there is an odd concentration about her <u>which I do not understand</u>.

   restrictive, *concentration*

6. At last I pulled open a heavy door <u>which stood ajar</u>, and found myself in an old ruined chapel, <u>which had evidently been used as a graveyard</u>.

   1. restrictive, *door;* 2. nonrestrictive, *chapel*

7. With hands <u>that trembled with eagerness</u>, I unhooked the chains and drew back the massive bolts.

   restrictive, *hands*

8. The mouth was redder than ever, for on the lips were gouts of fresh blood, <u>which trickled from the corners of the mouth and ran over the chin and neck</u>.

   nonrestrictive, *blood*

9. This was the being <u>I was helping to transfer to London, where, perhaps, for centuries to come he might, amongst its teeming millions, satiate his lust for blood, and create a new and ever-widening circle of semi-demons to batten on the helpless</u>.

   Actually, there are two relative clauses in this sentence, one inside of the other. The first consists of the entire underlined structure, and is a restrictive clause modifying *being.* The second relative clause is nonrestrictive. It begins with *where* and continues to the end of the sentence. It is a modifier of *London,* and since *London* clearly belongs to the first relative clause, its modifiers belong to the same structure of which it is a part.

10. There was no lethal weapon at hand, but I seized a shovel <u>which the workmen had been using to fill the cases</u>, and lifting it high struck, with the edge downward, at the hateful face.

    restrictive, *shovel*

11. The last glimpse <u>I had</u> was of the bloated face, bloodstained and fixed with a grin of malice <u>which would have held its own in the nethermost hell</u>.

    1. restrictive, *glimpse;* 2. restrictive, *grin (of malice)*

12. Last night one of my post-dated letters went to post, the first of that fatal series <u>which is to blot out the very traces of my existence from the earth</u>.

    restrictive, *series*

13. It was barely furnished with odd things, <u>which seemed to have never been used</u>.

    nonrestrictive, *things*

14. There, in one pile of the great boxes, <u>of which there were fifty in all</u>, on a pile of newly dug earth, lay the Count.

    nonrestrictive, *boxes*

15. You English have a saying <u>which is close to my heart</u>, for its spirit is that <u>which rules our *boyars*</u>.

    1. restrictive, *saying;* 2. restrictive, *that* (used here as a demonstrative pronoun). The second relative clause is interesting in that some grammarians consider it to be the source for many content clauses beginning with *what.* That is, they consider the *what* in those cases to be a combination of the demonstrative pronoun *that* and the relative pronoun *which* (e.g., its spirit is what rules our *boyars*). Thus they hold that these content clauses are actually relative clauses *that incorporate their head noun.* It should be clear that I do not share this opinion, although I do not say it is erroneous. It is another way of conceptualizing English structure.

16. The last <u>I saw</u> of Count Dracula was his kissing his hand to me, with a red light of triumph in his eyes, and with a smile <u>that Judas in hell might be proud of</u>.

    1. restrictive, *last;* 2. restrictive, *smile*

17. Lord, help me, and those <u>to whom I am dear</u>.

    restrictive, *those*

18. The Szgany and the Slovaks <u>of whom the Count had spoken</u> were coming.

    restrictive, *the Szgany and the Slovaks.* This sentence provides an exceptional case of a restrictive clause modifying a proper NP. However, a close reading of the sentence indicates that a common noun interpretation of the conjoined proper NPs is in order. The writer intends us to understand not all members of the named tribes of people, but just those particular individuals mentioned by the Count.

19. With a last look around and at the box <u>which contained the vile body</u>, I ran from the place and gained the Count's room.

    restrictive, *box*

20. Then there came the sound of many feet tramping and dying away in some passage <u>which sent up a clanging echo</u>.

    restrictive, *passage*

Distinguishing Between Content Clauses and Relative Clauses

You cannot distinguish between content clauses and relative clauses on the basis of the appearance of specific words. Sometimes clauses introduced by *whose, who, when,* and *where* may function as content clauses, and of course *that* may be either a complementizer or a relative pronoun in addition to having a demonstrative function. The only way to decide which kind of *that* occurs in a given subordinate clause is to examine the entire structure of the clause and determine the role that *that* plays in that structure. When *that* is a complementizer introducing a content clause, it is a meaningless element playing no direct role in the structure of the subordinate clause. It actually is external to the clause, and therefore does not serve any syntactic function outside of its role as a marker of subordination. Because of this feature, a content clause introduced by *that* could in some other context appear as an independent sentence if the *that* were stripped away. For example, if we remove *that* from the content clause of (46), taken from *The Ascent of Man,* the result is the independent clause provided in (47). As you can see, the complementizer serves no syntactic function in the clause; it is not a subject or any kind of object:

46. Pythagoras had proved <u>that the world of sound is governed by exact numbers</u>.

47. The world of sound is governed by exact numbers.

When *that* functions as a relative pronoun, however, it is an integral part of the subordinate clause, and although it is omissible if its function is that of object in the relative clause, the relative clause stripped of this pronoun cannot stand alone. Examples (48) and (49) from *The Ascent of Man* illustrate this fact nicely. Sentence (49), a truncated subordinate clause based on the relative clause of (48), clearly is ungrammatical (compare the complete acceptability of 47 above):

48. In the world of vision, then, in the vertical picture plane <u>that our eyes present to us,</u> a right angle is defined by its fourfold rotation back on itself.

49. *our eyes present to us.

Another consideration to keep in mind when determining the nature of a subordinate clause is that the word *what* <u>never</u> introduces a relative clause.

Exercise 8.3

Underline the finite subordinate clauses in each of the following sentences taken from Bram Stoker's *Dracula*. Then, in the space that follows each sentence, describe each underlined clause as one of the following:

a. restrictive relative clause (give head noun of NP it modifies)

b. nonrestrictive relative clause (head noun)

c. content clause, sentence subject

d. content clause, direct object of VP (provide specific VP)

e. content clause, object of preposition

Be sure to write out your answers; you may abbreviate, however. When more than one finite subordinate clause occurs in a given sentence, follow the procedure for each.

1. The only light was the flickering rays of our own lamps, in which the steam from our hard-driven horses rose in a white cloud.

2. The time I waited seemed endless, and I felt doubts and fears crowding upon me.

3. We Transylvanian nobles love not to think that our bones may be amongst the common dead.

4. It is strange that as yet I have not seen the Count eat or drink.

5. I rushed up and down the stairs, trying every door and peering out of every window I could find; but after a little the conviction of my helplessness overpowered all other feelings.

6. It is odd that a thing which I have been taught to regard with disfavour and as idolatrous should in a time of loneliness and trouble be of help.

7. What I saw was the Count's head coming out from the window.

8. In any case I could not mistake the hands which I had had so many opportunities of studying.

9. I thought it was some trick of the moonlight, some weird effect of shadow; but I kept looking, and it could be no delusion.

10. It was evident that up to lately there had been a large notice-board in front of the balcony; it had, however, been roughly torn away, the uprights which had supported it still remaining.

11. Behind the rails of the balcony I saw there were some loose boards, whose raw edges looked white.

12. I think that through the cloudiness of his insanity he saw some antagonism in me, for he at once fell back on the last refuge of such as he—a dogged silence.

13. After a short time I saw that for the present it was useless to speak to him.

14. The effect I desired was obtained, for he at once fell from his high-horse and became a child again.

15. The old physicians took account of things which their followers do not accept, and the professor is searching for witch and demon cures which may be useful to us later.

16. I sometimes think we must all be mad and that we shall wake to sanity in strait-waistcoats.

17. The minutes during which we waited passed with fearful slowness.

18. I had a horrible sinking in my heart, and from Van Helsing's face I gathered that he felt some fear or apprehension as to what was to come.

19. I dreaded the words that Renfield might speak.

20. I looked at my companions, one after another, and saw from their flushed faces and damp brows that they were enduring equal torture.

21. At last there came a time when it was evident that the patient was sinking fast; he might die at any moment.

22. Her face was ghastly, with a pallor which was accentuated by the blood which smeared her lips and cheeks and chin; from her throat trickled a thin stream of blood.

23. Then she put before her face her poor crushed hands, which bore on their whiteness the red mark of the Count's terrible grip, and from behind them came a low desolate wail which made the terrible scream seem only the quick expression of an endless grief.

24. The other hand was locked in that of her husband, who held his other arm thrown round her protectingly.

25. It seems to me that her imagination is beginning to work.

Answers to Exercise 8.3

1. The only light was the flickering rays of our own lamps, <u>in which the steam from our hard-driven horses rose in a white cloud</u>.

   nonrestrictive relative clause *(rays)*

2. The time <u>I waited</u> seemed endless, and I felt doubts and fears crowding upon me.

   restrictive relative clause *(time)*

3. We Transylvanian nobles love not to think <u>that our bones may be amongst the common dead</u>.

   content clause, direct object of *not to think*

4. It is strange <u>that as yet I have not seen the Count eat or drink</u>.

   content clause, sentence subject

5. I rushed up and down the stairs, trying every door and peering out of every window <u>I could find</u>; but after a little the conviction of my helplessness overpowered all other feelings.

   restrictive relative clause *(window)*

6. It is odd <u>that a thing</u> <u>which I have been taught to regard with disfavour and as idolatrous should in a time of loneliness and trouble be of help</u>.

   1. content clause, sentence subject

   2. restrictive relative clause *(thing)*

7. <u>What I saw</u> was the Count's head coming out from the window.

   content clause, sentence subject

8. In any case I could not mistake the hands <u>which I had had so many opportunities of studying</u>.

   restrictive relative clause *(hands)*

9. I thought <u>it was some trick of the moonlight, some weird effect of shadow</u>; but I kept looking, and it could be no delusion.

   content clause, direct object of *thought*

10. It was evident <u>that up to lately there had been a large notice-board in front of the balcony</u>; it had, however, been roughly torn away, the uprights <u>which had supported it</u> still remaining.

    1. content clause, sentence subject

    2. restrictive relative clause *(uprights)*

11. Behind the rails of the balcony I saw <u>there were some loose boards, whose raw edges looked white</u>.

    content clause, direct object of *saw*

    nonrestrictive relative clause *(boards)*

12. I think <u>that through the cloudiness of his insanity he saw some antagonism in me</u>, for he at once fell back on the last refuge of such as he—a dogged silence.

    content clause, direct object of *think*

13. After a short time I saw <u>that for the present it was useless to speak to him</u>.

    content clause, direct object of *saw*

14. The effect <u>I desired</u> was obtained, for he at once fell from his high-horse and became a child again.

    restrictive relative clause *(effect)*

15. The old physicians took account of things <u>which their followers do not accept</u>, and the professor is searching for witch and demon cures <u>which may be useful to us later</u>.

    1. restrictive relative clause *(things)*

    2. restrictive relative clause *(witch and demon cures)*

16. I sometimes think <u>we must all be mad</u> and <u>that we shall wake to sanity in strait-waistcoats</u>.

    content clause, direct object of *think*

    content clause, direct object of *think*

17. The minutes <u>during which we waited</u> passed with fearful slowness.

    restrictive relative clause *(minutes)*

18. I had a horrible sinking in my heart, and from Van Helsing's face I gathered <u>that he felt some fear of apprehension as to what was to come</u>.

    1. content clause, direct object of *gathered*

    2. content clause, object of preposition

19. I dreaded the words <u>that Renfield might speak</u>.

    restrictive relative clause *(words)*

20. I looked at my companions, one after another, and saw from their flushed faces and damp brows <u>that they were enduring equal torture</u>.

    content clause, direct object of *saw*

21. At last there came a time <u>when it was evident that the patient was sinking fast</u>; he might die at any moment.

    1. restrictive relative clause *(time)*

    2. content clause, subject of *was evident*

22. Her face was ghastly, with a pallor <u>which was accentuated by the blood which smeared her lips and cheeks and chin</u>; from her throat trickled a thin stream of blood.

    1. restrictive relative clause *(pallor)*

    2. restrictive relative clause *(blood)*

23. Then she put before her face her poor crushed hands, <u>which bore on their whiteness the red mark of the Count's terrible grip</u>, and from behind them came a low desolate wail <u>which made the terrible scream seem only the quick expression of an endless grief</u>.

    1. nonrestrictive relative clause *(hands)*

    2. restrictive relative clause *(wail)*

24. The other hand was locked in that of her husband, <u>who held his other arm thrown round her protectingly</u>.

    nonrestrictive relative clause *(husband)*

25. It seems to me <u>that her imagination is beginning to work</u>.

    content clause, sentence subject

Terms Used in Chapter Eight

complementizer: a word that has no meaning but serves the syntactic function of introducing a subordinate clause. The usual complementizer in content clauses is *that*.

content clause: a finite subordinate clause that can serve functions limited to NPs in basic sentences, such as subject and object.

extraposed: the characteristic of a content clause or an infinitive clause of being located at the end of a matrix clause, regardless of the grammatical function of the subordinate clause.

finite subordinate clause: a subordinate clause whose VP is either tensed or has a modal. Unlike nonfinite clauses, a finite clause always will have an overt subject.

fronted: the characteristic of a syntactic element of occurring at the beginning of its clause, regardless of its grammatical function.

matrix: the clause into which a subordinate clause is inserted.

mental experience verb: a verb whose meaning involves psychological states, e.g., *know, think, feel,* etc.

nonrestrictive: the property of providing additional, but nonessential information.

referent: the real-world event or object to which a particular word points.

relative clause: a finite subordinate clause that serves as an adjectival modifier in an NP and that typically begins with a relative pronoun.

relative pronoun: the words *who, whom, whose, which* and *that* when they are used to introduce a relative clause.

restrictive: the characteristic of modifiers that allows them to limit or restrict the meaning of the heads they modify.

speech act verb: a verb whose action involves speaking, e.g., *ask, say, tell, promise, urge,* etc.

Chapter Quiz

The following sentences come from Anne Rice's *Interview with the Vampire.* Underline every *finite* subordinate clause and, in the space following each sentence, identify the kind of finite subordinate clause you have underlined (i.e., content clause or relative clause). Content clauses must be additionally labeled as to function (e.g., *subject, direct object, object of a preposition*); relative clauses must be additionally labeled *restrictive* or *nonrestrictive*. If more than one finite subordinate clause occurs in any sentence, number the clauses and assign the corresponding numbers to your written responses. Be careful; some are nested inside of others. The point value given in parentheses following each sentence indicates how many finite subordinate clauses occur in the sentence.

1. His eyes moved slowly over the finely tailored black coat he'd only glimpsed in the bar, the long folds of the cape, the black silk tie knotted at the throat, and the gleam of the white collar that was as white as the vampire's flesh (2).

2. I don't think I ever heard him complain of anything, but I knew how he felt (2).

3. People who cease to believe in God or goodness altogether still believe in the devil (1).

4. His gray eyes burned with an incandescence, and the long white hands which hung by his sides were not those of a human being (1).

5. He had human problems, a blind father who did not know his son was a vampire and must not find out (2).

6. This was the open door through which Lestat had come on both the first and second occasion (1).

7. Candles burned in the upstairs parlor, where we had planned the death of the overseer (1).

8. [Lestat] was the sow's ear out of which nothing fine could be made (1).

9. I opened the door of my brother's oratory, shoving back the roses and thorns which had almost sealed it, and set the coffin on the stone floor before the priedieu (1).

10. It was obvious that a great gulf existed between father and son, but how it came about, I could not quite guess (2).

11. I suspected that beneath his gentleman's veneer he was painfully ignorant of the most simple financial matters (1).

12. [New Orleans] was filled not only with the French and Spanish of all classes who had formed in part its peculiar aristocracy, but later with immigrants of all kinds, the Irish and the German in particular (1).

13. And then there were the Indians, who covered the levee on summer days selling herbs and crafted wares (1).

14. I presume you know sugar was refined in Louisiana (2).

15. I could see by her face that she had heard every word (1).

16. But in seventeen ninety-five these slaves did not have the character which you've seen in films and novels of the South (1).

17. They were not soft-spoken, brown-skinned people in drab rags who spoke an English dialect (1).

18. Slavery was the curse of their existence; but they had not been robbed yet of that which had been characteristically theirs (1).

19. The slave knew now we were not ordinary mortals (1).

20. I immediately rang for Daniel, the slave to whom I'd given the overseer's house and position (1).

Chapter Nine

Adjectivals, Appositives, and the Fuzziness of Categories

Introduction

In previous chapters we have encountered adjectivals in the form of prepositional phrases, participle clauses, and relative clauses. But these three types of structures are not the only candidates for the adjectival slot. In fact, any adjective phrase that has internal structure (i.e., more than a chain of descriptive words) may fill the adjectival slot following a noun. Take, for example, the following sentences from Louise Erdrich's *The Beet Queen:*

1. I smelled the air, peppery and warm from the sausage makers.
2. Her flat black eyes were shaded by thick lashes, soft as paintbrushes.
3. The tiny birds, light as moths, hovered in the trumpet flowers.

The adjective phrases following the head nouns of the NP in (1)–(3) are all nonrestrictive, providing nonessential descriptive information. This factor allows such phrases to occur in positions that precede or are *not* contiguous to the NP, as the following sentences illustrate. Such behavior of nonrestrictive adjectivals will be familiar to you from your study of participle clauses:

4. Large and anxious, [the dog] flew forward in great bounds.
5. Karl turned his head away, sullen.
6. The shock of it made me bend to my cookie cutting, speechless.

However, even restrictive adjectival phrases that have internally complex structure (e.g., the modification of the adjective by a prepositional phrase) will immediately follow rather than precede their head noun, and they will do so without an intervening comma, as the following sentence from Michael Dorris's *A Yellow Raft in Blue Water* suggests:

7a. For a place full of sick people, it's too silent.

Notice that *full of sick people* restricts and follows the noun *place*. When adjectives such as *full* are modified in this fashion, they may not occur as left-handed modifiers:

7b. *a full of sick people place

In some sentences, we find the coordination of post-noun adjective phrases with other kinds of adjectival elements. This combination demonstrates the functional equivalence of adjective phrases to other sorts of adjectivals. Take, for example, Sentence (8) from *The Beet Queen,* in which the coordinated adjectival elements following *man* include two adjectives and a subject-bearing participle clause:

8. Below the words there was a picture of a man, sleek, moustachioed, his orange scarf whipping in a breeze.

In other cases, a coordination may occur that suggests functional equivalence between a nonrestrictive adjective and a nonrestrictive **appositive** NP, with the result that the dividing line between apparently different kinds of elements becomes fuzzy indeed. In (9), for example, the nonrestrictive adjective *weak* is conjoined to the appositive phrase *a scratch of light against the gray of everything else:*

9. Small trees were planted in the yards of a few of these houses, and one tree, weak, a scratch of light against the gray of everything else, tossed in a film of blossoms.

Reassessing the Status of Adjectives

The ability of English adjectives to function in slots ordinarily reserved for modificational *clauses* may seem at first surprising to you, but even more surprising is the fact that English adjectives start to look a lot like verbs (and vice versa) when we examine them further. For one thing, we know that present and past participles of verbs can be simple adjectives when they occur to the left of nouns, so phrases such as *the barking dog* or *the torn dress* seem not in the least unusual. Moreover, there are occasions when a sentence that is apparently passive may be analyzed as a copular verb with a copular complement, even though the complement in question happens to be a verb participle. For example, think about the following sentence from Alice Walker's *The Color Purple:*

10. The children <u>were stunned</u> by their mother's death.

The underlined phrase in (10) looks just like a true passive, but before we pass judgment too quickly, let us ask ourselves why a passive construction should appear in this sentence. First of all, you should be aware that this sentence occurs in a letter that one character in the novel—Nettie—writes to her sister, the protagonist Celie. Ordinarily, we do not use passive constructions much in personal communications. Why, then, does such a construction occur here? It occurs precisely because no agent has actively done anything to the children to cause their shock. Thus, the passive version allows us to focus on the state of the children, and one might, in spite of the evidence of the *by* phrase, be inclined to call *stunned* an adjective rather than a verb. The sentence does seem to be passive in form, however.

But let us examine another sentence from the same novel:

11. As he neared the coast, [the chief] <u>was stunned</u> to see hundreds and hundreds of villagers much like the Olinka clearing the forests on each side of the road, and planting rubber trees.

Now look at this occurrence of *stunned.* Do we have a passive VP? One might imagine an implicit *by* in front of *to see* (compare the participle clause equivalent: *by seeing hundreds and hundreds of villagers . . .*) but here again the notion of an agent having an intention to act upon something is altogether lacking. In fact, it is the chief's own perceptions that stun him. Whether we have a passive sentence here or a stative adjective predicated of the subject is indeterminate.

But let us examine another sentence from the same novel and compare it to (11):

12. My sister was glad to see Olivia with you.

The parallelism of *was glad to see . . .* with *was stunned to see . . .* is striking. And in (12), the decision is clear: *Glad* is *not* a verb; clearly it is an adjective serving as the copular complement of the sentence. But something else about this sentence is problematic. If *glad* is an adjective, what function then does the infinitive clause *to see Olivia with you* serve? Your first answer may be that it is an adverbial, modifying an adjective, but before you make your decision, consider the following sentence from Tina Marie Freeman-Villalobos's "The Way It Was":

13. I was glad he stayed there.

In (13), instead of an infinitive clause following the adjective *glad,* we have a finite content clause that appears to relate to the adjective in the same way. What are we to make of this, since all the content clauses we have thus far encountered have been subjects or objects?

Let us examine this phenomenon further by examining another pair of sentences, this time from *The Beet Queen:*

14. She trotted just to the side of the road, and I was <u>afraid</u> she'd be hit.

15. I <u>fear</u> that something has gone wrong with it.

In (14), a finite content clause follows the adjective *afraid;* in (15) a finite content clause follows the verb *fear*. We know that the content clause in (15) is the direct object of *fear,* and that fact makes us wonder about *was afraid* in (14). Would the sentence mean anything different if we substituted *feared* for *was afraid*? And would (15) change in meaning if *am afraid* replaces *fear*?

In fact, the adjective and the verb forms of the predicates in (14) and (15) are interchangeable, and that fact leads us to the conclusion that some adjectives, at least, behave like verbs *and take objects*! This is indeed a startling conclusion if we are wedded to the idea that adjectives and verbs constitute radically different categories, but a little reflection over all the facts we have just considered should convince us they are not. To be a bit conservative and not rattle too many people who have not had the opportunity to consider all the evidence, however, we shall refrain from designating as objects those infinitive clauses and content clauses that complement adjectives, and refer to them instead as **adjective complements.**

In fact, a number of adjectives besides *stunned, glad,* and *afraid* take content clause and infinitive clause complements. Like verbs taking such complements, such adjectives typically describe mental states or experience, as illustrated by the following sentences from Linda Hogan's short story, "Aunt Moon's Young Man":

16. Even the women who had watched the stranger all that night were *sure* <u>he was full of demons.</u>

17. But Margaret Tubby was still *angry* <u>that her husband had lost money to the stranger.</u>

18. I was *surprised* <u>that I didn't feel sad</u>.

Interesting examples of nonrestrictive adjectival phrases consisting of an adjective and its complement come from Clifford E. Trafzer's *Cheyenne Revenge:*

19. *Furious* <u>that he had missed his prey</u> and *angered* <u>that his comrade had fallen under the lance,</u> the Bluecoat chased after Lone Wolf.

NP Complements

We have just seen that content clauses actually serve more functions than we had previously determined. So, in addition to being subjects and objects of verb phrases (i.e., complements of verb phrases), we have found that content clauses may also complement adjectives. We will now find that content clauses can complement NPs. To prove to ourselves that this contention is true and to illustrate the analogy of **NP complements** to VP and adjective complements, let us compare two sentences we have already seen, (14) and (15),

14. She trotted just to the side of the road, and I was *afraid* <u>she'd be hit</u>.

15. I *fear* <u>that something has gone wrong with it</u>.

with (20), from the same book:

20. I had *a fear* <u>they would make an examination, search the house, find what's left of [the pills] floating in the toilet tank, in the waterproof container Louis used to keep his matches in whenever he went out to the field to gather botanical specimens</u>.

In the above sentences, all the material following the concept of fear constitutes a content clause serving as a complement. In (14), the content clause is a complement to an adjective, in (15) it is a complement to a VP, and in (20) it is a complement to the noun—an appositive, in fact.

We have already met NP complements in Chapter One, in the form of appositives that complete the meaning of the NPs to which they are appended. All of the appositives we met back then were NPs complementing other NPs. Given how often content clauses slip into NP slots, it should come as no surprise that content clauses often fill the "appositive" slot next to an NP (we know that infinitive clauses may also complement NPs as appositives; see Chapter Four to review this topic). As examples of content clauses as appositives, consider Sentences (21) and (22) below from Bronowski's *The Ascent of Man*. The content clauses are underlined:

21. The idea <u>that science is a social enterprise</u> is modern, and it begins at the Industrial Revolution.

22. And he was a genius, in the sense <u>that a genius is a man who has *two* great ideas</u>.

The underlined content clause in (21) is an appositive to the noun *idea*. Notice that the clause actually tells what the idea is; it doesn't simply restrict its meaning, as a relative clause may. The content clause in (22) restricts and completes or "fleshes out" the meaning of *sense*. Contrast (21) and (22) to a sentence such as (23), which contains the noun *thought* modified by a restrictive relative clause:

23. The thought <u>that Einstein had had in his teens</u> was this: 'What would the world look like if I rode on a beam of light?'

Notice that the relative clause in (23), *that Einstein had had in his teens,* does not reveal the character of the thought, and in addition the subordinate indicator *that* is here a bona fide relative pronoun, and not a complementizer. Recall that a complementizer is a meaningless element that does not take part in the constituent structure of the content clause; in fact, if the content clause in (21) were removed from the sentence in which it serves as modifier and stripped of its complementizer, it could stand as an independent sentence, as in (24):

24. Science is a social enterprise.

However, a different fate awaits the relative clause; because the relative pronoun functions as an essential element within the relative clause itself, a relative clause stripped of its pronoun cannot stand:

25. *Einstein had had in his teens

Sentence (25) shows us that the relative pronoun *that* in (23) functions as the direct object of *had had.*

Another way of thinking about finite appositive clauses is to imagine an implicit *be* between the NP and the appositive clause. Thus the relationship between the noun *idea* and the content clause that describes it is an implicitly copular one, as (26) illustrates:

26. The idea *is* that science is a social enterprise.

Of course there is a big difference between the grammatical function of the copular complement and that of the appositive clause. Their relationship is a logical one, yet the two are not syntactically equivalent. In example (27), also from *The Ascent of Man,* the underlined subordinate clause provides an example of a content clause functioning as a copular complement because the copula *is* is explicit:

27. The fact of the matter is <u>that our conception of science now, towards the end of the twentieth century, has changed radically</u>.

Another point needs to be added, and that is that sometimes an NP bearing an appositive clause will function in its entirety as a copular complement; in this case, the subordinate clause is not by itself the copular complement. Rather, it is the appositive of the NP. In turn, the entire NP—appositive and all—functions as the copular complement. Such a copular complement occurs in (28), where the finite content clause functions as appositive to the head noun of the copular complement, *conviction:*

28. What drove [these men] was the conviction that every man is master of his own salvation.

And finally, it will help you to understand that just as in the case of verbs and adjectives, not all nouns will admit this sort of complementation by content clauses. In particular, nouns that describe mental experience such as *fact, idea, notion, concept, belief, fear, thought,* and so on often take complements, most of which are restrictive. (NP complements, like other appositives, may be restrictive or nonrestrictive, and the usual rule about commas applies.) In addition, nouns that describe speech acts, such as *expression, saying, promise,* and so on, may admit NP complements. As you will recall, these nouns are analogous to the verbs that will admit content clauses as objects in the predicate phrase and to adjectives admitting clausal complements.

Exercise 9.1

The following sentences come from *The Queen's Physician* by Edgar Maass. Underline every *finite* subordinate clause and, in the space following each sentence, identify the kind of finite subordinate clause you have underlined (i.e., content clause or relative clause). In addition, label content clauses according to function (e.g., *subject, direct object, object of preposition, copular complement, appositive, adjective complement*); label relative clauses as *restrictive* or *nonrestrictive*. If more than one finite subordinate clause occurs in any sentence, number the clauses and assign the corresponding numbers to your responses. Be careful; some are nested inside of others.

1. The Doctor had an odd feeling that he knew the neighborhood, but could not place it.

2. The coachman told Struensee that he doubted a wheelwright could be found so late in the day.

3. A sun-dial of gray stone stood in the middle of the unmown lawn, which was heavily sprinkled with yellow dandelion blooms and populous with fat thrushes in search of worms.

4. Then he went directly up the path to the house, the door of which was also ajar.

5. He awoke with a little start and saw by the warm flecks of sun playing on the bedcovers that the forenoon was already well along.

6. The two shook hands on it and walked through the spring morning to the road, where the carriage, its wheel repaired, was drawn up waiting for the Doctor.

7. Opportunities were rather scarce for the reason that everyone with any power was incompetent and lazy.

8. He could not rid his inner being of the barbs she had carefully planted there.

9. Besides the humiliations heaped on her by her husband, she had to accept a cloudy future for the son she had borne the King.

10. The upshot was that both Christian and Sperling were ordered to get on their knees before Reventlau, two shattered sinners, and take solemn oath on the Bible that never again would they experiment with the girls.

11. He was sure he was being carried off to his death, apparently somewhere on the island of Amager.

12. Shaking with apprehension he asked the Swiss what he should do.

13. On one occasion he had a seizure during which he tried to smash his brains out on the marble of the fireplace.

14. The poor of Copenhagen, who even in normal times lived pretty much from hand to mouth, no longer had even a crust to eat.

15. I feel certain that with your usual adroitness you can overcome any obstacles that may conceivably arise.

16. It was obvious that he must settle down to business and earn more money than ever.

17. There were times when he thought over the teachings of Leibniz, those arguing that elemental monads underlie reality.

18. Struensee's grandfather alone had not despaired, even in the face of what seemed to be certain death.

19. The main difference between him and his grandfather was that he had no experience in handling men.

20. Nonetheless Struensee was confident that in time he would learn the ropes and develop sea-sense.

21. On this particular winter evening the Doctor was riding over a road skirting the sea, not too far from the place where he had first met Brandt.

22. The catch was that the Queen did not arrive.

23. Lili and Mimi knew for certain that the Queen was wearing a rose-colored costume richly decorated with lace, a lilac velvet jacket and a cap of the same hue.

24. Then someone brought notice that the Queen, after eating a brief lunch in City Hall, intended at once to take a coach to the capital.

25. It was felt that perhaps the many new impressions and the influence of foreign princes might waken in him a now dormant sense of royal responsibility.

Answers to Exercise 9.1

1. The Doctor had an odd feeling <u>that he knew the neighborhood</u>, but could not place it.

   content clause, appositive to *feeling*

2. The coachman told Struensee <u>that he doubted a wheelwright could be found so late in the day</u>.

   1. content clause, direct object of *told*

   2. content clause, direct object of *doubted*

3. A sun-dial of gray stone stood in the middle of the unmown lawn, <u>which was heavily sprinkled with yellow dandelion blooms and populous with fat thrushes in search of worms</u>.

   nonrestrictive relative clause

4. Then he went directly up the path to the house, <u>the door of which was also ajar</u>.

   nonrestrictive relative clause

5. He awoke with a little start and saw by the warm flecks of sun playing on the bedcovers <u>that the forenoon was already well along</u>.

   content clause, direct object of *saw*

6. The two shook hands on it and walked through the spring morning to the road, <u>where the carriage, its wheel repaired, was drawn up waiting for the Doctor</u>.

   nonrestrictive relative clause

7. Opportunities were rather scarce for the reason <u>that everyone with any power was incompetent and lazy</u>.

   content clause, appositive to *reason*

8. He could not rid his inner being of the barbs <u>she had carefully planted there</u>.

   restrictive relative clause

9. Besides the humiliations heaped on her by her husband, she had to accept a cloudy future for the son <u>she had borne the King</u>.

   restrictive relative clause

10. The upshot was <u>that both Christian and Sperling were ordered to get on their knees before Reventlau, two shattered sinners, and take solemn oath on the Bible that never again would they experiment with the girls</u>.

    1. content clause, copular complement

    2. content clause, appositive to *oath*

11. He was sure <u>he was being carried off to his death, apparently somewhere on the island of Amager</u>.

    content clause, adjective complement *(sure)*

12. Shaking with apprehension he asked the Swiss <u>what he should do</u>.

    content clause (embedded question), direct object of *asked*

13. On one occasion he had a seizure <u>during which he tried to smash his brains out on the marble of the fireplace</u>.

    restrictive relative clause

14. The poor of Copenhagen, <u>who even in normal times lived pretty much from hand to mouth</u>, no longer had even a crust to eat.

    nonrestrictive relative clause

15. I feel certain <u>that with your usual adroitness you can overcome any obstacles that may conceivably arise</u>.

    1. content clause, adjective complement *(certain)*

    2. restrictive relative clause

16. It was obvious <u>that he must settle down to business and earn more money than ever</u>.

    content clause, extraposed subject

17. There were times <u>when he thought over the teachings of Leibniz, those arguing that elemental monads underlie reality</u>.

    1. restrictive relative clause

    2. content clause, direct object of *arguing*

18. Struensee's grandfather alone had not despaired, even in the face of <u>what seemed to be certain death</u>.

    content clause, object of preposition *of*

19. The main difference between him and his grandfather was <u>that he had no experience in handling men</u>.

    content clause, copular complement

20. Nonetheless Struensee was confident <u>that in time he would learn the ropes and develop sea-sense</u>.

    content clause, adjective complement *(confident)*

21. On this particular winter evening the Doctor was riding over a road skirting the sea, not too far from the place <u>where he had first met Brandt</u>.

    restrictive relative clause

22. The catch was <u>that the Queen did not arrive</u>.

    content clause, copular complement

23. Lili and Mimi knew for certain <u>that the Queen was wearing a rose-colored costume richly decorated with lace, a lilac velvet jacket and a cap of the same hue.</u>

    content clause, direct object of *knew*

24. Then someone brought notice <u>that the Queen, after eating a brief lunch in City Hall, intended at once to take a coach to the capital.</u>

    content clause, appositive to *notice*

25. It was felt <u>that perhaps the many new impressions and the influence of foreign princes might waken in him a now dormant sense of royal responsibility.</u>

    content clause, extraposed subject

Exercise 9.2

The following sentences come from Louise Erdrich's *The Beet Queen*. Examine the underlined element in each, and in the space below, give its structure (e.g., infinitive clause, content clause, relative clause, adjective phrase, etc.) and its function (e.g., subject, direct object, appositive, nonrestrictive adjectival modifier, etc.)

1. No, the river is not the marvel of clean water from a spout, <u>hot and wild</u>, buoying me up with this strange illusion that I'm well.

2. No, the river is not the marvel of clean water from a spout, hot and wild, <u>buoying me up with this strange illusion that I'm well</u>.

3. No, the river is not the marvel of clean water from a spout, hot and wild, buoying me up with this strange illusion <u>that I'm well</u>.

4. <u>That I made a good cup of coffee at age eleven and fried eggs</u> was a source of wonder to my aunt and uncle, and an outrage to Sita.

5. He was proud <u>that she'd left her children and her whole life, which he gathered had been comfortable from her fine clothes and jewelry, for a bootlegger with nothing to his name but a yellow scarf and an airplane held together with baling wire.</u>

6. He was proud that she'd left her children and her whole life, <u>which he gathered had been comfortable from her fine clothes and jewelry</u>, for a bootlegger with nothing to his name but a yellow scarf and an airplane held together with baling wire.

7. He was proud that she'd left her children and her whole life, which he gathered had been comfortable from her fine clothes and jewelry, for a bootlegger with nothing to his name but a yellow scarf and an airplane <u>held together with baling wire</u>.

8. Now Sita was ready <u>to explode</u>.

9. "I'm so goddamn glad <u>I'm getting out of here</u>," she whispered.

10. The idea of robots, <u>which is current in magazines,</u> has taken root in her mind along with other things.

11. I was not sure <u>I liked it</u>.

12. "I'm awfully glad <u>to see you</u>, Sita. It's been a long time."

Answers to Exercise 9.2

1. adjective phrase; nonrestrictive adjectival modifier
2. participle clause; nonrestrictive adjectival modifier
3. content clause; appositive
4. content clause; subject
5. content clause; adjective complement
6. relative clause; nonrestrictive adjectival modifier
7. participle clause; restrictive adjectival modifier
8. infinitive clause; adjective complement
9. content clause; adjective complement
10. relative clause; nonrestrictive adjectival modifier
11. content clause; adjective complement
12. infinitive clause; adjective complement

Exercise 9.3

The following sentences come from a newspaper article entitled "Thawing Europe's Bronze Age" (*San Jose Mercury News,* October 2, 1991), by Brenda Fowler. Underline every *finite* subordinate clause, and in the space following each sentence, identify the kind of finite subordinate clause you have underlined (i.e., content clause or relative clause). Content clauses must be additionally labeled as to function (e.g., *subject, direct object, object of preposition, copular comple-ment, adjective complement, appositive*); relative clauses must be additionally labeled *restrictive* or *nonrestrictive*. If more than one finite subordinate clause occurs in any sentence, number the clauses and assign the corresponding numbers to your written responses. Be careful; some are nested inside of others.

1. The ax is of a well-known type that appears exclusively from the Early Bronze Age, which in Europe started about 2000 B.C.

2. Scientists who study glaciers say the ice that encased the man, who died hunched over on his knees on solid rock, is the oldest ever found in the Alps.

3. It is not yet understood why the body did not melt out during the last warm period.

4. He believes this eliminates the possibility that someone could recently have planted the body, which was found encased in ice.

5. Egg, who examined the body, believes the man was either hunting or looking for minerals like copper, which were plentiful in the Alps.

Answers to Exercise 9.3

1. The ax is of a well-known type <u>that appears exclusively from the Early Bronze Age, which in Europe started about 2000 B.C.</u>

   1. restrictive relative clause

   2. nonrestrictive relative clause

2. Scientists <u>who study glaciers</u> say <u>the ice that encased the man, who died hunched over on his knees on solid rock, is the oldest ever found in the Alps.</u>

   1. restrictive relative clause

   2. content clause, direct object of *say*

   3. restrictive relative clause

   4. nonrestrictive relative clause

3. It is not yet understood <u>why the body did not melt out during the last warm period.</u>

   content clause, extraposed subject

4. He believes <u>this eliminates the possibility that someone could recently have planted the body, which was found encased in ice.</u>

   1. content clause, direct object of *believed*

   2. content clause, appositive to *possibility*

   3. nonrestrictive relative clause

5. Egg, <u>who examined the body</u>, believes <u>the man was either hunting or looking for minerals like copper, which were plentiful in the Alps</u>.

   1. nonrestrictive relative clause

   2. content clause, direct object of *believes*

   3. nonrestrictive relative clause

Terms Used in Chapter Nine

adjective complement: an infinitive clause or a content clause that serves as object to an adjective.

appositive: an NP, content clause, or infinitive clause that serves to name or completely identify an NP.

NP complement: an infinitive clause or a content clause that serves as an appositive to an NP.

Chapter Quiz

The following sentences come from *Dreaming in Cuban* by Cristina Garcia. Underline every *finite* subordinate clause and, in the space following each sentence, identify the kind of finite subordinate clause you have underlined (i.e., content clause or relative clause). In addition, label content clauses according to function (e.g., *subject, direct object, object of preposition, copular complement, appositive, adjective complement*); label relative clauses as *restrictive* or *nonrestrictive*. If more than one finite subordinate clause occurs in any sentence, number the clauses and assign the corresponding numbers to your responses. Be careful; some are nested inside others. The point value inside parentheses indicates how many clauses you should find.

1. Separation is familiar, too familiar, but Celia is uncertain she can reconcile it with permanence (1).

2. Pilar, her first grandchild, writes to her in a Spanish that is no longer hers (1).

3. Celia knows that Pilar wears overalls like a farmhand and paints canvases with knots and whorls of red that resemble nothing at all (2).

4. Lourdes tries for nearly an hour to telephone her mother in Santa Teresa del Mar, but the operator tells her that the rains have knocked out the phone lines on the northwest coast of Cuba (1).

5. Her father's last weeks were happy ones under the care of Sister Federica, whose devotion to a bewildering array of saints did not lessen her duty to cleanliness (1).

6. Lourdes knew that the little nun, with her puckish face and faint mustache, reminded her father of his barber in Havana, of the smell of his tonics and pomades, of the cracked red leather and steel levers of his enameled chairs (1).

7. She tells me she loves me (1).

8. She said that artists are a bad element, a profligate bunch who shoot heroin (2).

9. Store-bought ice cream is cheap, but for Felicia, making ice cream from scratch is part of the ritual that began after her husband left in 1966 (1).

10. Celia rests in the interior patio of the plaza, where royal palms dwarf a marble statue of Christopher Columbus (1).

11. The only problem is that the entire Puente tribe practically lives at his house (1).

12. Two of my aunts are conferring in the bathroom but I can't hear what they're saying (1).

13. Felicia knew that her mother, who stayed at home reading her books and rocking on the porch swing, had an instinctive distrust of the ecclesiastical (2).

14. Celia leaves, confident that the intolerable season is over (1).

15. In January, Hilario and Vivian Ortega, who live down the street from Celia, will defend themselves against charges that they have been illegally renting by the hour two rooms of their beachfront home (2).

16. Celia fears that the citizens of Santa Teresa del Mar once again will consider the court as hardly more than occasion for a live soap opera (1).

17. Abuela Celia tells us that before the revolution smart girls like us usually didn't go to college (1).

18. Lourdes misses the birds she had in Cuba (1).

19. Cuba has become the joke of the Caribbean, a place where everything and everyone is for sale (1).

20. His name is Rufino Puente, and despite the fact that he comes from one of the wealthiest families in Havana, he's a modest young man (1).

21. I'm glad they're going back to boarding school tomorrow (1).

Chapter Ten

Adverbial Subordination

Introduction

The final type of English subordinate structure we shall examine is the **adverbial subordinate clause.** Luckily for those of us who are feeling somewhat overwhelmed by all the varieties of subordination we have thus far encountered, adverbial subordinate clauses are relatively easy to identify, since in most cases they begin with a particular member of a very small set of elements known as "subordinating conjunctions." In general, backgrounded details of time, cause, condition, concession, and purpose are expressed in adverbial subordinate clauses, most of them finite.

Temporal Adverbial Subordinate Clauses

A **temporal** (i.e., associated with time) **adverbial clause** expresses an event occurring in sequence with or simultaneously to the matrix clause, but does so by setting the subordinate clause as the time reference for the matrix event. The most common conjunctions introducing temporal clauses are: *after, before, since, until, when, while,* and *as.* These clauses may occur in front of or following or even in the middle of the matrix clause they modify, with a comma often, but not always, separating an introductory or medial adverbial clause from the rest of the sentence. As you already know, this kind of movability is typical of adverbials in general.

After, before, until, and *since* are conjunctions introducing clauses whose event occurs prior or subsequent to the event specified in the matrix clause. As is typical of adverbial clauses, *after* clauses, which describe events occurring prior to the matrix event, may precede or follow matrix clauses. The following sentences from Paula Gunn Allen's short story, "Deer Woman" illustrate an *after* clause preceding the matrix:

1a. <u>After they'd traveled for an hour or so</u>, Linda suddenly pointed to a road that intersected the one they were on.

1b. <u>After maybe half an hour had passed</u>, the old man addressed the young men again.

However, *after* clauses also may occur following the clause they modify, as (2), from Clifford E. Trafzer's *Cheyenne Revenge* demonstrates:

2. Lone Wolf lay quietly <u>after Silas had gone</u>.

Likewise, adverbial clauses beginning with *before,* which typically provide events following the matrix event, also may occur in sentence-initial position, as (3) from "Deer Woman" demonstrates:

3. But <u>before they'd taken more than a few steps</u> Linda and Junella took their arms and led them away from the feast toward the doorway of one of the houses.

And they may occur sentence-finally, like the adverbial clause in (4) from Beth Brant's "Swimming Upstream":

4. She smoked a cigarette sitting in the parking lot, wondering where to go, where to stop and turn the cap that would release the red, sweet smell of the wine <u>before the taste would overpower her and she wouldn't have to wonder anymore</u>.

Before is a particularly interesting conjunction in that it sometimes introduces a clause whose event does *not* occur because the matrix clause precludes it, as shown in (5), from Louise Erdrich's *The Beet Queen:*

5. She picked up a coffee cup, poured it shakily full, and he reached forward to take it from her hands <u>before it spilled</u>.

Clauses introduced by *until* have the same kind of positional freedom as *after* and *before* clauses, but often they follow the matrix clause because the event of the subordinate clause typically terminates the matrix event, as sentences (6a) and (6b) from *The Beet Queen* demonstrate:

6a. [The pain] coiled and uncoiled like a big steel spring, out and in, <u>until it suddenly shrank and collapsed into a black button</u>.

6b. I didn't know how badly off we were <u>until my mother stole a dozen heavy silver spoons from our landlady, who was kind, or at least harbored no grudge against us, and whom my mother counted as a friend</u>.

Sometimes the *until* clause provides a result of the matrix clause, which naturally follows the matrix event in time, as (7), also from *The Beet Queen,* illustrates:

7. After Christmas, the winter turned nasty and the pressure dropped <u>until by January a blizzard was taking shape</u>.

Sentence (7) also is notable for the phrase *after Christmas,* which of course is not a subordinate clause at all, but a prepositional phrase. Many of the temporal conjunctions have alter egos as prepositions, and their prepositional use should not be confused with their clausal use.

Though it would seem that an *until* clause would always follow the matrix clause, the adverbial nature of the clause allows it to occur first in the sentence, as illustrated by (8), from Robert Fulghum's *All I Really Need to Know I Learned in Kindergarten:*

8. <u>Until you have experienced raccoons mating underneath your bedroom at three in the morning</u>, you have missed one of life's more sensational moments.

When the conjunction *since* (or sometimes *ever since*) is used to introduce a temporal clause, the clause typically gives the event or point in time that initiates the matrix event. The following sentence from Anne Rice's *The Mummy* provides an example:

9. But [the photographers] had been at his side for months now—<u>ever since the first artifacts had been found in these barren hills, south of Cairo</u>.

When Clauses

The most common temporal conjunction in English is *when,* which sometimes expresses sequences of events, as (10) from Alice Walker's *The Color Purple* shows:

10. <u>When we reached the shore</u> they didn't bother to help us alight from the boat and actually set some of our supplies right down in the water.

and sometimes expresses simultaneous events, as in (11), which is also from *The Color Purple:*

11. They want to know what Olivia and Tashi do in my hut <u>when all the other little girls are busy helping their mothers</u>.

Examples (10) and (11) demonstrate the positional freedom enjoyed by many *when* clauses, but this freedom does not extend to all occurrences. In particular, a *when* clause may be used to express a sudden shift of attention to another event. In such cases, illustrated in (12) from James Baldwin's *Go Tell It on the Mountain,* the *when* clause always occurs at the end of the sentence:

12. The door had but barely closed behind the women <u>when one of the elders . . . laughed and said, referring to Deborah, that there was a holy woman all right</u>!

Sometimes subordinating words other than *when* are used to introduce temporal clauses that could be *when* clauses. In particular, clauses addressing the sequence of events may be expressed by *once,* as in (13) from *The Beet Queen* or by *as soon as,* as in (14) from Thomas King's "A Seat in the Garden":

13. My dress is unbearable, a prickling mess that I strip off <u>once we walk into the house.</u>

14. <u>As soon as the men stripped the cart and sat down on the ground,</u> Red got to his feet and stretched.

In the case of recurring events, the conjunction for certain temporal clauses will be *whenever* instead of *when.* This state of affairs appears in (15), from *The Beet Queen* and in (16a), from *The Color Purple:*

15. <u>Whenever Celestine came into his mind</u> he put her out of it.

16a. <u>Whenever they see her</u> they talk about the day when she will become their littlest sister/wife.

Example (16b) also is notable for its *when* clause, which in this case is *not* an adverbial:

16b. Whenever they see her they talk about the day <u>when she will become their littlest sister/wife.</u>

The underlined *when* clause in (16b) is a restrictive relative clause modifying *day.* Another example of such a relative clause occurs in (17), again from *The Color Purple:*

17. Nobody could remember a time <u>when roofleaf did not exist in overabundant amounts.</u>

We previously encountered such relative clauses in Chapter Eight. Remember that *when* is sometimes a relative pronoun and sometimes not. The fact that we are currently examining adverbial functions of *when* clauses does not negate the possibility of their serving as adjectival clauses in other circumstances.

The Simultaneous Temporal Conjunctions, *While* and *As*

The temporal conjunctions *while* and *as* introduce a clause whose **durative** event (i.e., one not taking place at a single point in time, but over an interval) occurs simultaneously with the matrix clause. *While* clauses are freely positionable within the sentence, as Sentences (18) from *The Color Purple* and (19) from *The Beet Queen* demonstrate:

18. <u>While the second child was still a baby</u>, a stranger appeared in the community, and lavished all his attention on the widow and her children; in a short while, they were married.

19. We spent all night on that train <u>while it switched and braked and rumbled toward Argus</u>.

As also expresses simultaneous events, but in this case the two events together form a unified whole, with one event being a part of or emerging out of the other. The following examples from *The Color Purple* (20) and *The Beet Queen* (21 and 22) demonstrate this property:

20. And <u>as they struggled to put up roofs of this cold, hard, glittery, ugly metal</u> the women raised a deafening ululation of sorrow that echoed off the cavern walls for miles around.

21. <u>As he sat there, waiting</u>, the picture of Celestine in the slip, shadowed in the narrow hall, full and outcurved like the prow of a boat, rose in his mind.

22. <u>As I drove</u> I began to link other people with that moment too, even people I thought I had left behind forever, like my sister.

Although the temporal clauses in (20)–(22) all occur in sentence-initial position, temporal *as* clauses also may occur in sentence-final position, as demonstrated by (23), from Gloria Bird's "Turtle Lake":

23. The air was chilled, and their breath became clouds <u>as it left their mouths</u>.

Causal Adverbial Clauses

Adverbial clauses expressing notions of cause or reason may be introduced by the conjunctions *because* or *since*. Even though in spoken English *because* clauses generally occur following the matrix clause, in the written language they are freely positionable in the sentence, as the following sentences from *The Color Purple* (24 and 25) and *The Beet Queen* (26 and 27) demonstrate:

24. <u>Because he was chief at the time</u>, he gradually took more and more of the common land, and took more and more wives to work it.

25. I was thinking about teeth a lot on the voyage over, <u>because I had toothache nearly the entire time</u>.

26. <u>Because they were loaded on sloe gin and schnapps</u>, they argued on everything and nothing.

27. The major was the mayor of Argus <u>because he never completely lost his footing in any crisis, but could always be counted on to respond with dull remarks</u>.

The conjunction *since* may also be used causally, as the following passages from *The Color Purple* attest:

28. [S]ince she already has five boy children she can now do whatever she wants. She has become an honorary man.

29. Since the Olinka no longer own their village, they must pay rent for it, and in order to use the water, which also no longer belongs to them, they must pay a water tax.

Conditional Adverbial Clauses

Adverbial clauses stating the conditions that make something possible are called conditional adverbial clauses, and generally they begin with the conjunction *if*, and occasionally *provided* or *provided that* and *unless:* Example (30a), which provides a hypothetical condition, and (30b), which provides a possible condition, both come from *All I Really Need to Know . . .* and nicely illustrate the adverbial functioning of *if* clauses:

30a. If dandelions were rare and fragile, people would knock themselves out to pay $14.95 a plant, raise them by hand in greenhouses, and form dandelion societies and all that.

30b. [I]f you blow just right and all those little helicopters fly away, you get your wish. Magic. Or if you are a lover, they twine nicely into a wreath for your friend's hair.

An example of *provided* used as a conditional conjunction occurs in (31), from *The Ascent of Man,* where it introduces a clause in sentence-final position:

31. We feel that Darwin would really have liked to die before he published the theory, provided after his death the priority should come to him.

The conjunction *unless* is like *if,* but it contains an implicit negative, so it is equivalent to *if not,* as this example from *The Color Purple* shows:

32. About a month ago, Corrine asked me not to invite Samuel to my hut unless she were present. (Compare: *if she were not present.*)

In some instances a conditional adverbial notion can be expressed without any subordinating conjunction whatsoever, as the following examples from Maurice Kenny's "Wet Moccasins" (33) and William James's *Varieties of Religious Experience* (34) attest:

33. Winter was out there somewhere. You could practically see it. Were the windows opened you could probably smell it on the night.

34. Were one asked to characterize the life of religion in the broadest and most general terms possible, one might say that it consists of the belief that there is an unseen order, and that our supreme good lies in harmoniously adjusting ourselves thereto.

Notice that the conditional intent of these clauses is brought about by the interchanging of the subject and auxiliary (**subject/auxiliary inversion**) in the adverbial clause, with the auxiliary *be* expressed in the **subjunctive** (also seen in 32), a form indicating that the action or state expressed is possible rather than actual or contingent on hypothetical events. Though *were* appears past and plural in the preceding examples, it is actually an invariant form that signals neither tense nor number.

When Is an *If* Clause Not a Conditional Clause?

The answer to the question posed in the section heading above is quite simple: An *if* clause is not a conditional clause when it functions as an embedded **yes/no question.** Examine the following sentences from *The Color Purple:*

35a. Samuel asked <u>if they'd ever seen the white woman missionary twenty miles farther on</u>, and he said no.

36a. He said the woman wanted to know <u>if the children belonged to me or to Corrine or to both of us</u>.

37a. She wanted to know <u>if I was also Samuel's wife</u>.

We can make several observations about (35a), (36a), and (37a). First, the actual verbal transactions reported in these sentences must have been something like the *yes/no* questions (those expecting—in general—either a yes or a no for an answer) given in the (b) versions of these sentences, none of which are conditional:

35b. Have you ever seen the white woman missionary who lives twenty miles from here?

36b. Do the children belong to you, or to Corrine, or to both of you?

37b. Are you Samuel's wife, too?

Second, the word *if* appearing in the (a) versions of these examples can be changed readily to *whether,* another indicator of *yes/no*-question subordination, as (38), also from *The Color Purple,* clearly shows:

38. Corrine had asked me once <u>whether I was running away from home</u>.

Finally, you can see for yourself that the subordinate clauses given in all these sentences are not movable in the way that adverbials generally are, and any attempt to move them to sentence-initial position will result in unacceptable strings:

39. *If they'd ever seen the white woman missionary twenty miles farther on Samuel asked

In fact, the pseudo-conditional clauses discussed in this section are all content clauses of the embedded question type.

Concessive Adverbial Clauses

Concessive adverbial clauses provide a kind of condition that would lead one to expect the opposite of what actually happens in the main clause, as in (40), from *The Color Purple:*

40. <u>Even though they are unhappy and work like donkeys</u> they still think it is an honor to be the chief's wife.

The conjunctions that mark this category of adverbial include *even though, although,* and *though.* Examples (41) from *The Beet Queen* and (42) from *The Color Purple* demonstrate the operation of *although* and *though:*

41. <u>Although her eyes have gotten ever harsher and brighter</u>, she has aged like an ordinary enough person.

42. <u>Though the Olinka no longer ask anything of us, beyond teaching their children—because they can see how powerless we and our God are—</u> Samuel and I decided we must do something about this latest outrage, even as many of the people to whom we felt close ran away to join the *mbeles* or forest people, who live deep in the jungle, refusing to work for whites or be ruled by them.

Sentence (42) is interesting too for its demonstration that a subordinating conjunction may be modified by an adverb to its left:

43. <u>even as</u> many of the people to whom we felt close ran away to join the *mbeles* or forest people, who live deep in the jungle, refusing to work for whites or be ruled by them.

and that one adverbial subordinate clause may occur within another:

44. Though the Olinka no longer ask anything of us, beyond teaching their children—<u>because they can see how powerless we and our God are</u>.

Adverbial Clauses of Purpose

Adverbial clauses of purpose introduced by *so* and *so that,* like other adverbials, are movable, but in general they occur in sentence-final position. The following examples from Tina Marie Freeman-Villalobos's "The Way It Was" (45 and 46) and from *Cheyenne Revenge* (47) demonstrate this tendency:

45. All good little Indian girls have nice braids—without tangles—and they sit still <u>so their Grandmas can make them look pretty</u>.

46. I held the tiny ant up close to my face <u>so I could get a good look at him</u>.

47. He repeated the name of the officer over and over <u>so that he would always remember it</u>.

The only difficulty with identifying adverbial clauses of purpose is that you may confuse them with coordinated clauses of result, which begin with the <u>coordinating conjunction</u> *so*. To help you distinguish between the two, let us examine the following sentence from William Zinsser's "On Writing Well":

48. Perhaps the writer has switched pronouns in mid-sentence, or has switched tenses, <u>so</u> the reader loses track of who is talking or when the action took place.

Notice that in (48) the writer in question has no intention that the reader should lose track of what is going on. Instead, the writer's carelessness leads to this *result*. In (45)–(47), on the other hand, the actors in the main clause behave in a certain way with a *purpose* in mind—the one given in the subordinate adverbial clause. This distinction between intentional purpose (a subordinate notion) and generally unintentional result represents the distinction between subordinate and coordinate uses of *so*.

Adverbial Clauses of Extent

Now that you feel comfortable identifying subordinate structures, you may not have too much difficulty identifying yet another kind of subordinate clause. Examine the following passages:

49. I buy an ice cream sandwich for dinner. It's so cold <u>that the wrapper is frozen to the cookie part</u>, and I have to pick ragged scraps off the end of my tongue [Michael Dorris, *A Yellow Raft in Blue Water*].

50. I had lost so much and suffered so badly from the grief and cold <u>that I'm sure what I saw was quite natural, understandable, although it was not real</u> [*The Beet Queen*].

51. His stomach is shaved and tracked with stitches, and his skin is so transparent <u>that even the most delicate veins are visible</u> [Cristina Garcia, *Dreaming in Cuban*].

How do the underlined content clauses differ from content clauses we have seen previously? To answer this question, we must first rule out the possibility of subject, object, or NP or adjective complement status for these clauses, and, I think, that feat is easily accomplished. Next, we notice that each content clause is preceded by some intensification of an element in the clause being modified, through the use of *so* modifying an adjective or adverb (this *so* is an adverb and not a conjunction). In each case the underlined content clause gives the *extent* to which the modified element is intensified, and so we can call these content clauses **adverbial clauses of extent.**

Truncated Adverbial Clauses

Sometimes adverbial clauses introduced by subordinating conjunctions occur in truncated (or shortened) form. The result is generally a nonfinite subordinate clause, adverbial in function, as these examples from Toni Morrison's *Beloved* attest:

52. Sethe never came to her, never said a word to her, never smiled and worst of all never waved goodbye or even looked her way <u>before running away from her.</u>

53. She had married the blackest man she could find, had five rainbow-colored children and sent them all to Wilberforce, <u>after teaching them all she knew right along with the others who sat in her parlor.</u>

Sometimes—and this fact will undoubtedly come as a shock—the truncated clause may actually be *verbless.* Indeed such things are possible (and you thought clauses had to have verbs), as this example from Martin Luther King, Jr.'s "Letters from Birmingham Jail" shows:

54. In your statement you assert that our actions, <u>even though peaceful,</u> must be condemned because they precipitate violence.

Another example of a verbless adverbial clause appears in the familiar proverb "When in Rome, do as the Romans do."

Sometimes adverbial clauses are not truncated versions of full-blown finite clauses marked with conjunctions, but are shortened versions of content clauses functioning as adverbials of extent; these truncated clauses typically occur as infinitive clauses, as in (55a) from Richard Rodriguez's *Hunger of Memory* and (56a) from Debra Earling's "The Old Marriage":

55a. He knew a Catholic priest who promised to get money enough <u>to study full time for a high school diploma.</u>

56a. He was too shy and too stupid <u>to actively do anything.</u>

Notice the occurrence of the intensifying words *enough* and *too* in the modified clauses, and the inherent negation in the infinitive clause in (56a). In addition, notice that the removal of the intensifier may result in an ungrammatical string:

56b. *He was shy and stupid to actively do anything.

Exercise 10.1

The following sentences come from Richard Rodriguez's *Hunger of Memory*. Underline each finite adverbial subordinate clause and, in the space following each sentence, write the term describing its *semantic* category (i.e., conditional, concessive, causal, temporal, etc.).

1. Until I was seven years old, I did not know the names of the kids who lived across the street.

2. When I was in high school, I admitted to my mother that I planned to become a teacher someday.

3. These discussions ended abruptly, though my mother remembered them on other occasions when she complained that our "big ideas" were going to our heads.

4. I was the first in my family who asked to leave home when it came time to go to college.

5. On other occasions I waited apprehensively while my mother read onion-paper letters airmailed from Mexico with news of a relative's illness or death.

6. To console myself for the loneliness I'd feel when I read, I tried reading in a very soft voice.

7. At the library I would literally tremble as I came upon whole shelves of books I hadn't read.

8. I had the idea that [books] were crucial for my academic success, though I couldn't have said exactly how or why.

9. If that core essence could be mined and memorized, I would become learned like my teachers.

10. According to Hoggart, the scholarship boy grows nostalgic because he remains the uncertain scholar, bright enough to have moved from his past, yet unable to feel easy, a part of a community of academics.

11. In twelve years of Catholic schooling, I learned, in fact, very little about the beliefs of non-Catholics, though the little I learned was conveyed by my teachers without hostility and with fair accuracy.

12. Even while grammar school nuns reminded me of my spiritual separateness from non-Catholics, they provided excellent *public* schooling.

13. During my first months in school, I remember being struck by the fact that—although they worshipped in English—the nuns and my classmates shared my family's religion.

14. The old mass proceeded with sure, blind pomp precisely because Catholics had faith in their public identity as Catholics; the old liturgy was ceremonial because of the Church's assumption that worship is a public event.

15. When I go to church on Sunday I am forced to recognize a great deal about myself.

16. When my family visited my aunt's house in San Francisco, my grandmother searched for me among my many cousins.

17. Once I learned public language, it would never again be easy for me to hear intimate family voices.

18. As I grew fluent in English, I no longer could speak Spanish with confidence.

19. Because I wrongly imagined that English was intrinsically a public language and Spanish an intrinsically private one, I easily noted the difference between classroom language and the language of home.

20. They were stories so familiar to me that I couldn't remember the first time I'd heard them.

Answers to Exercise 10.1

1. <u>Until I was seven years old,</u> I did not know the names of the kids who lived across the street.
   temporal adverbial clause

2. <u>When I was in high school,</u> I admitted to my mother that I planned to become a teacher someday.
   temporal adverbial clause

3. These discussions ended abruptly, <u>though my mother remembered them on other occasions when she complained that our "big ideas" were going to our heads</u>.

   concessive adverbial clause (note: the *when* clause in this sentence is not adverbial)

4. I was the first in my family who asked to leave home <u>when it came time to go to college</u>.

   temporal adverbial clause

5. On other occasions I waited apprehensively <u>while my mother read onion-paper letters airmailed from Mexico with news of a relative's illness or death</u>.

   temporal adverbial clause

6. To console myself for the loneliness I'd feel <u>when I read</u>, I tried reading in a very soft voice.

   temporal adverbial clause

7. At the library I would literally tremble <u>as I came upon whole shelves of books I hadn't read</u>.

   temporal adverbial clause

8. I had the idea that [books] were crucial for my academic success, <u>though I couldn't have said exactly how or why</u>.

   concessive adverbial clause

9. <u>If that core essence could be mined and memorized</u>, I would become learned like my teachers.

   conditional adverbial clause

10. According to Hoggart, the scholarship boy grows nostalgic <u>because he remains the uncertain scholar, bright enough to have moved from his past, yet unable to feel easy, a part of a community of academics</u>.

    causal adverbial clause

11. In twelve years of Catholic schooling, I learned, in fact, very little about the beliefs of non-Catholics, <u>though the little I learned was conveyed by my teachers without hostility and with fair accuracy</u>.

    concessive adverbial clause

12. <u>Even while grammar school nuns reminded me of my spiritual separateness from non-Catholics</u>, they provided excellent *public* schooling.

    temporal adverbial clause

13. During my first months in school, I remember being struck by the fact that—<u>although they worshipped in English</u>—the nuns and my classmates shared my family's religion.

    concessive adverbial clause

14. The old mass proceeded with sure, blind pomp <u>precisely because Catholics had faith in their public identity as Catholics</u>; the old liturgy was ceremonial because of the Church's assumption that worship is a public event.

    causal adverbial clause (the second occurrence of *because* is a prepositional use)

15. <u>When I go to church on Sunday</u> I am forced to recognize a great deal about myself.

    temporal adverbial clause

16. <u>When my family visited my aunt's house in San Francisco</u>, my grandmother searched for me among my many cousins.

    temporal adverbial clause

17. <u>Once I learned public language</u>, it would never again be easy for me to hear intimate family voices.

    temporal adverbial clause

18. <u>As I grew fluent in English</u>, I no longer could speak Spanish with confidence.

    temporal adverbial clause

19. <u>Because I wrongly imagined that English was intrinsically a public language and Spanish an intrinsically private one</u>, I easily noted the difference between classroom language and the language of home.

    causal adverbial clause

20. They were stories so familiar to me <u>that I couldn't remember the first time I'd heard them</u>.

    adverbial clause of extent

Exercise 10.2

The following sentences are the same ones you encountered in Exercise 10.1. This time, underline each finite subordinate clause that is not an adverbial and, in the space following each sentence, write the term describing its *structure* (content clause or relative clause) and *grammatical function* (i.e., subject, direct object, restrictive relative clause, appositive, etc.).

1. Until I was seven years old, I did not know the names of the kids who lived across the street.

2. When I was in high school, I admitted to my mother that I planned to become a teacher someday.

3. These discussions ended abruptly, though my mother remembered them on other occasions when she complained that our "big ideas" were going to our heads.

4. I was the first in my family who asked to leave home when it came time to go to college.

5. To console myself for the loneliness I'd feel when I read, I tried reading in a very soft voice.

6. At the library I would literally tremble as I came upon whole shelves of books I hadn't read.

7. I had the idea that [books] were crucial for my academic success, though I couldn't have said exactly how or why.

8. In twelve years of Catholic schooling, I learned, in fact, very little about the beliefs of non-Catholics, though the little I learned was conveyed by my teachers without hostility and with fair accuracy.

9. During my first months in school, I remember being struck by the fact that—although they worshipped in English—the nuns and my classmates shared my family's religion.

10. The old mass proceeded with sure, blind pomp precisely because Catholics had faith in their public identity as Catholics; the old liturgy was ceremonial because of the Church's assumption that worship is a public event.

11. Because I wrongly imagined that English was intrinsically a public language and Spanish an intrinsically private one, I easily noted the difference between classroom language and the language of home.

12. They were stories so familiar to me that I couldn't remember the first time I'd heard them.

Answers to Exercise 10.2

1. Until I was seven years old, I did not know the names of the kids <u>who lived across the street</u>.

   restrictive relative clause

2. When I was in high school, I admitted to my mother <u>that I planned to become a teacher someday</u>.

   content clause, direct object of *admitted*

3. These discussions ended abruptly, though my mother remembered them on other occasions <u>when she complained that our "big ideas" were going to our heads</u>.

   1. restrictive relative clause

   2. content clause, direct object of *complained*

4. I was the first in my family <u>who asked to leave home when it came time to go to college</u>.

   restrictive relative clause

5. To console myself for the loneliness <u>I'd feel when I read</u>, I tried reading in a very soft voice.

   restrictive relative clause

6. At the library I would literally tremble as I came upon whole shelves of books <u>I hadn't read</u>.

   restrictive relative clause

7. I had the idea <u>that [books] were crucial for my academic success</u>, though I couldn't have said exactly how or why.

   content clause, appositive

8. In twelve years of Catholic schooling, I learned, in fact, very little about the beliefs of non-Catholics, though the little <u>I learned</u> was conveyed by my teachers without hostility and with fair accuracy.

   restrictive relative clause

9. During my first months in school, I remember being struck by the fact <u>that—although they worshipped in English—the nuns and my classmates shared my family's religion</u>.

   content clause, appositive

10. The old mass proceeded with sure, blind pomp precisely because Catholics had faith in their public identity as Catholics; the old liturgy was ceremonial because of the Church's assumption <u>that worship is a public event</u>.

    content clause, appositive

11. Because I wrongly imagined <u>that English was intrinsically a public language and Spanish an intrinsically private one</u>, I easily noted the difference between classroom language and the language of home.

    content clause, direct object of *imagined*

12. They were stories so familiar to me that I couldn't remember the first time <u>I'd heard them</u>.

    restrictive relative clause

Exercise 10.3

This time examine the sentences for nonfinite clauses. Underline each nonfinite subordinate clause and, in the space following each sentence, write the term describing its *structure* (infinitive clause or participle clause) and *grammatical function* (e.g., subject, direct object, adverbial, etc.).

1. When I was in high school, I admitted to my mother that I planned to become a teacher someday.

2. I was the first in my family who asked to leave home when it came time to go to college.

3. On other occasions I waited apprehensively while my mother read onion-paper letters airmailed from Mexico with news of a relative's illness or death.

4. To console myself for the loneliness I'd feel when I read, I tried reading in a very soft voice.

5. According to Hoggart, the scholarship boy grows nostalgic because he remains the uncertain scholar, bright enough to have moved from his past, yet unable to feel easy, a part of a community of academics.

6. During my first months in school, I remember being struck by the fact that—although they worshipped in English—the nuns and my classmates shared my family's religion.

7. When I go to church on Sunday I am forced to recognize a great deal about myself.

8. Once I learned public language, it would never again be easy for me to hear intimate family voices.

Answers to Exercise 10.3

1. When I was in high school, I admitted to my mother that I planned <u>to become a teacher someday</u>.

   infinitive clause, direct object of *planned*

2. I was the first in my family who asked <u>to leave home</u> when it came time to go to college.

   infinitive clause, direct object of *asked*

3. On other occasions I waited apprehensively while my mother read onion-paper letters <u>airmailed from Mexico</u> with news of a relative's illness or death.

   past participle clause, restrictive adjectival

4. <u>To console myself for the loneliness I'd feel when I read</u>, I tried <u>reading in a very soft voice</u>.

   1. infinitive clause, adverbial

   2. present participle clause, direct object of *tried*

5. According to Hoggart, the scholarship boy grows nostalgic because he remains the uncertain scholar, bright enough <u>to have moved from his past</u>, yet unable <u>to feel easy, a part of a community of academics</u>.

   1. infinitive clause, adverbial of extent

   2. infinitive clause, adjective complement

6. During my first months in school, I remember <u>being struck by the fact that—although they worshipped in English—the nuns and my classmates shared my family's religion</u>.

   present participle clause, direct object of *remember*

7. When I go to church on Sunday I am forced <u>to recognize a great deal about myself</u>.

   infinitive clause, predicate complement

8. Once I learned public language, it would never again be easy <u>for me to hear intimate family voices</u>.

   subject-bearing infinitive clause, extraposed subject

Terms Used in Chapter Ten

adverbial clause of extent: a subordinate clause that functions to give the extent to which the information given in the matrix clause is true.

adverbial subordinate clause: a subordinate clause that modifies the matrix clause by providing certain details of time, cause, condition, concession, purpose, or extent. As with other adverbials, the adverbial subordinate clause has more freedom of movement than other structures.

causal adverbial clause: a subordinate clause that provides the cause or reason for the state of affairs in the matrix clause.

conditional adverbial clause: a subordinate clause that gives the condition under which the matrix clause event may occur.

durative: the characteristic by which an event continues over a period of time.

semantic: pertaining to meaning.

subject/auxiliary inversion: the interchanging of the subject and the auxiliary verb in questions and several other constructions with negative or conditional impact.

subjunctive: a form of the verb indicating that the action or state expressed in the predicate phrase is possible rather than actual or contingent on hypothetical events.

temporal adverbial clause: a subordinate clause that provides the time reference for the matrix clause.

yes/no question: a question characterized in syntactic terms solely by subject/auxiliary inversion and requiring only a yes or no for answer, e.g. *Are they leaving?*

Chapter Quiz

All of the following sentences come from *Go Tell It on the Mountain,* by James Baldwin. Examine each sentence carefully and, in the space below each, write a label that best describes the structure and function of the underlined subordinate clause. Keep in mind that all kinds of subordinate clauses—finite and nonfinite—are represented in these selections. The *structures* that may occur include: adverbial clauses, content clauses, relative clauses, infinitive clauses, and participle clauses. The functions that may occur include: subject, direct object, object of preposition, appositive, adjectival, adverbial (give semantic category for a finite clause), copular complement, predicate complement.

1. In this pause, <u>if it was good weather</u>, the old folks might step outside a moment to talk among themselves.

2. In this pause, if it was good weather, the old folks might step outside a moment <u>to talk among themselves</u>.

3. <u>To sweep the front room</u> meant, principally, to sweep the heavy red and green and purple Oriental-style carpet that had once been that room's glory, but was now so faded that it was all one swimming color, and so frayed in places that it tangled with the broom.

4. To sweep the front room meant, principally, <u>to sweep the heavy red and green and purple Oriental-style carpet that had once been that room's glory, but was now so faded that it was all one swimming color, and so frayed in places that it tangled with the broom</u>.

5. To sweep the front room meant, principally, to sweep the heavy red and green and purple Oriental-style carpet <u>that had once been that room's glory, but was now so faded that it was all one swimming color, and so frayed in places that it tangled with the broom</u>.

6. To sweep the front room meant, principally, to sweep the heavy red and green and purple Oriental-style carpet that had once been that room's glory, but was now so faded <u>that it was all one swimming color</u>, and so frayed in places that it tangled with the broom.

7. To sweep the front room meant, principally, to sweep the heavy red and green and purple Oriental-style carpet that had once been that room's glory, but was now so faded that it was all one swimming color, and so frayed in places <u>that it tangled with the broom</u>.

8. He looked straight ahead, down Fifth Avenue, <u>where graceful women in fur coats walked</u>, looking into the windows that held silk dresses, and watches, and rings.

9. He looked straight ahead, down Fifth Avenue, where graceful women in fur coats walked, looking into the windows <u>that held silk dresses, and watches, and rings</u>.

10. Once, one winter <u>when he had been very sick with a heavy cold that would not leave him</u>, one of his teachers had brought him a bottle of cod liver oil, especially prepared with heavy syrup so that it did not taste so bad.

11. Once, one winter when he had been very sick with a heavy cold <u>that would not leave him</u>, one of his teachers had brought him a bottle of cod liver oil, especially prepared with heavy syrup so that it did not taste so bad.

12. Once, one winter when he had been very sick with a heavy cold that would not leave him, one of his teachers had brought him a bottle of cod liver oil, <u>especially prepared with heavy syrup so that it did not taste so bad</u>.

13. Once, one winter when he had been very sick with a heavy cold that would not leave him, one of his teachers had brought him a bottle of cod liver oil, especially prepared with heavy syrup <u>so that it did not taste so bad</u>.

14. They were kind—he was sure <u>they were kind</u>—and on the day that he would bring himself to their attention they would surely love and honor him.

15. They were kind—he was sure they were kind—and on the day <u>that he would bring himself to their attention</u> they would surely love and honor him.

16. She laughed at him <u>because he was a cripple</u>.

17. She had fallen from that high estate <u>which God had intended for men and women</u>, and she made her fall glorious because it was so complete.

18. She had fallen from that high estate which God had intended for men and women, and she made her fall glorious <u>because it was so complete</u>.

19. John walked into his parents' bedroom and picked up the squalling baby, <u>who was wet</u>.

20. <u>As they sang</u>, they clapped their hands, and John saw that Sister McCandless looked about her for a tambourine.

21. As they sang, they clapped their hands, and John saw <u>that Sister McCandless looked about her for a tambourine</u>.

22. The word was fulfilled one morning, <u>before she was awake</u>.

23. Soon it occurred to her <u>that there was no longer any reason to tarry here</u>.

24. Soon it occurred to her that there was no longer any reason <u>to tarry here</u>.

25. And, after the beating, his pants still down around his knees and his face wet with tears and mucus, Gabriel was made <u>to kneel down while his mother prayed</u>.

26. And, after the beating, his pants still down around his knees and his face wet with tears and mucus, Gabriel was made to kneel down <u>while his mother prayed</u>.

27. Tears stood suddenly in her own eyes, <u>though she could not have said what she was crying for</u>.

28. Tears stood suddenly in her own eyes, though she could not have said <u>what she was crying for</u>.

29. And he feared <u>to make a vow before Heaven</u> until he had the strength to keep it.

30. And he feared to make a vow before Heaven <u>until he had the strength to keep it</u>.

31. And he feared to make a vow before Heaven until he had the strength <u>to keep it</u>.

32. He understood <u>that she was sorry for him because he was always worried</u>.

33. He understood that she was sorry for him <u>because he was always worried</u>.

34. He stole the money <u>while Deborah slept</u>.

35. Sometimes he was certain <u>she had discovered that the money was missing and knew that he had taken it</u>.

36. Sometimes he was certain she had discovered <u>that the money was missing</u> and knew that he had taken it.

37. Sometimes he was certain she had discovered that the money was missing and knew <u>that he had taken it</u>.

38. It would surely be believed <u>that they were plotting vengeance</u>.

39. And yet, tonight, in her great confusion, she wondered <u>if she had not been wrong</u>.

40. And Elizabeth was checked by the fear <u>that if her aunt should discover how things stood between her and Richard she would find . . . some means of bringing about their separation</u>.

41. And Elizabeth was checked by the fear that <u>if her aunt should discover how things stood between her and Richard</u> she would find . . . some means of bringing about their separation.

42. And Elizabeth was checked by the fear that if her aunt should discover <u>how things stood between her and Richard</u> she would find . . . some means of bringing about their separation.

43. And Elizabeth was checked by the fear that if her aunt should discover how things stood between her and Richard she would find . . . some means of <u>bringing about their separation</u>.

44. But <u>since he was going to school at night and made very little money,</u> their marriage . . . was planned for a future that grew ever more remote.

45. But since he was going to school at night and made very little money, their marriage . . . was planned for a future <u>that grew ever more remote</u>.

46. <u>While Elizabeth stood trembling and indecisive in the hall</u>, two white policemen entered.

47. She believed him <u>when he said that God had sent him to her for a sign</u>.

48. She believed him when he said <u>that God had sent him to her for a sign</u>.

49. He wanted to obey the voice, <u>which was the only voice that spoke to him</u>.

50. He wanted to obey the voice, which was the only voice <u>that spoke to him</u>.

Appendixes

Appendix A

Summary of Syntactic Tests

Transitivity Test

When in doubt about the transitivity of certain VPs, we can apply the passive rule to the sentence. Since only transitive verbs may undergo the passive rule, a successful (i.e., *grammatical*) result indicates that the VP so tested is transitive. For example, the VP of one of the following sentences is transitive, whereas the VP of the other is not:

a. We sang a song.

b. We walked a long time.

If we attempt to make (a) passive, the result is:

A song was sung (by us).

This result is acceptable, and so the VP *sang* is transitive in sentence (a). However, the application of the same rule to (b) yields different results:

*a long time was walked (by us).

This result clearly is unacceptable, and we have good evidence that the VP *walked* is not transitive in Sentence (b).

Indirect Object Test

In simple sentences, often it is possible to determine the indirect object status of an NP by inserting the preposition *to* in front of the first of two sequential NPs in the predicate phrase and moving the resulting PP to the end of the sentence. If what results is an acceptable paraphrase of the original sentence, then the NP converted into an object of the preposition *to* is an indirect object. The lack of acceptable results generally indicates that it is not. In Example (a) below, the first of the two NPs in the predicate phrase is indeed an indirect object, since it passes the indirect object test:

a. The mother read the child a book.

   The mother read a book to the child.

However, in Sentence (b), the unacceptable result of the application of the indirect object test indicates that the first of the two predicate phrase NPs is not an indirect object:

b. The mother called her child a genius.

   *The mother called a genius to her child.

The altered version of Sentence (b) might be acceptable in certain circumstances, but clearly the meaning is significantly altered over the original version.

The Predicate Complement Test

In simple sentences in which an NP-NP string or an NP-PP string occurs in the predicate phrase, often it is possible to determine the predicate complement status of the second NP or of the PP by removing the string in question from the sentence and inserting a form of the verb *be* between the two elements. If what results is an acceptable copular paraphrase of the gist of the original sentence, then the element following *be* in the new sentence is the predicate complement of the original. The lack of acceptable results generally indicates that it is not. In example (a) below, the second of the two NPs in the predicate phrase is indeed a predicate complement since it passes the test:

a. The mother called her child a genius.

   Her child *is* a genius.

However, the second NP in (b) clearly is not a predicate complement because it fails:

b. The mother read her child a book.

   *Her child is a book.

The same results will occur with a PP:

c. The mother put the book on the shelf.

The book *is* on the shelf.

Testing for Infinitive Clause Functions

This set of tests has been systematically laid out in the decision procedure on page 107.

Distinguishing Between Appositive Clauses and Relative Clauses

Remember that both appositive clauses and relative clauses may begin with *that*. However, in the case of the relative clause, the *that* must serve a grammatical function: It must be the subject of the relative clause or some kind of object within the relative clause itself. As a consequence, a relative clause whose pronoun is *that* requires its pronoun to complete the grammatical pattern of the subordinate clause. To make this factor clear, it helps if we try to substitute a true relative pronoun such as *which, who,* or *whom* for the *that*. If the result is an acceptable clause, then the original structure is indeed a relative clause; if the result is gibberish, then the clause probably is an appositive. In addition, there is frequently a copular relationship between a noun and the appositive clause that modifies it. Thus, in Sentence (a) below, the subordinate clause is an appositive:

a. The thought <u>that summer vacation was just around the corner</u> guided us through the darkest days of final examinations.

The thought *was* that summer vacation was just around the corner.

Note however that Sentence (a) would not be grammatical if *which* were substituted for *that:*

*The thought which summer vacation was just around the corner guided us through the darkest days of final examinations.

Sentence (b) does contain a relative clause because the substitution of *which* results in a perfectly acceptable sentence *and* there is no copular relationship between the head noun and the subordinate clause:

b. The belief <u>that dominated his thinking</u> may explain his hesitation about taking the job.

The belief which dominated his thinking may explain his hesitation about taking the job.

*The belief *is* that dominated his thinking.

Appendix B

Pronoun Paradigms

Inflections still are maintained in the English pronoun system, but there are some obvious "gaps." Most pronouns have a case distinction. That is, there are differing forms for a pronoun serving as a subject (subjective case) and a pronoun serving as an object (objective case). However, only one form exists for the third person neuter singular pronoun *(it)*. In addition, there is no distinction between singular and plural forms of the second person pronoun *(you),* except in the reflexive form. Gender distinctions exist only in third person singular personal and possessive pronouns. Thus, there is a subjective/objective distinction in the third person plural, but the same forms are used for masculine, feminine, and neuter antecedents. Within the class of relative pronouns, there is a gender distinction, but it is not the traditional break into masculine, feminine, and neuter categories. Instead, the distinction is between human and nonhuman. These facts are systematically presented in the paradigms on pages 256 and 257.

English Personal Pronouns

		Subjective Case	Objective Case
First person			
	singular	I	me
	plural	we	us
Second person		you	
Third person			
	masculine singular	he	him
	feminine singular	she	her
	neuter	it	
	plural (all genders)	they	them

Possessive Pronouns

		Determiner Function (precedes noun)	Noun Function (stands alone)
First person			
	singular	my	mine
	plural	our	ours
Second person		your	yours
Third person			
	masculine singular	his	his
	feminine singular	her	hers
	neuter singular	its	
	plural	their	theirs

Reflexive Pronouns

First person

singular	myself
plural	ourselves

Second person

singular	yourself
plural	yourselves

Third person

masculine singular	himself
feminine singular	herself
neuter	itself
plural	themselves

Relative Pronouns

Subjective case (human)	who
Objective case (human)	whom
Nonhuman	which
Possessive (determiner function only)	whose

Appendix C

Glossary of Syntactic Terms

absolute phrase: a term used for subject-bearing participle clauses that modify NPs nonrestrictively.

active voice: a form of the VP of particular verbs that have subjects serving as agents acting upon another sentence entity.

adjectival: a phrase or clause that may or may not contain an adjective but that functions to modify a noun.

adjective: a word that modifies a noun.

adjective complement: an infinitive clause or a content clause that serves as object to an adjective.

adverb: a word that modifies a verb, adjective, or another adverb.

adverbial: a PP, NP, or adverb phrase that serves to modify the VP of a sentence.

adverbial clause of extent: a subordinate clause that functions to give the extent to which the information given in the matrix clause is true.

adverbial subordinate clause: a subordinate clause that modifies the matrix clause by providing certain details of time, cause, condition, concession, purpose, or extent. As with other adverbials, the adverbial subordinate clause has more freedom of movement than other structures.

affected participant: the usual semantic role of the direct object—i.e., the entity acted upon.

agent: the role played by the subjects of active verbs. An agent causes a change of state in some person or thing.

agree: a verb is said to agree with its subject, and a pronoun is said to agree with its antecedent. These statements mean that the forms of verbs and subjects and of pronouns and antecedents match in an important way.

agreement: the grammatical process by which a verb phrase carries a plural inflection if its subject is plural, and a singular inflection it its subject is singular.

antecedent: the NP that a pronoun replaces in subsequent mentions of the NP.

anticipatory pronoun: the pronoun *it* that holds the place for a subordinate clause moved to the end of the sentence. An anticipatory pronoun has no antecedent.

appositive: an NP, content clause, or infinitive clause that serves to name or completely identify an NP.

article: one of the function words *the* and *a (an)* that often begin noun phrases.

aspect: a grammatical category, usually associated with verbs in English, that indicates the nature of an event, e.g., whether it is ongoing or whether it occurs at a single point in time.

asterisk notation: the use of an asterisk in front of a string of words to show that the string does not constitute an acceptable phrase or sentence.

auxiliary: a helping verb that has little inherent meaning.

causal adverbial clause: a subordinate clause that provides the cause or reason for the state of affairs in the matrix clause.

causative construction: a construction that indicates that the subject brings about a state of affairs causing the object to experience something or to be located somewhere other than its starting position. *Make* is the best example of a causative verb.

clausal coordination: the connection of two or more independent clauses through the process of coordination or conjunction.

clause: a construction containing a subject (though sometimes implied rather than overt) and a predicate phrase. The very basic sentences studied in Chapter One are single clauses.

complement: a structure that serves as a companion to the VP in the predicate phrase of a sentence and that "completes" the predicate phrase. NPs and APs sometimes take complements as well.

complementizer: a word that has no meaning but serves the syntactic function of introducing a subordinate clause. The usual complementizer in content clauses is *that;* in infinitive clauses, the complementizer *to* generally appears.

conditional adverbial clause: a subordinate clause that gives the condition under which the matrix clause event may occur.

conjuncts: the elements connected through the process of coordination.

content clause: a finite subordinate clause that can serve functions usually limited to NPs in basic sentences, such as subject and object.

coordinating conjunctions: members of the small, closed class of function words that bring about coordination in English—*for, and, nor, but, or, yet, so.*

coordination: the fusion of two or more of any sentence elements of the same status through the use of coordinating conjunctions.

copular verb: a verb that sets up a kind of equation between its subject and its complement. The complement either assigns the subject to a class (when the complement is an NP) or assigns an attribute to the subject (when the complement is an adjective).

correlative conjunctions: conjunctions made up of two separate words, each marking the start of a conjunct, e.g., *both . . . and, either . . . or.*

dangling participle: a participle clause used in a sentence lacking the NP needed to serve as the implicit subject of the participle, e.g., *Riding in the car, the countryside seemed more colorful than ever.*

demonstrative: one of the function words *this* and *that* or their plural forms *these* and *those.*

determiner: those function words such as articles and demonstratives that introduce noun phrases.

detransitivized verb: a transitive verb that has undergone the passive rule.

durative: the characteristic by which an event continues over a period of time.

extraposed: the characteristic of a content clause or an infinitive clause of being located at the end of a matrix clause, regardless of the grammatical function of the subordinate clause.

extraposition: the movement to the end of the sentence of certain subject or object subordinate clauses from the position typical of these functions.

finite subordinate clause: a subordinate clause whose VP is either tensed or has a modal. Unlike nonfinite clauses, a finite clause always will have an overt subject.

finite verb: a verb inflected for tense.

finite VP: a VP that is inflected for tense or contains a modal auxiliary—e.g., *were riding, may leave, jumped.*

free NP: an NP that is not caught up in a prepositional phrase or some other structure, making it available to interact directly with the VP of a sentence as a subject, object, or complement.

fronted: the characteristic of a syntactic element of occurring at the beginning of its clause, regardless of its grammatical function.

function: the use to which any given structure is put in a particular sentence, e.g., subject.

function shift: the use of a word from a particular word class (e.g., a noun) as some other word class (e.g., a verb). The word thus shifts its function from noun to verb.

function word: a word signaling primarily grammatical information, such as a preposition or a conjunction.

gapping: the omission of repeated material from within a conjunct.

Germanic: the language subfamily to which English belongs. Other languages in this group include German, Dutch, and Norwegian. Languages belonging to the same family have a common ancestor language.

gerund: the term used in traditional grammar for a present participle functioning as a noun.

gerundive: the term used in traditional grammar for a present participle clause functioning as a modifier.

gerund phrase: the term used in traditional grammar for a present participle clause serving a function filled by an NP in a basic English sentence.

head: the chief element in a phrase or clause. An N, for example, is the head of an NP.

implicature: a logical assumption derived from the supposition that writers or speakers have some intent to communicate in mind when they use the language, even though that intent may not be explicit in the communication.

implicit coordination: the connection of two or more elements of equal status through the process of coordination, but without the use of an expressed coordinating conjunction.

indefinite pronoun: a pronoun without a specific antecedent, e.g., *someone, anyone.*

infinitive: the uninflected or base form of a verb.

infinitive clause: a clause whose VP is the infinitive form of the verb.

inflected: the property of a word that allows it to indicate its function, usually via a suffix.

inflection: a suffix indicating grammatical information such as person, number, and tense—e.g., *-ed* indicates past tense in English.

intransitive verb: a verb that is followed by no free NPs that are not adverbials.

lexical verb: the verb within a verb phrase that indicates a specific action or state.

matrix clause: the clause into which a subordinate clause is inserted.

mental experience verb: a verb whose meaning involves psychological states, e.g., *know, think, feel,* etc.

modal auxiliary: the verbs *can, could, will, would, shall, should, may, might,* and *must;* the verb that follows a modal must appear in the infinitive form.

modifier: a word or phrase that limits or describes another word or phrase.

nonfinite verb: any verb form that is not inflected for tense—infinitives and participles.

nonrestrictive: the property of providing additional, but nonessential information. Only modifiers may be nonrestrictive.

noun phrase (NP): a phrase whose head element is a noun. It may also include a determiner and adjectives.

NP complement: an infinitive clause or a content clause that serves as an appositive to an NP.

number: markings on verbs, nouns, and pronouns that indicate whether the form in question is singular or plural.

object: a noun phrase or its equivalent that enters into a relationship with a preceding verb or preposition.

objective case: an inflection, now limited to English pronouns, that typically indicates that the pronoun serves as the object of some other sentence element. The pronouns *me, us, her, him,* and *them* all are in the objective case.

obligatory element: a sentence element that must be present to ensure the grammatical acceptability of a sentence.

optional element: a sentence element that can be omitted without affecting grammatical acceptability, even though it may contain information important to communication.

participle clause: a nonfinite subordinate clause headed by a participle verb form and generally lacking an overt subject.

passive: the voice of the VP in a sentence in which the subject is not the instigator of the action but the affected participant. The auxiliary *be* occurs in the VP with the past participle of the lexical verb.

passive voice: the form of the VP indicated by the combination of the auxiliary *be* and the past participle of the lexical verb. Only inherently transitive verbs have passive forms in English.

past participle: one of the principle parts of the verb, the past participle usually ends in *-ed* or *-en,* and when part of the VP of the predicate phrase, it is accompanied by an auxiliary.

past tense: the form of the verb signaling past time, most often indicated by *-ed.*

perfective aspect: a VP made up of *have* and the past participle of the lexical verb.

person: an indication in a verb or pronoun as to whether the subject of the verb or the antecedent of the pronoun is the speaker, the addressee, or whatever is spoken about.

phrasal coordination: the connection of two or more plural elements through the process of coordination or conjunction.

phrase: a sequence of words functioning as a unit.

phrase structure tree: a schematic representation of a sentence.

possessive case: an inflection found on English nouns and pronouns indicating that the NP "possesses"—sometimes only in a loose sense—the NP that follows it. On nouns, the possessive inflection is - *'s.*

possessive pronoun: a pronoun inflected to show that the pronoun possesses the noun that follows, e.g., *his, its, their.*

pragmatics: the study of how language is used to get things done in the world.

predicate: when used as a verb (i.e., *to predicate*), to predicate is to assert an action or a quality of an entity.

predicate phrase: the part of the sentence that includes the verb, its auxiliaries and modifiers, and any noun phrases or other constructions required by the verb.

preposition: a word or group of words functioning as a unit that signals a relationship of time, space, or association between the noun phrase that follows it and some other entity in the sentence.

present participle: a verb form ending in *-ing.*

primary auxiliary: the verbs *be, have,* and *do* in their function as helpers preceding another verb.

primary conjunctions: the most important and frequent coordinators—*and, but, or.*

progressive aspect: signaled by *be* plus the present participle of the lexical verb.

pronoun: a function word that replaces a noun phrase on subsequent mention of the noun phrase.

referent: the real-world event or object to which a particular word points.

reflexive pronoun: a pronoun form ending in *-self.* It cannot serve as the subject of a sentence.

relative clause: a finite subordinate clause that serves as an adjectival modifier in an NP and that typically begins with a relative pronoun.

relative pronoun: the words *who, whom, whose, which* and *that* when they are used to introduce a relative clause.

restrictive: the characteristic of modifiers that allows them to limit or restrict the meaning of the heads they modify.

semantic: pertaining to meaning.

semantics: the meaning component of language.

sentence constituents: the major structural divisions within a sentence.

speech act verb: a verb whose action involves speaking, e.g. *ask, say, tell, promise, urge,* etc.

strong verb: a verb that forms its past tense by changes inside the base form, usually a vowel change.

structure: a particular coherent grouping of elements in a sentence that can be described in terms of the components that comprise it, e.g., NP.

subject: a free NP—or something else that behaves like one—that occurs before the verb, making it the first element in a declarative sentence. Typically, the subject NP is the element that performs the action in an active transitive sentence or experiences the event or state in an intransitive sentence.

subject/auxiliary inversion: the interchanging of the subject and the auxiliary verb in questions and several other constructions with negative or conditional impact.

subject-bearing participle clause: a participle clause that contains an explicit and overt subject.

subjective case: the inflection on a pronoun indicating that the pronoun is the subject of a finite verb. The pronouns *I, we, she, they* all are in the subjective case.

subjunctive: a form of the verb indicating the action or state expressed in the predicate phrase is possible rather than actual, or contingent on hypothetical rather than factual events.

subordinate clause: a clause that cannot stand as an independent sentence in its own right, but rather serves a particular grammatical function (e.g., subject, object, complement, or modifier) in another "matrix" clause.

subordinating conjunction: a function word that introduces a clause that is subordinate to another structure—*because* is a good example.

syntax: the arrangement of words in a sentence.

temporal adverbial clause: a subordinate clause that provides the time reference for the matrix clause.

tense: the time reference of a verb—in English, past or present.

transitive verb: a verb followed by a free NP that does not identify the subject. Usually the subject acts upon this free NP.

verb phrase: a structural unit containing a lexical verb and any auxiliaries or particles associated with it.

verbal particle: a word, usually selected from the class of prepositions, that has lost its prepositional function and behaves instead as a component of the verb phrase.

voice: an inflection on a transitive VP that indicates whether the VP is active or passive.

weak verb: a verb that forms its past tense by adding *-ed*. The vast majority of English verbs are weak verbs.

yes/no question: a question characterized in syntactic terms solely by subject/ auxiliary inversion and requiring only a yes or no for answer; e.g., *Are they leaving?*

Works Cited in *Grammar in Many Voices*

Allen, Paula Gunn. "Deer Woman." *Talking Leaves: Contemporary Native American Short Stories*. Ed. Craig Leslie. New York: Laurel-Dell, 1991. 1–11.

Baldwin, James. *Go Tell It On the Mountain*. New York: Laurel-Dell, 1981.

---. *Going to Meet the Man*. New York: Dial Press, 1965.

Bird, Gloria. "Turtle Lake." *Talking Leaves: Contemporary Native American Short Stories*. Ed. Craig Leslie. New York: Laurel-Dell, 1991. 12–21.

Brant, Beth. "Swimming Upstream." *Talking Leaves: Contemporary Native American Short Stories*. Ed. Craig Leslie. New York: Laurel-Dell, 1991. 22–30.

Bronowski, Jacob. *The Ascent of Man*. Boston: Little, Brown, 1973.

Chang, Jung. *Wild Swans*. New York: Simon & Schuster, 1991.

Cosby, Bill. *Fatherhood*. New York: Berkley Books, 1986.

Dorris, Michael. *A Yellow Raft in Blue Water*. New York: Henry Holt, 1987.

Earling, Debra. "The Old Marriage." *Talking Leaves: Contemporary Native American Short Stories*. Ed. Craig Leslie. New York: Laurel-Dell, 1991. 61–9.

Erdrich, Louise. *The Beet Queen*. New York: Henry Holt, 1986.

---. *The Bingo Palace*. New York: HarperCollins, 1994.

---. *Love Medicine: New and Expanded Version*. New York: Henry Holt, 1993.

Flexner, Stuart Berg, and Harold Wentworth. *Dictionary of American Slang*. 2nd ed. New York: Crowell, 1975.

Fowler, Brenda. "Thawing Europe's Bronze Age." *San Jose Mercury News* 2 Oct. 1991: A2.

Freeman-Villalobos. Tina Marie, "The Way it Was." *Talking Leaves: Contemporary Native American Short Stories*. Ed. Craig Leslie. New York: Laurel-Dell, 1991. 100–17.

Fulghum, Robert. *All I Really Need to Know I Learned in Kindergarten*. New York: Ivy/Ballantine-Random House, 1988.

Garcia, Cristina. *Dreaming in Cuban*. New York: Ballantine-Random House, 1992.

Ghiglieri, Michael. "War Among the Chimps." *Discover* Nov. 1987: 66–70+.

Highwater, Jamake. *The Primal Mind: Vision and Reality in Indian America*. New York: Harper & Row, 1981.

Hogan, Linda. "Aunt Moon's Young Man." *Talking Leaves: Contemporary Native American Short Stories*. Ed. Craig Leslie. New York: Laurel-Dell, 147–69.

James, William. *The Varieties of Religious Experience, A Study in Human Nature*. New York: Modern Library, 1936.

Kenny, Maurice. "Wet Moccasins." *Talking Leaves: Contemporary Native American Short Stories*. Ed. Craig Leslie. New York: Laurel-Dell, 1991. 173–83.

King, Martin Luther Jr. "Letter from Birmingham Jail, April 16, 1963." *Why We Can't Wait*. New York: Harper & Row, 1963.

King, Thomas. "A Seat in the Garden." *Talking Leaves: Contemporary Native American Short Stories*. Ed. Craig Leslie. New York: Laurel-Dell, 1991. 184–94.

Lee, Gus. *China Boy*. New York: Plume-Penguin, 1991.

Maass, Edgar. *The Queen's Physician*. New York: Charles Scribner's Sons, 1948.

Maranto, Gina. "Earth's First Visitors to Mars." *Discover* May 1987: 28–31+.

McCartney, James, and Dan Meyers. "President Loses Fight on Tax Plank." *San Jose Mercury News* 15 Aug. 1984: A1+.

Miller, Sue. *The Good Mother*. New York: Dell, 1986.

Morrison, Toni. *Beloved*. New York: Plume-Penguin, 1987.

Moser, Penny Ward. "All the Real Dirt on Dust." *Discover* Nov. 1986: 106–12+.

Murdoch, Iris. *A Word Child*. New York: Viking, 1975.

Nixon, Richard. *In the Arena: A Memoir of Victory, Defeat, and Renewal*. New York: Simon & Schuster, 1990.

Poe, Edgar Allan. *The Fall of the House of Usher*. New York: Cheshire House, 1931.

Rice, Anne. *Interview With The Vampire*. New York: Ballantine-Random House, 1976.

---. *The Mummy or Ramses the Damned*. New York: Ballantine-Random House, 1989.

---. *The Witching Hour*. New York: Knopf, 1990.

Rodriguez, Richard. *Hunger of Memory: The Education of Richard Rodriguez*. Toronto: Bantam, 1982.

Sacks, Oliver. *A Leg to Stand On*. New York: Perennial-Harper & Row, 1984.

Seuss, Dr. *The Five Hundred Hats of Bartholomew Cubbins*. New York: Vanguard, 1938.

Silko, Leslie Marmon. *Ceremony*. New York: Viking, 1977.

Stoker, Bram. *The Annotated Dracula: Dracula by Bram Stoker*. Ed. Leonard Wolf. New York: Ballantine, 1975.

Tan, Amy. *The Joy Luck Club*. New York: Ivy-Ballantine, 1989.

Taubes, Gary. "Everything's Now Tied to Strings." *Discover* Nov. 1986: 34–6+.

Tolkien, J. R. R. *The Annotated Hobbit: The Hobbit , or, There and Back Again*. Ed. Douglas A. Anderson. Boston: Houghton Mifflin, 1988.

Trafzer, Clifford E. *Cheyenne Revenge*. *Talking Leaves: Contemporary Native American Short Stories*. Ed. Craig Leslie. New York: Laurel-Dell, 1991. 267–83.

Walker, Alice. *The Color Purple*. New York: Pocket Books, 1982.

Zinsser, William. *On Writing Well: An Informal Guide to Writing Nonfiction*. 3rd ed. New York: Harper & Row, 1976.

Index